Fort Meade, 1849–1900

T0357506

Main Street, Fort Meade, in 1887. (From Polk Co., Florida, *1887)*

Fort Meade
1849–1900

CANTER BROWN JR.

The University of Alabama Press

Tuscaloosa

Copyright © 1995
The University of Alabama Press
Tuscaloosa, Alabama 35487–0380
All rights reserved

Library of Congress Cataloging-in-Publication Data

Brown, Canter.
Fort Meade, 1849–1900 / Canter Brown, Jr.
p.   cm.
Includes bibliographical references (p.   ) and index.
ISBN 0-8173-0763-X (alk. paper)
1. Fort Meade (Fla.)—History.   I. Title.
F319.F73B76   1995
975.9'67—dc20   94-25623

With love and appreciation
to my brother,
John Eugene Brown

Contents

Illustrations

Maps

Figures

Preface

Fort MEADE IS THE OLDEST TOWN in interior south Florida. It lies on
Peace River about fifty miles east of Tampa and ten miles south of
Polk County's seat of Bartow. Nearby are the better-known, but much
younger, cities of Lakeland, Winter Haven, Plant City, and Lake Wales.
Fort Meade was founded in 1849 as a military outpost, although for
generations the site had served as a center or Seminole and Tallahassee Creek Indians. During the first half century that followed the fort's
construction, the community that it fostered, including the neighboring settlement six miles north at Homeland, withstood every demand
that a frontier environment could place upon it, as well as the bitterly
violent Civil War, the ravages of nature, economic depression, and corporate treachery. Despite the challenges and despite the costs, the town
survived the nineteenth century and endured to the present day.

Because of its relative longevity and early social and commercial
importance, Fort Meade and its residents played key roles in Florida's
history during the middle and late nineteenth century. The fort and
its experience also helped to mold the military careers of numerous
individuals who came to prominence during the Civil War, including
George G. Meade, Ambrose Powell Hill, Thomas J. "Stonewall" Jackson, William H. French, William F. Barry, and Thomas Williams. The
early village, in turn, became the center for southwest Florida's cattle
industry, a fact that caused its destruction by locally recruited Union
forces in 1864 and its subsequent prosperity. Through its streets during
the postwar era passed many of the settlers who pioneered the Peace,
Kissimmee, and Caloosahatchee river valleys and adjacent areas.

Later in the century the Fort Meade community hosted numerous
families of southern and midwestern farmers looking for new opportunity on one of the nation's few remaining frontiers. Eventually they
were joined by many of the blacks who built and operated south Florida's railroads and phosphate mines and by English colonists who
sought to recreate their British lifestyles on the remote southern edge
of United States settlement. The diversity led to situations and events

that defy stereotypes associated with the period. At Fort Meade and Homeland, for example, armed whites defended the rights of local blacks to vote and to expect protection of the laws; Union and Confederate veterans jointly celebrated the Fourth of July; Protestant citizens rewarded Jewish social and commercial leadership; and Cracker cowhunters enjoyed cricket matches, foxhunts, lawn tennis, and jockey club races.

Given its geographical location, the circumstances of its founding and growth, and the complexity of its experience, Fort Meade's story is unique. Nonetheless, an examination of its early history offers a contribution to our understanding of frontier communities and their significance. That subject has concerned historians since Frederick Jackson Turner in 1893 expressed his theories on the importance of the frontier to the development of American character and democracy.[1] It particularly came to the fore after 1954, however, when Stanley Elkins and Eric McKitrick presented the first theoretical model by which the impact of communities on frontier life and the rise of democratic political institutions might be measured.[2]

In the four decades since Elkins and McKitrick published their model, studies of frontier communities have flourished. For the most part, though, they have concentrated on towns and cities in the Old Northwest, the Southwest, and the West. Second, they have focused primarily upon settlements that not only endured but grew into cities.[3] The southern frontier in Florida, and towns that were important while the frontier persisted but that declined or else failed to grow substantially once it had passed, were neglected. Yet such towns likely represented the majority of frontier communities.

Fort Meade's early history contributes to filling this scholarly void. While its story may not have been typical of frontier towns in other areas, events occurring and factors important there offer fresh perspectives by standing in contrast. Among other things its experience illustrates how very complex, interwoven, and interdependent were the forces that affected the birth, growth, and decline of one frontier town, including geography, government policies, war, isolation, weather, disease, the subtleties of immigration and emigration, interracial friction and cooperation, human emotions, personal ambitions, corporate greed, land availability, animosities stemming from conflicting lifestyles and backgrounds, and rivalries between communities. It also emphasizes that the development of an overriding sense of community and its concomitant, mutual interdependence, were often essential to survival on the frontier; that the uncertainties of frontier life could persist for decades in a town and continually call that survival into question; and that this sense of community and interdependence could—and often had to—overcome day-to-day conflict and even greater challenges.

Naturally, any sense of a frontier town's experience requires a broader context, which I have attempted to provide in Fort Meade's case with *Florida's Peace River Frontier*. That book offers a framework and background materials for understanding regional history in the nineteenth century, and I encourage readers to refer to it.

While I believe that Fort Meade's history deserves careful attention on its own merits, I must confess prejudice. Fort Meade is my hometown, and in many ways, I still consider it my home. My great-great-grandfather John Richard Brown patrolled its riverbank in 1849. Another great-great-grandfather, Sherod E. Roberts, arrived in 1869, while great-grandfather Arthur B. Canter settled there in 1885. My roots are deep there, and they have been a source of strength throughout my life.

As much as possible, I have attempted to present this history in the words of persons who lived it. In this regard, I have several regrets. First, I would have liked to explore much further the experience of Indians who lived at the town of Talakchopco, which lay at the site of Fort Meade prior to 1836. The history of that settlement and its destruction, as far as I have been able to piece it together, is presented in *Florida's Peace River Frontier*, and I felt that its repetition would serve no valid purpose. Readers should keep in mind, though, that the Indians' former presence continued to be evident throughout the nineteenth century. Through the 1850s, if not longer, the ruins of the vicinity's several towns and villages were plainly visible, and in later years artifacts were often unearthed.

I truly regret that I have not been able to represent the lives and experiences of blacks and of women more fully. Unfortunately, primary source materials are extremely limited or else unavailable. Almost everything that I have found is included in this book, in *Florida's Peace*

River Frontier, or in both. I sincerely hope that these publications will prompt individuals and families who possess letters, diaries, and journals to realize their importance and to share them with the community.

I am able to present this story at all thanks to the work of many individuals. Particularly important were accounts left by pioneer settlers including Francis A. Hendry, George W. Hendry, Francis C. M. Boggess, Edward J. Hilliard, Pearl Thompson, Ernest B. Simmons, and Ben Johnson. The work of local historians Walter Crutchfield, Robert M. White, Spessard Stone, Kyle S. VanLandingham, and Louise K. Frisbie also deserves special recognition. I am indebted to the individuals mentioned in the preface to *Florida's Peace River Frontier* and also deeply appreciative for the personal assistance and contributions of John E. Brown, Katharine E. Brown, Vernice Williams, Margaret Durrance, Sallie Robinson, Winnifred T. Brown, Leland M. Hawes, and Peter A. Krafft.

Mention should be made of a number of technical matters. Documentation of material in footnotes is the same as that for the text unless otherwise indicated. Incorrect spellings and usage within direct quotations appear as they do in the original; I have avoided using "[*sic*]." Finally, responsibility for the interpretation of events and for errors of fact is mine alone.

Fort Meade, 1849–1900

Captain George Gordon Meade, USA, c. 1859.
(Courtesy of the U.S. Military History Institute)

1

"It was one vast wilderness"

Lieutenant Meade's Reward

THE MORNING of December 13, 1849, found George Gordon Meade unhappy and apprehensive. A "gaunt, thin man, with a hatchet face and a prominent aquiline nose," the thirty-four-year-old army lieutenant had spent the previous two damp, cool months slogging across south Florida swamps and prairies in an attempt to site the route of a military road intended eventually to link Florida's west coast at Tampa with the Atlantic coast at Fort Pierce.[1] That day, in particular, the burden of Meade's fatigue weighed ever more heavily as he surveyed the status of his military career. Although honored three years previously "for gallant conduct in the several conflicts at Monterey, Mexico," he still held the permanent rank of a lowly second lieutenant, a position that had been his since graduation from the United States Military Academy in 1835. To make matters worse, Meade suspected that his commanding officer, General David Emanuel Twiggs, harbored a grudge due to "some unpleasant passages" occurring between them during the Mexican War.[2]

The events that drew Meade and Twiggs together in south Florida had been sparked the previous summer when a small Indian band emerged from remote havens near Lake Okeechobee to attack a settlement on Indian River. Thereafter the party had crossed the peninsula to rob and burn the main trading station for Florida's Indians, established that spring at Peace River near modern Bowling Green. In its ashes the body of George Payne, clerk of the Indian store, was found. With it was the corpse of Payne's assistant, Dempsey Whidden, a son

---

of James W. Whidden, who headed the vicinity's only white settlement. Wounded during the attack were Dempsey's sister, Nancy, and her twenty-eight-year-old husband, William McCullough. The Whidden homestead, located six miles to the north on a creek already bearing Whidden's name, was also fired upon, and another of his sons was wounded. Within a very short time, the creek adjacent to the store had been renamed Paynes Creek, and the site itself became known as "Chokonikla," the Creek and Seminole word for "burned house."[3]

James W. Whidden should not have been living on Whidden Creek when his family was attacked. Since 1845, by order of President James K. Polk, American settlement had been prohibited within twenty miles west of the Indian nation's boundary, which lay to the east and south of Peace River. Within months prior to the attack at Chokonikla, however, Whidden had entered the vicinity, as had at least one family in the area just north of modern Bartow. Most south Florida frontier residents remained to the west, beyond Hooker's Prairie, at Alafia, Itchepuckesassa (Plant City), and Thonotosassa. Their cattle, though, ranged south to the Myakka and as far east as Peace River.[4]

The Chokonikla attack panicked frontier settlers, who believed that the episode signaled a general Indian uprising and feared for their lives. Although military authorities considered the attack an isolated incident, settler fears were whipped to a fever pitch by Tampa merchants and politicians desirous of an Indian war as well as by cattlemen anxious to acquire the vast range lands that lay to the east and south of Peace River. These individuals demanded expulsion of all Indians from south Florida or, barring that, their extermination. Cooler heads ultimately prevailed. By mid-October 1849, President Zachary Taylor, at the urging of Twiggs and Indian agent John C. Casey, decided that, if the Indians complied with their promises to surrender the murderers, removal would not be forced upon them.

To separate frontiersmen and those Indians who chose not to emigrate, Twiggs proposed the construction of a line of military posts from the head of navigation on the Manatee River to the Atlantic coast. Linked by a reliable, well-designed road capable of supporting heavy artillery wagons during all seasons of the year, these posts would protect inhabitants on both sides of the Indian boundary. By mid-December 1849, Lieutenant Meade had been working on this road for the previous two months. The project had created a problem for Meade, however, and the lieutenant in turn had been forced to lay the problem in Twiggs's lap.

Meade's dilemma involved telling Twiggs that the general had made a mistake. Tampa merchant John Darling, an owner of the Peace River trading store, was also one of the prime supporters of an Indian war. Darling had chosen the site for the store and now was adamant that the new line of posts should be anchored there. To placate the influential merchant, Twiggs in mid-October had ordered the construction of Fort Chokonikla. The action apparently was conditioned upon Darling's assurance that the site lay well north of the Indian boundary.[5]

The problem was, as Meade had discovered, that Darling's designated boundary line, the Big Charlie Apopka Creek, was not the Indian nation's true northern limit. The lieutenant's examination had disclosed, to the contrary, that the line ran up Bowlegs Creek on the river's eastern side just north of the mouth of Whidden Creek. As if that news were not bad enough, Meade also had concluded that the route Twiggs had selected for the road, a course running from the Manatee River to Chokonikla, was poorly suited to military purposes. If Meade's findings were correct, the road would have to be shifted at least ten miles north of its originally intended route, and the post at Chokonikla—so recently and laboriously constructed—would have to be abandoned.[6]

Not anxious to suffer Twiggs's temper, Meade held one card that he could play to soften the general's adverse reaction. The lieutenant believed that he had found a much better site for the new road and for a fort to protect its crossing of Peace River. Accordingly he informed Twiggs of his conclusions and, on that morning of December 13, 1849, was preparing to depart from Chokonikla with the general and his aides to present the new site. Meade's career seemingly tottered in the balance.

The reconnaissance party departed Fort Chokonikla at 6:00 A.M. Twiggs, Casey, Meade, Lieutenant Darius Couch, and others directed their horses to the north, along a route surveyed by Meade just two weeks previously. Three and one-half hours later they arrived at a swamp and hammock that, in the future, would be called Kendrick Branch. Located three miles above Whidden Creek on the river's west side, the branch formed a crescent running south to east. Enclosing an area approximately one-half mile square dotted with pine and oak trees, the location promised shade from summer sun and protection from winter winds.[7]

The Kendrick Branch area offered other advantages as well. Nearby a grove of sour orange trees thrived, indicating soil fertility. Stretching for several miles to the north were the ruins and abandoned fields of Talakchopco, a Seminole and Creek town destroyed in April 1836 during the Second Seminole War's opening months. The riverbanks immediately above the branch were high and firm and overlooked an ancient Indian ford that had given generations of Creeks and Seminoles access to south Florida hunting grounds. The river coursed by with a stream only forty to fifty yards in width. Across its usually placid waters, the opposing or eastern bank opened, after a short passage through river hammocks, into high, open land almost denuded of living trees. This area, which ran roughly northeast to southwest with a width of seven to eight miles and a length considerably greater, was called "the Deadening."[8]

As Twiggs examined Meade's chosen site, his desire to placate Darling and his natural reluctance to undo the construction work of two months was overcome by delight at the beautiful location and its superiority to Chokonikla. So pleased was he that Twiggs turned to a surprised and relieved Meade and, in the words of Meade's son, "[confirmed] Lieutenant Meade's selection, and as a recognition of his judgement in the special case, and of his general good service and conduct, he caused the post to be named Fort Meade."[9] The party quickly returned to Chokonikla, and within hours, Meade transmitted to his commanding officer a personally drawn map of the region that stretched from Lake Hancock on the north to below Chokonikla on the south and extended eastward to the Kissimmee River. On the chart, signed "Geo. G. Meade, Lt. Topogl. Engineers, Chokko-nikla, Decr. 13th 1849," Meade carefully delineated the new route of a military road leading to the east. As its anchor on Peace River, the lieutenant boldly inked in the location of the new post, and for the first time, the name "Fort Meade" was committed to writing.[10]

4

Brigadier General David Emanuel Twiggs, USA, 1849. (From Charles J. Peterson, The Military Heroes of the War With Mexico, *1849)*

The First Fort

Four days after Twiggs's designation of Fort Meade as a military post, Lieutenant Henry Bainbridge, with two companies of the Seventh Infantry, was ordered to begin construction of the new fort and to garrison it. Arriving on December 19, Bainbridge was greeted with orders to "cut down the banks and make a good crossing for wagons over Peas Creek as soon as possible" and "with all dispatch to put up light frame houses and cover them in with clapboards, for the stores which will be collected at that place."[11] In addition he was instructed to employ available troops "in opening the road some four miles, by the trail from Peas Creek to Hatche-thlocco [Bowlegs Creek]."[12] Falling to the effort Bainbridge's men constructed Fort Meade on a bluff overlooking the Peace River ford and within the crescent of Kendrick's Branch. Within four days additional elements of the Seventh Infantry, as well as companies of the First, Third, and Fourth Artillery presented themselves. At month's end the post boasted a complement of twenty-two officers and 397 men.[13]

The decade of the 1850s opened with feverish activity at Fort Meade, aimed primarily at completion of the military road from Tampa to the Atlantic coast. Eastward along that route passed Fort Meade garrison

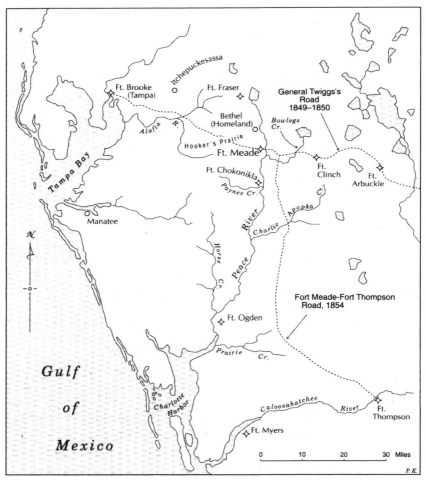

Tampa Bay and Peace River Areas, c. 1850s

troops ordered to establish additional posts between the Peace and Kissimmee rivers. Sited by Meade and built by soldiers under Lieutenant Ambrose Powell Hill's command, the new forts were named Clinch and Arbuckle. As efforts were continued to induce voluntary emigration by the remaining natives, Indian delegations from west of the Mississippi also passed through the post. In turn, parties of natives resigned to a departure from their Florida homes gathered at the new Peace River camp to await transportation west.

The Indian scare of 1849 and its attendant excitement waned in 1850. In short order most of Twiggs's new military posts were closed. Fort Arbuckle, for instance, fell victim to the trend on May 15, 1850, and Fort Clinch followed on June 8. When Chokonikla was abandoned on July 18, Fort Meade remained the only garrisoned post in interior south Florida east of the Manatee River.[14]

Fort Meade during that summer of 1850 was not a fort in the traditional sense of a blockhouse or palisaded enclosure. Rather, it contained a collection of wooden buildings clinging for the most part to Peace River's western bank astride the Tampa–Fort Pierce military road. On Kendrick Branch to the south the post's beef contractor had constructed a house and pens. Stables had been placed between the branch and river, and storehouses had been erected just to their north but south of the military road. Enlisted men's quarters were positioned above the road, and further north was located at least one cabin for an officer's family. A ferry operated at the ford near today's Peace River bridge, and a few hundred yards westward along the road, "officers sheds" could be found.[15]

A hospital, located 200 or 300 yards west of the officers' sheds, stood out as one of the post's most important facilities. It consisted of "one large room for the sick of all diseases," but however humble the hospital may have been, it proved to be sorely needed. Because of proximity to mosquito breeding grounds in the swamps and hammocks of the river and of Kendrick Branch, the garrison was struck by malaria and "intermittent fevers." During July, August, and September 1850 almost one-third of the outpost's 185 to 200 men fell sick. At least two privates died. Because of health conditions, most of the garrison soon was transferred to recently commissioned Fort Myers ninety miles south on the Caloosahatchee River. By November, Fort Meade held only 42 men and 2 officers. The post still suffered from the sickness of 13 men.[16]

As health problems persisted in the closing months of 1850, it was apparent to all concerned that something had to be done about Fort Meade. On December 21 the post commander, Major William H. French, requested permission to move all quarters to a ridge about one mile west of the river. The site was higher than any other land for miles to the west and was surrounded on all sides by gentle slopes. The recommendation claimed General Thomas Childs's immediate attention. "You will immediately erect quarters at the point indicated, for officers and men," he ordered French on December 23. "In the position of the new quarters, you will have regard to symmetry and defence, when further additions are made, such as the removal to the new site of commissary, quartermaster and sutler's stores."[17] As will be seen, French quickly undertook the transfer. Under the supervision of Major Thomas J. Jackson, later called "Stonewall," the old buildings were dismantled and reerected upon the new site. The original Fort Meade had enjoyed a lifespan of only a little more than one year.

Before we leave the original Fort Meade, we should note that sickness was not the only danger at hand in the area. The weather could, on occasion, pose just as great a threat. An August 1850 letter from future Confederate general A. P. Hill well illustrates that fact. Hill, who thought Fort Meade "a very pretty post," wrote: "The lightning came near extinguishing my youthful aspirations yesterday. Coming from Fort Meade a violent storm passed over, such a one as you read of in books but never see except in these tropical latitudes, in which the trees are seen skylarking in the air. Jupiter Tonans hurled a bolt at my head, but being too quick for him I dodged it and a tree by my side was mangled shockingly 'I was not kilt, but spacheless.' My eyes haven't stopped blinking yet—Oh for an iced Julep!"[18]

Stonewall Jackson

A. P. Hill was not the only future Confederate general who ran into problems at Fort Meade, and the fort's relocation in late 1850 and early 1851 provided the context within which the most famous such officer was compelled to retire from the United States Army. The story began on December 18, 1850, when thirty-five-year-old William H. French and twenty-seven-year-old Thomas J. Jackson arrived together at the frontier station. The two men had been friends and fellow officers during the Mexican War. Both carried the rank of brevet major derived from gallant action in Mexico, and both had ambitions for successful military careers. When French assumed the post command, Jackson was designated commissary and quartermaster officer.[19]

Life at Fort Meade during French's and Jackson's stay was ex-

Brevet Major Thomas Jonathan (later "Stonewall") Jackson, USA, 1851.
(Courtesy of the University of Virginia Library)

tremely difficult for the roughly fifty officers and men serving at the post. The position was an isolated one. No civilian settlers lived within ten miles, and the boredom and routine of garrison duty were relieved only by occasional scouts to the lake country of the Kissimmee River valley. Basically restricted to the fort's immediate vicinity, the camp's occupants suffered through winter's damp cold and summer's sweltering heat. Only officers' families could live at the fort. French was married and had his family with him. Jackson was single.

At first French and Jackson maintained a good—even friendly— relationship. Within a few months, however, each man began to bristle at supposed slights on the part of the other. Tensions mounted until they exploded in March 1851 over the question of which of the two officers had authority over construction of the second fort's buildings. Most persons might presume that the commander of an isolated frontier outpost would have ultimate authority over all normal activities at his station, but Jackson argued for an extremely literal interpretation of army regulations and demanded complete control over construction. As the two men attempted to work around one another, the situation deteriorated into open hostility. Jackson, who had fallen ill at about the time the controversy arose, and who was already entertaining thoughts of leaving the army for a teaching position at the Virginia Military Institute, displayed a clearly insubordinate attitude toward French.

The conflict between Fort Meade's two top officers burst into plain view in the spring of 1851. On March 23 Jackson appealed the issue of his authority to Florida army headquarters and, within a week, received his reply. Overruling Jackson's interpretation of regulations and reprimanding the young officer, the commanding general bluntly informed him, "A difference of opinion amongst officers, may honestly occur, on points of duty.—It ought never to degenerate into personalities, or to be considered a just cause for withholding the common courtesies of life so essential in an Officer & to the happiness & quiet of garrison life."[20]

Unable or unwilling to learn the lesson of his reprimand, Jackson quickly intensified the personal aspects of his quarrel with French. Vague rumors had come to Jackson's attention suggesting that French and a nurse in the employ of the major's family had been involved in an improper relationship. Asserting that his conscience compelled him to prove the truth of the rumors, Jackson on April 12 began interviewing enlisted men who supposedly had witnessed the indiscretions. The men proved unwilling to provide Jackson with fuel for his suspicions. Instead they got word of the interviews to French, and the post commander had Jackson arrested for "Conduct Unbecoming an Officer and a Gentleman." Jackson then filed the same charges against French and demanded an official court of inquiry.[21]

At this point in the drama, French and Jackson seemingly lost all sense of objectivity, although Jackson's actions may be explained in part by the mid-April receipt of his acceptance as a "Professor of Natural and Experimental Philosophy and Artillery Tactics" at Virginia Military Institute (VMI).[22] Both men filed petty allegations and countercharges to the extent that General Twiggs, by then serving as departmental military commander, rejected all charges and ordered both men to forget the whole thing. Jackson, who had accepted his appointment to VMI on April 22, was released from arrest on May 15 and departed six days later. He never again served on active duty in the United States Army. French was not so easily handled. Feeling his honor had been impugned, he appealed the matter without success all the way to the secretary of war. In October 1851, his own patience with the affair exhausted, Twiggs relieved French of his command, and the major departed Fort Meade for a subordinate position elsewhere.[23]

The New Fort

Despite the turmoil surrounding the French-Jackson feud, a new Fort Meade slowly rose on its ridge one mile west of Peace River. By December 1851, even with a reduced garrison of only thirty-two men and four officers, the frontier station contained a number of substantial buildings as well as an assortment of minor facilities and outbuildings. Post commander Samuel K. Dawson described them for his superior:

> The officers Quarters consist of three separate buildings—all framed, one covered, on the sides, with clap boards—one covered on one side, with board, on the other sides with shingles—and one covered entirely

with shingles. The first building is 46 feet long, by 20 feet wide contains two rooms, with a passage between them 8 feet wide, one room is lined with shingles, and ceiled partly with puncheons and partly with canvass—has a fire-place, with a mud chimney—the other room is neither lined or ceiled—the floors are of a very inferior kind—being made of pine board (neither planed or grooved) laid down while green and as they become seasoned, enlarge the Chinks between them. The second building is 40 feet long by 20 feet wide, contains two rooms, with a passage between them, 8 feet wide—the rooms are neither lined or ceiled—the floors of these quarters appear to have been made of boards, that were seasoned, but they are neither planed or grooved—

The third building is 34 feet long by 14 feet wide, contains two rooms, with an open passage between them, 7 feet wide—the rooms are not ceiled, but lined at one end—the floors are like those of the second building—each of these buildings have a rough porch in front, and rear of them—six feet wide and a small building a short distance in rear, which can be used—for Kitchens—one a log building, 26 feet long by 15 feet wide—the other 12 feet by 10 wide. These buildings may be called indifferent quarters—for the want of lining and ceiling—they do not afford a very good protection against the heat or the cold—Their principal recommendation is they are very Cheap.

The Barracks for the soldiers is a log building 180 feet long, by 21 feet wide—good quarters, except when the northers prevail—when the soldiers suffer very much from the cold. The commissary store is a log building 38 feet long, by 30 feet wide and protects the stores very well in dry weather.

The Clothing Store is a log building, 20 feet long by 14 feet wide—The Guard house is a log building 45 1/2 feet long by 9 1/2 feet wide—The Cook house is a log building, 16 feet long, by 13 feet wide—has just been built—There is a shed near the Barracks, 40 feet long by 20 feet wide, which serves as a mess room for the soldiers—two shingle houses one 27 feet by 14 feet, and the other 15 feet long, by 10 feet wide, complete the number of buildings at the Post—these shingle houses are occupied, one by a Sergeant, the other by a soldier and his family—

There is a small bakehouse and bake oven—and a shed—for the horses & mules—[and] about a half mile from the post is the Hospital, a large frame building, 50 feet long by 25 feet wide, with a Piazza on four sides, 12 feet wide—this is an excellent building and the best at the Post, but like all the others, cold when Northers prevail, and there is no means of warming it.[24]

Captain Dawson's repeated references to "Northers" and "the cold" proved accurate within a matter of days after he put them to paper. "[The] winter of 1851–'52 was an exceedingly cold one for the latitude; the formation of ice being no uncommon occurrence," reported Assistant Surgeon Jonathan Letherman the following fall. "Officers and men suffered much from the cold," he continued, "the quarters being entirely inadequate for their protection. The buildings are very inferior; those of the men are no more than sheds, which afford but little protection from the rain or cold. Being placed upon posts several feet high, and situated upon the highest ground in the vicinity, and no trees of any size near, they are necessarily much exposed to the winds, which frequently, during the winter, blow strong and cold."[25]

Throughout 1852 increased demands upon the fort's facilities due to Indian alarms and a garrison that more than tripled by May—coupled with renewed dissention between the fort's commander, officers, and men—resulted in a marked deterioration of the post. When Colonel Harvey Brown assumed command in October, he was shocked by its condition. "The Post," he reported, "is very far from being what in my opinion it should be, whether its defense & security or the health and comfort of the men be considered." Taking the initiative Brown advised headquarters, "I propose, at once, to employ the command in putting the barracks in a more comfortable condition."[26]

Harvey Brown commanded Fort Meade, with one short interruption, from October 16, 1852, to May 30, 1853. During that period it reached its peak as a military installation. "The Garrison was neat and clean as a new pin," remembered one early resident, "and the very best of military order was fastidiously maintained."[27] Another particularly recalled the evening dress parades. "Drum and fife with glistening bayonets, all in full uniform, afforded an interesting sight to me," he recalled, "one worth looking at."[28]

A further sense of the fort's military pageantry and order is suggested by the "beats and calls" known to have been observed within the compound. On a typical day they included:

"Reveille"	Dawn of Day
"Fatigue Call"	20m after reveille
"Peas upon trencher"	7½h A.M.

Log building constructed in the early 1850s, originally used as officers' quarters at the second Fort Meade. (Courtesy of the Florida State Archives)

"Surgeons Call"	8 ——
"Guard Mtg"	9 ——
"1st Sgts. Call"	12 m
"Dinner d°"	12½ PM
"Fatigue Call"	2 h PM
"First Retreat Call"	10ᵐ before Sunset
"Tattoo"	8½ P.M.[29]

The post, as it evolved from the efforts of William H. French and Thomas J. Jackson and the refinements of Harvey Brown, was based upon the principle of a quadrangle. The buildings were centered upon a square or parade ground of "five or six" acres within the area now bounded on the east and west by Orange and Cleveland avenues and on the north and south by Third and First streets northeast. The post's main facilities formed a square around and faced toward the parade ground. "Officers quarters," according to a visitor, "were on the south [side of the quadrangle,] with commissary, stables, etc., on part of the east [and] with common log buildings scattered on the north and west. There was no picket enclosure or other special defense."[30]

The compound included structures designed for varied purposes. "A large commissary store was kept within the Garrison, in which was stored and regularly issued all manner of military stores and supplies," one man recollected. "A settlers [sutler's] store was kept there by permission, and under the regulations of the Commandant, from which all ordinary goods common to the mercantile line could be purchased. There was a wagon yard, a wagon master, mules, horses and wagons galore." The post's water supply was the spring that fed Kendrick Branch, located southeast of the fort. "The water supply for the Garrison," the man added, "was conveyed by a large mule and tank cart operated by Jack, a big awkward German. Every day that cart made the rounds through the camp, turning the hose into the water tanks conveniently arranged to receive it."[31]

The First Permanent Settlers

An early fall 1852 Fort Meade report could still note, "There are no inhabitants in the immediate vicinity of this post." A suggestion that this was not the whole truth, though, was carried in the report's very next sentence. "Those that live in the interior," commented the observer, who was clearly unused to the general appearance of frontier settlers, "are afflicted with intermittent and remittent fevers as the chief diseases." He continued, " 'Dirt eaters' are said to be not uncommon. I have seen no one in the act of gratifying this morbid propensity; yet the sallow countenance, the tumid abdomen, and the impression vividly conveyed of premature senility, suggest at once malaria and clay. The common remedy is said to be whisky or cider in which nails have been steeped."[32]

Who were the settlers about whom so much medical concern was expressed? Frontier families had just begun entering the Peace River valley's upper reaches at the time of the 1849 Indian scare. One or perhaps several homesteads lay north of modern Bartow, and James W. Whidden's family had moved to a location on Whidden Creek some miles below Fort Meade. As the 1849 tensions subsided, the Bartow-area residents returned to their homes, but the Whiddens remained near their relations at Alafia.

Although the exact timing is uncertain, in the months prior to October 1851 a train of oxen-drawn wagons coursed the sand tracks of interior south Florida from what became Sumter County to the vicinity of present-day Homeland. The arrival of those carts marked the real beginnings of civilian settlement in the Fort Meade area. The new residents were the families of the brothers Durrance, Francis M. and John Rufus. With Francis M. Durrance also came three black slaves whose names are unknown. Two of these black pioneers were men aged about forty and fifteen, and the third was a woman of about sixteen. The Durrance homesteads lay some four to six miles northwest of the second fort. The families were in the cattle business.[33]

For a year the Durrances remained the lone civilians in the area. Then in October 1852 a disastrous hurricane struck Tampa and the countryside to the west of Peace River. In the storm's aftermath nineteen-year-old Francis Asbury Hendry, known as "Berry," pulled up roots from his mother's homestead at Alafia and set out with his seventeen-year-old bride of only a few months, Ardeline Ross Lanier, to a new home. "I first lived within the Garrison of Fort Meade . . . ," Hendry recalled. "The officers and men were very kind to me, and socially it was very pleasant to live among them. Some of the officers and soldiers had their wives and children with them, and made it very pleasant for my wife, who was then in her teens."[34] At Fort Meade, Hendry butchered beef for the garrison and, more important, moved his cattle and those of his father-in-law, Louis Lanier, to ranges east of the river. Soon he and Ardelia settled on "a pretty little stream" two miles northwest of the fort, and thereafter the stream was known as Berry Hendry Branch. Fifty years and many moves later Hendry would still say, "That place today is precious and sacred in my memory."[35]

The pace of settlement remained slow in the year after the Hendrys' arrival, but others slowly came upon the scene. By March 1853 twenty-seven-year-old James Lawrence Whidden, son of James W. Whidden, and his bride Amelia Hall, had built a house two miles west of the fort. Almost immediately Whidden fell afoul of the post's commander by selling whiskey to the garrison's men—a trade the military was unable to disrupt. Five months later Louis Lanier, whose Alafia home had been a main resting point on the Tampa–Fort Meade road and who held a contract to supply beef at Fort Myers and Fort Meade, built a

Representative of rural homesteads near Fort Meade, this photo portrays the Bennett Whidden family at "Old Whidden Homestead" west of Fort Meade, c. 1890. Bennett Whidden was the son of James W. Whidden and brother of James L. Whidden. (Courtesy of the Florida State Archives)

dwelling to the fort's east on the original hospital site. Considering Lanier's settlement an intrusion, post commander William F. Barry attempted to remove him. To Barry's frustration his superior officers declined to permit the expulsion short of an "order of the Secretary of War to the U.S. Marshal." Such an order was not forthcoming.[36]

With Louis Lanier's family came the only other settler known to have arrived in 1853, Berry Hendry's fourteen-year-old brother, George Washington Hendry. As an old man Hendry reminisced about how this new world appeared to its early settlers.

It was one vast wilderness with no human being to occupy or see its beauties and grandeur, as the Seminoles occupied the more central portions of the peninsula—the Arbuckle and Kissimmee sections. Hence, game was unmolested and the whole face of the earth was alive with deer, turkeys, bear, wolves, and other wild beasts; a few panthers, catamounts and other smaller animals, with the lakes, streams and all bodies of water teeming with fish of many species, mostly bass, drum and channel catfish. Wild honey in great abundance, and the elements alive with fowls, whooping cranes, heron, egrets, ganites, pink curlews, limpkins, ducks and thousands of other varieties that would fill a page to enumerate. The range was in its pristine glory, no herds of cattle having grazed upon it.[37]

Fort Meade was founded in December 1849 because of its strategic location on firm, high ground overlooking one of the best Peace River fords. During its first four years of existence, the fort developed into a substantial military installation representing the army's presence in interior south Florida. Just as the military had been drawn to Fort Meade by its strategic location, by the early 1850s cattlemen and their families had begun settling, lured by the magnet of immense cattle ranges in their "pristine glory." Before that dream could be fully realized, however, a bloody Indian war would come to Fort Meade, and out of its suffering and loss would be born the first town in interior south Florida.

2

"We're in a village of sorts"

A Town Is Born

FORT MEADE SERVED from 1849 to 1854, in great part, to keep white frontiersmen and Florida Indians apart. While the attempt more often than not succeeded, pressures continued to mount among settlers residing between Peace River and Tampa Bay for the expulsion of all Indians from south Florida. When efforts to achieve voluntary emigration collapsed in late 1853 and early 1854, the United States government adopted an aggressive policy aimed at pressuring the natives to leave the state. Central to this new policy was the opening for settlement of lands along Peace River as far south as modern Hardee County. Government teams were ordered into these areas with instructions to push land surveys deep into the Indian nation. Army troops were assigned to protect the work crews.[1]

The government's new policy more than doubled the size of Fort Meade's garrison. For the several months prior to April 1854, the post's roster stood roughly at 60 men and 7 or 8 officers. For the next seven months the number of enlisted men never stood at fewer than 118. Patrols constantly were on the move to reopen roads, rebuild bridges, examine new routes, and protect survey crews. The fort became so active that in May its commander, Major Lewis G. Arnold, requested that a military reserve two miles square or larger be created. The reserve was to center on the flagstaff at the post's parade ground, and the action, among other things, would have caused the expulsion of the Francis A. Hendry and Louis Lanier families from their homes. Secretary of War Jefferson Davis approved the plan and requested that the secretary of the interior reserve the area from sale when "the public lands in the vicinity of Fort Meade, Fla. shall have been surveyed."[2] Before the lands had been surveyed, however, the situation changed dramatically.

During the summer of 1854, government officials decided to further their plans for pressuring the Indians by establishing a military outpost near their home villages. Fort Meade garrison officers, particularly Lieutenants Henry Benson and George L. Hartsuff, with the assistance of Francis A. Hendry and Louis Lanier as guides, scoured south Florida for an appropriate site. Eventually Fort Thompson, a Second Seminole War post on the Caloosahatchee River's headwaters, was rebuilt. With only a limited number of troops available in the area, the army relocated Fort Meade's garrison to the new post.[3]

Beginning in late November and extending into December 1854, soldiers and government properties slowly were transferred from Peace River to Fort Thompson. Fort Meade's buildings were sold to another of Louis Lanier's sons-in-law, thirty-two-year-old cattleman John I.

John Irving Hooker, 1822–1862.
(Courtesy of the Hillsborough County Historical Museum and Library)

Hooker, who held a contract to supply beef to Fort Myers. For $200 Hooker received possession of all post facilities, and on December 1, 1854, he took up residence with his twenty-one-year-old wife, Cuthbert Wayne Lanier, in "a splendid double-penned log house" that had been used as officers' quarters.[4] Moving into the abandoned fort also were five black slaves of the Hooker family, including a woman, Charlotte, and two men, Augustus and Henry.[5]

An Onrush of Settlers

Fort Meade's December 1854 abandonment, together with ongoing government land surveys, opened the door for numerous new settlements within the vicinity. Since completion of the survey was a prereq-

Typical frontier "double-pen" log cabin of the John Wiley Hill family near modern Homeland. (From DeVane's Early Florida History, *vol. 1, 1978)*

uisite for posting a valid private claim to public land, those who wanted to stake out the best of the newly opened lands, if they were not already present and "squatting" on the land, followed closely in the surveyor's wake.

Florida survey techniques divide the state into "townships," an area six miles square. Each township is identified by its distance north or south of the state's "prime meridian" near the state capitol at Tallahassee. Township 30 South, for example, lies 180 miles south of an east-west line drawn through the prime meridian, a distance derived by multiplying the number of the township (30) by its length (six miles). Similarly, the township is identified by its "range," which is its distance east or west of the prime meridian, determined by multiplying the number of the range by the width of the township (six miles). Each township, in turn, is divided into thirty-six "sections," each approximately one mile square.

Fort Meade and Homeland lie in Township 31 South, Range 25 East. While the township's exterior boundaries were marked in August 1854, it was not sectioned until May 1855. The original survey plat, which was finalized the following August, indicates the location of homesteads existing at the time of the survey. A similar plat for the township just to the south (Township 32 South, Range 25 East) does the same, but the plat of the township immediately to the north (Township 30 South, Range 25 East) does not illustrate settlements. Fortunately, a military map published in April 1856 sheds light on settlements just to the north of Homeland and also on homesteads established in the entire area between August and December 1855. From these sources, the location and arrival of new settlers may be traced. As mentioned, most of the newcomers arrived within a month or two after completion of the survey.[6]

In the Homeland area in 1855 were the families of Alderman Carlton; Joseph Lemuel, Francis M., Jesse H., Joseph L., John R., and William H. Durrance; William Parker; Eli English; and John C. Oats. North of Homeland resided Thomas Ellis and George T. Durrance, while to the east of Peace River was the settlement of John L. Skipper (also known by the name John L. Pearce). One of the Durrance families lived just to the south of Skipper, and perhaps two miles below them, on what became known as Poole Branch, were the homesteads of John Green and Joseph Underhill.

Some farms and homesteads were located below and to the west of Fort Meade. A little less than three miles south-southwest of the fort was William McCullough's settlement, sited on a Whidden Creek tributary that was known thereafter as McCullough Creek. A short walk southeast of McCullough's led to David Russell's home. By December 1855 the family of Willoughby Tillis, a brother-in-law of the Durrances, was building a house in the same area. About four and one-half miles south of the fort, on the eastern side of Peace River, lived the family of William P. Brooker. North of McCullough's on McCullough Creek was the Francis C. M. Boggess homestead, and three-quarters of a mile further along the stream, the well-established James L. Whidden settlement lying two and one-quarter miles due east of the fort. Between Whidden's and the fort was the Julius C. Rockner home. The locations of the residences of Francis A. Hendry, John I. Hooker, and Louis Lanier have been mentioned previously.

The new settlements served as a catalyst for the development of the fundamental institutions so necessary to the beginning of civilized life on a frontier. In January 1855, for example, the Hillsborough county commission (modern Polk County was a part of Hillsborough until 1861) ordered the establishment of a school "at Fort Meade School House." Alderman Carlton, Francis M. Durrance, and James L. Whidden were appointed trustees, and thirty-six dollars were dedicated to its purposes. At year's end, the commission continued the school, and Carlton, John C. Oats, and John I. Hooker held the position of trustee.[7] The first school sessions were probably held in an empty fort building. An old tradition suggests that in the early days classes met in good weather in the shade of the huge oak tree in front of the home at 613 Northeast Sixth Street. The tree lies in close proximity to the fort, and a post outbuilding may have stood on the property. Frank Boggess likely was the first teacher.[8]

Hand in hand with schools came elections and politics. Fort Meade in 1855 was declared a voting precinct, and a poll return for December lists Francis M. Durrance, Joseph Durrance, John I. Hooker, Francis A. Hendry, and Francis C. M. Boggess as the earliest voters. Two months previously the area had already exercised political clout by the election of Democrat Francis M. Durrance to the county commission. At about the same time the basics of law enforcement were also established by the creation of a justice of the peace district. Francis M. Durrance and John C. Oats first held that office.[9]

The Billy Bowlegs War

The powder keg that had been primed by repeated military penetrations of Indian havens in and near the Everglades exploded upon the south Florida frontier on December 20, 1855. A Seminole band led by Billy Bowlegs attacked a survey crew under Lieutenant Hartsuff's command. Four men were killed and four, including the lieutenant, wounded. Word of the attack arrived at Fort Meade on Christmas Day and struck pioneer settlers, in Francis A. Hendry's words, "[like] a veritable clap of thunder from a clear sky." Hendry remembered, "The people were excited and quickly congregated for self-protection."[10]

The fort's buildings offered frontier settlers an ideal haven, and John I. Hooker immediately made them available. "Mr. Hooker, with his great, large, generous heart, opened the doors of the Government buildings, most of which being still habitable, and invited the whole community to come and take shelter," Hendry recalled. "Fort Meade at once assumed the attitude of a military camp, with hundreds of frightened women and children as guests, and soon became the central point of extensive movements against Billy Bowlegs and his wily braves."[11]

Area residents responded to the war news by preparing for their defense. Within four days Francis M. Durrance had organized a volunteer company of almost 100 frontiersmen, and the men had taken station at the fort. A "strong long block-house" was erected, and, as recollected by James Dallas Tillis, "around this building were grouped the various families in their roughly built homes where they had gathered for temporary protection." Soon other volunteer companies arrived on the frontier, and all were organized under the command of John I. Hooker's brother, cattleman William Brinton Hooker.[12]

After the initial rush of excitement, wartime life quickly settled into routine. Military patrols came and went, while refugees grappled more with the need for supplies than with an Indian menace. Simeon L. Sparkman reported of the "forted up" frontier families, "I don't know what will become of some of them if there should be a protracted war—they are generally very poor and some of them have not been living on their places long enough to make bread for their families, and must quit the country or starve without speedy relief (or at least suffer for bread, meat they have)."[13] The first months of 1856 passed particularly slowly, as Fort Meade's occupants were kept indoors and miserable due to torrential rains, which were promptly dubbed "the flood of '56."[14] Occasionally the tedium was relieved when word arrived of a clash or sudden ambush elsewhere, but the post compound seemed relatively safe, so that many settlers relaxed their vigilance and began to think of returning home. Willoughby Tillis acted upon the thought and lived to regret it.

The Battle of Peace River

Many versions of the attack of June 14, 1856, on the Tillis family and the subsequent Battle of Peace River have been published and make

Willoughby Tillis, 1808–1895.
(Courtesy of the Polk County Historical Quarterly, *June 1983)*

compelling reading. Contemporary reports were filed by William B. Hooker and Francis M. Durrance. J. D. Tillis later prepared an account of the experience that he endured as a six-year-old child, and Frank Boggess also published his recollections.[15] The accounts agree on many particulars, but each contains factual errors. Perhaps the most moving description of the events appeared in a Tampa newspaper twenty-one years later. Written as a letter by a Fort Meade man pen-named Sanko, the narrative reflects a highly romantic style and suffers from errors and critical omissions. Still, it provides an interesting and fresh perspective:

Fate of the Seminole Sub-Chief Oxian.

All brave men appreciate the manly courage and the heroic valor even of a vindicative foe, while cowardice and poltroonery is sneered and hissed at by cowards themselves. Hundreds of brave officers and soldiers have fought, bled, and died whose names together with their acts, have sunk into eternal oblivion, unrecorded in the world's history. Such is the fate of our brave sub-chief Oxian.

In 1856–57 there was a war between the whites and the Seminoles under Billy Bowlegs. There was a sub-chief named Oxian accompanied by about 18 warriors that ranged during, and even before the war, north of the Caloosahatchee river, and around the Istokpoga Lake. Frequently making raids far into the interior of the settlements to the annoyance and danger of the inhabitants. It was always impossible to get any clue as to his directions or whereabouts, or even conjecture where he might next turn up. His party was in the true sense of the word a "surprise party." Notwithstanding his shrewdness, his sagacity and his bravery, he was alike subject to misfortunes, and reverses, and as a context to his last engagement the sequence of which resulted in his final quietness and afforded a transport to his eternal hunting land, a place to which all good Indians expect to go—we pen the following detail,

One morning in June . . . Oxian and his daring banditti arose and silently arrayed themselves in the habiliments of battle. Just one mile from their camp-fire, which burned dimly in the fastness and denseness of Peace Creek swamp, resided Capt. Willoughby Tillis and family, for which place they struck up their line of march perhaps in Indian file. No doubt their hearts were buoyant with a hope of a complete surprise and a glorious victory[. J]ust as the dawn of light had spread its broad expanse all around, they had reached near the cattle pen under cover of a high fence. . . .

[A]t this juncture Mrs. Tillis with some of her little boys repaired to the cattle pen to replenish their dairy. . . . But a manifest uneasiness among the cattle which indicated the scent of something with which they were not familiar, attracted Mrs. Tillis's attention, when she spied a group of dark brown savage-like objects making ready for a volley. She being one of those strong minded old ladies who could not be scared out of her wits by trifles, took leave of speedy absence from that place, leaping high fences with the agility of an athlete and succeeded in reaching the house unhurt notwithstanding the missiles of death flew fast and thick on every side.

This was the prelude to an attack upon the dwelling which was continued perhaps two hours without resulting in any serious injury, either to its inmates or to the Indians. This place was 3¼ miles south of Ft. Meade. . . . The report of the firing was heard at the Fort and created considerable excitement among the people. Six brave men under command of Lieut. Alderman Carlton, mounted and under whip and spur sped for the scene of action. The Indians discovered their approach and in double quick time made for a swamp, and while in their confused state before they reached the swamp these brave seven volunteers rushed pellmell into the center of the group. The Indians took protection behind trees, stumps, logs, bushes and some squatted in the grass like rabbits. The work of carnage began—the contest was short and deathly.

In a few minutes Lieut. Carlton, Wm. [Parker] and Lot Whidden lay struggling in death. Daniel Carlton, John H. Hollingsworth, and John C. Oates wounded, and Wm. McCullough the only one escaping injury, had just ended a deadly grapple fisticuff with one of his deadly antagonists, his fate for weal or woe was suspended by a fibre and depended on pluck and physical manhood, but with the assistance of Daniel Carlton (though wounded) they succeeded in . . . cutting his throat from ear to ear with a pocket knife. After which [the volunteers] abandoned the bloody conflict and repaired to the house of Capt. Willoughby Tillis leaving their dead in possession of their antagonists.

The number of Indians killed was not known in this engagement, but it was evident that old Oxian still lived. A courier was immediately dispatched to Fort [Fraser] a distance of 18 miles north of Ft. Meade and a reinforcement of about 15 men under command of Lieut. Streaty Parker was immediately instituted but precautionary action was necessary as ambushing was one of the prerogatives of Indians in our war and to avoid such a disaster required prudence in a commander as well as bravery. In this instance, however, the maneuvering was so skillfully executed on the following day that the Indians instead were surprised and the doom of Oxian was forever sealed.

[Oxian] had proceeded 3 or 4 miles below the battle ground of the preceding day under cover of the swamp and penetrated to the bank of the river, crossed over to the east side leaving a portion of his men on the west—the side where he expected the attack if pursued and attacked at all. But fate ordered it otherwise. Lieut. Parker and his brave band crossed the river and made their search on the east side. In the denseness of the swamp near the bank of the river he came in contact with a sentinel of old Oxian's. No doubt at this juncture Oxian was sitting crouched over his dinner fire recounting the incidents of former engagements, his silvery locks dangling over his keen piercing eyes which flashed with a spirit of revenge evincing that determination so characteristic of the Indian race—undaunted, undiscouraged, brave, tall and erect in stature, the heretofore invincible old veteran sat surrounded by a brave band who were willing to live and die by his side.

Alas! the peace and quiet of his camp was disturbed by the vigorous clanking of U.S. yagers discharged at the sentry as he went bounding through the swamp, hurly burly, pell-mell over logs, through brush and briers. Without disorder or confusion sallied forth Lieut. Parker with his brave men into the center of their camp. The bluff was of medium height for such a river and the water shallow at the brink. The Indians roiled promiscuously and headlong down the bluff and took protection under the bank, halted and gave desperate battle. The reckless or to use a milder term, the heedless and fearless commander with his men rushed to the bluff, while just beneath and within 6 or 8 feet stood the red man ready for the combat. Smoke and bullets gushed forth in angry fury while those on the opposite bank poured volleys into their ranks.

It was not the object of the whites to merely whip, but to kill and they in like manner with cool nerve and steady aim sent the missiles of death among them with terrible fury. [The Indians] were routed from their strong-hold under the bank and notwithstanding the fearful fire to which they exposed themselves were forced to swim the river. The carnage was fearful. As the deep current of water moved slowly out in its silent grandeur the body of the brave sub-chief sank from sight in death. . . . Not Oxian alone, but the band except 3 or 4 met this same fate. The casualties of Lieut. Parker's command were Robt. Prine and George Howell killed, Wm. [Brooker], J. L. Whidden and John L. Skipper wounded. . . .

Thus passed away a brave sub-chief who was a dupe of his cowardly superiors, and a victim to his own intrepid ambition.[16]

Shortly after the Battle of Peace River, the bodies of Alderman Carlton, Lott Whidden, William Parker, Robert F. Prine, and George Howell were returned to Fort Meade and buried in a common grave. Seventy-five years after the event, Oregon Hendry Blount could still remember the "solemn" faces of the soldiers as they slowly entered the fort's grounds. As Mrs. Blount stated, the faces "told of death in their ranks."[17]

A few qualifications should be made to Sanko's account, and a few details added. The author was attempting to tell a good story. In the process he omitted certain significant details and, of course, explained others from a biased perspective. For example, Thomas Underhill, who was living with the Tillis family at the David Russell place near McCullough Creek, helped the Tillises to defend themselves. More important, Sanko omitted all reference to Aunt Line, a Tillis family slave who was with Mrs. Tillis when the Indians attacked. Aunt Line subsequently was "painfully wounded" in the forehead as she sought the protection of the Russell cabin after Mrs. Tillis and her sons Dallas and Calhoun had entered it. The circumstances suggest that Aunt Line put their safety ahead of her own.[18]

Other omissions are also important. Concerning motivation for the incident, quite likely the attack on the Tillis family was personal rather than random. Frank Boggess, who was on the scene, recorded that Willoughby Tillis knew the Indian chief Oscen (Oxian) Tustenuggee well. Tillis and Oscen had bad blood between them arising out of incidents going back to the Second Seminole War, and possibly Oscen intended to settle his affairs with Tillis once and for all.[19] Second, the hostiles were apparently keeping tabs on events at the fort from a position in an old oak tree four miles to the east atop "Lookout Hill." They could thus have timed the attack when most volunteer defenders were absent. The warrior Tallahassee told early settler J. M. Van Hook that the tree was often used as a lookout post. "[When] I said to him that it was quite a distance to the fort," Van Hook related, "he said he had a field glass that he had taken from a dead officer and he went to the tree and showed me the rusty remains of some of the nails that he had fastened the cleats to the tree."[20]

The respect and even admiration for Oscen Tustenuggee and other members of his party evidenced in Sanko's letter were shared by survivors of the conflict. Frank Boggess later encountered Oscen's brother, Micco Tustenuggee, at Fort Ogden. An onlooker told the story. "An old warrior, Micko," he observed, "met here the man who wounded him in the battle of Pease creek, when Oxian was killed. Lieut. Boggess was the person, the leader of the whites in that engagement. They had quite a talk over the old days, and pledged each other (rather too many times, I fear, for mutual advantage), in fire water. 'Enemies we then were, but friends now,' was about all I could hear from them, when I sought quieter quarters."[21]

A Village Emerges

The Battle of Peace River occurred June 14–16, 1856. Less than two years later, on May 7, 1858, Billy Bowlegs and 164 of his fellow Indians left Florida forever, ending the Billy Bowlegs War.[22] During the two-year interval the violence of war did not again touch Fort Meade. Apart from the handling of prisoners, the only significant report of Indian activity in the area occurred in September 1856, when Willoughby Tillis reported that his farm had again been visited and that some potatoes and items of personal property had been stolen.[23]

Despite the absence of violence, the war's continuation had a tremendous impact at Fort Meade. It remained a key staging area and supply depot servicing thousands of army troops and Cracker volunteers and was garrisoned throughout the period. At times the number of troops present was so great that overflow camps were established just across Peace River near the beautiful spring on Sink Branch. During March–September 1857 the fort was recommissioned a United States Army installation with a complement of regular troops.[24]

A score or more of families remained "forted up" at Fort Meade throughout the conflict primarily because many of their men were serving elsewhere in volunteer companies. Unable to plant crops, the family members became dependent upon the government as well as more accustomed to the amenities available at the outpost. "All or nearly all the inhabitants are mustered as volunteers," reported one man in March 1857. "They perform very little duty," he noted, "but are paid and provisioned by government for retaining their homes in the interior. Without this assistance from the government [when] the war is over and [when] the troops [are] withdrawn the people will almost starve."[25]

While the war continued and the troops remained, food became increasingly plentiful and easily available. One officer arriving in August 1857 from garrison duty on the Kissimmee River wrote his wife: "Oh, Moddie dear: what a good dinner I sat down to soon after my arrival. *Luxuries!* Roast chicken; fresh butter; *sweet* potatoes; light-fresh, sweet bread; & fresh beans in a sort of succotash;—in the evening about 6½ oclock, a cup of *good* black tea, & fresh bread & butter. By the way, I haven't enumerated all the good things at dinner; we had, for desert, a large, well flavored musk-mellon."[26] At the same time John I. Hooker employed himself as a sort of roving grocer for troops garrisoning remote posts, offering among other items "Porter (London Stout)" and "high priced champagne."[27]

Alcoholic spirits were so easily available on the frontier that their consumption and its aftereffects continually caused problems. "The Sergt. (Jackson) just came in & reported a row between some of our men & citizens of Ft. Meade [,] cause—whiskey," reported post commander Major Thomas Williams on August 15, 1857. He added, "I told him to shut up all the whiskey in the guardhouse." Three months later the Tampa newspaper reported: "Fatal Rencounter.—Information from Ft. Meade states that Levi Long was killed in an affray with Benjamin Oglesby, near that place, by stabbing him with a knife in the abdomen, on Monday last. Both were members of Capt. Wm. Kendrick's Company, Fla. M. Vs. Cause—King Alcohol!"[28]

Despite such problems the civilian families began to develop a real sense of community. Joys and sorrows, fears and triumphs all were shared as the war slowly ground to its conclusion. Happy events such as the wedding of Lott Whidden and Caroline Crews or the births of Benjamin Franklin Moody, Lewis W. Hooker, Joseph C. Pearce, and Mary Ellen Hooker offered opportunities for celebration and for the bonds of shared experience. The children particularly could forget the cares of the day and enjoy each other's company. "Life at the fort was

Fort Meade's last United States Army post commander, Major Thomas Williams, c. 1861. (Courtesy of the Library of Congress)

lots of fun," according to Oregon Hendry Blount. "[I] had plenty of companions to play with and everything was exciting and new."[29]

Just as celebration and joy played their roles, tragedy also drew the community together—a case in point being the death of William P. Brooker. Brooker was a well-regarded community leader and a wounded veteran of the Battle of Peace River, about which he loved

Lydia Carlton Hendry Moody, 1812–1898, and Benjamin Moody, 1811–1896.
(In possession of the author, courtesy of Eugenia Dillon Allen)

to reminisce in a good-humored manner. Major Williams humorously described Fort Meade's exaggerated memories of its June 1856 experiences and of Brooker's role as storyteller:

> About a year ago last June, a party of Indians variously reported to number from 50 to 100 warriors attacked the house of one Tillis living with his family some two miles south of this. After a conflict of many hour duration & according to volunteer report, unprecedented severity, & after the performance of feats of heroic valor, rivalled scarcely in the song of Troubadour, or in the achievement of a Coeur de Lion, the red men were defeated & driven off with a loss of *no* prisoners, & *two* found dead; tho', *authentic* history no doubt, states the number of the slain at not less than *25*!!! One of the heroes who led the Cracker *chiselry* told me yesterday, he recd two wounds himself, one thro' the thigh & one the left side, & that to this day there are to be seen in his *shirt of mail*, hung up for the inspection of the curious in this quarter:—*twenty one* ball holes!!! The narrations of this heroic man are regarded by the truthful, to be quite as reliable as those of the adventures, marvelous indeed, of the renowned & veracious *Muchausen*. So partial, indeed, is our hero, for

truth, *stripped* of every thing adventitious—the naked truth—that, on certain occasions of festive revelry, "at the Hall," it is his custom to divest himself of his garments & appear to his guests in all the *naked truth* of nature's own proportions—dancing & singing. Such is Mister Booker [Brooker] (aged 60), father to our chief cookress, the Lady, Widow Kennedy, aged, *they say*, 25![30]

One month after Williams penned his portrait of Brooker, tragedy common to the frontier struck at his subject. The Tampa newspaper reported the incident:

A Fatal Casualty.—A serious accident, resulting in the death of an old and respected citizen of this County, occurred, on Tuesday morning last, at Fort Meade, under the following circumstances: Wm. P. Broker, while engaged in pouring the powder from the horn, it ignited, and communicating with the horn, exploded, blowing out Mr. B's right eye the blaze went down his throat, severely burning him internally. The unfortunate man lived but a few hours in the greatest agony. He leaves many relatives to mourn his sad fate.[31]

Out of the forced concentration of settlers, the shared experiences, the tragic losses, and the flow of army dollars, a village slowly emerged at Fort Meade during the Billy Bowlegs War. To be sure, it retained a distinctly rural flavor. As Major Williams explained, "We're in a village of sorts & such is the crowing of roosters & cackling of hens, barking of dogs; & lowing of cattle, that one might easily imagine himself the inhabitant of a large farm-yard."[32] Still, the community held its charms. Surgeon Thomas A. McParlin could wistfully note, "[Fort Meade] is near Tampa & very healthy—some settlers & families."[33] He later added, "Tampa I find is very hot, quite a contrast with Fort Meade, so cool[,] airy and elevated."[34] Williams agreed. "Moddie dear," he insisted to his wife, "I've already told you, this place is considered to be among the most healthy in *all* Florida &, I here repeat it, that you may entertain no anxieties on the score of climate. It is dry, compared to Kissimmee & has *good* water, & something of a market, affording as much variety as is conducive to real good health. I hope to wax fat."[35]

The village was centered in 1857 and 1858 upon the fort's buildings but included new structures erected along the Tampa–Fort Meade road and upon a road leading from the fort northward to the homesteads at present-day Homeland and Bartow. Except for Louis Lanier's home near the Peace River ford and several residences north of modern Third Street Northeast between Lanier and Cleveland avenues, these buildings were concentrated within the area now bounded on the south and north by First and Fourth streets northeast and on the east and west by Perry and Polk avenues. In 1858 the army, almost as a parting gift, reconstructed and improved the road to Tampa and extended it across the river and south a considerable distance. A large commissary store was also built, and more important, a well-designed and solidly constructed wooden bridge was raised over the river ford. Thus, out of the tragedy of war was born the first town in interior south Florida.[36]

The Billy Bowlegs War came as an almost unbelievable shock to the not-yet-settled pioneers of the Fort Meade area, and it soon delivered death and destruction to their very doorsteps. Out of the destruction, pain, and death, however, came the seeds of town life that, with trials and tribulations, as we will see, has continued to the present day.

3

"Unpleasant relations which for years rankled in the heart"

Civil War

WHILE BILLY BOWLEGS prepared to leave Florida at the end of the Third Seminole War, Louis Lanier sat in his Fort Meade home to pen a few words to his sister in Georgia. Describing his world as it appeared in April 1858, Lanier wrote, "Our Country has a very bad appearance from the fact that people has been broken up nearly three years, and their places gone to rack besides some of our best citizens have been killed by the Savage Indians." He continued optimistically, "The Settlers have just commenced moving to their respective homes to commence anew." Lanier then added words that applied to only a few area men: "I have been liveing at home nearly all the time because there was troops Stationed near where I live."[1]

Pioneers returning to their homes and farms that spring ached for the peace that would permit them to resume normal lives. At Fort Meade, though, the peace was arbitrarily and violently delayed for months. "At the close of the Indian war," remembered George W. Hendry, "thousands of men were mustered out of service—a class of men no country would welcome or invite. Immediately, hordes of horse-jockies, gamblers, swindlers and cut-throats ran roughshod over the whole country from Fort Meade to Tampa." Fort Meade, Hendry insisted, became "one of the toughest places this side of pergatory, proportionate to population." He explained, "The town was run over and dominated by a class of men destitute of all moral restraint or conscientious impulses. This place was cursed with a grogshop in those days that brought about the murders, shootings, knockdowns and dragouts.

So bad were existing conditions that no self-respecting lady would venture on the streets unless some male friend accompanied her."[2] Although Hendry's memory exaggerated conditions, violence did beset the area. In the absence of effective law enforcement, settlers fell back upon the frontier tradition of the vigilance committee, the members of which were known in south Florida as "Regulators."[3]

South Florida's first Regulator band was born at Fort Meade in 1858, and soon the movement spread to Tampa and Hernando County. In the Fort Meade area actions were limited to threats and "thrashing," but Tampa Regulators turned to whipping women suspected of improper behavior and, more ominously, to lynchings.[4] Before more than a few had realized what was happening, Regulator force had been turned to political ends. One pioneer recalled, "Many wrongs were perpetrated and involved many of the best meaning people into unpleasant relations which for years rankled in the hearts." Still, the Regulators achieved their initial goal for, as the same old-timer put it, "The country was pretty well cleaned up of the worst element."[5]

As fears of lawlessness and violence eased, Fort Meade saw itself slowly transformed from frontier outpost to town. New settlers began staking out homesteads or else stopping for a while before continuing further south to newly opened lands in modern Hardee and DeSoto counties. By June 1860 the vicinity contained almost 400 residents, about 13 percent of the total population of old Hillsborough County. At least forty-nine of those present were black slaves.[6] To capitalize upon the change, Louis Lanier opened a general store, probably in the new commissary building constructed in 1858. In February 1860 Lanier supplemented the store with "one of the most complete sawmills" in Florida. The facility was constructed and operated by Christopher Q. Crawford, reportedly "one of the best steam saw mill men in the Southern States." Lanier's enterprise permitted residents the luxury of plank, rather than log, homes where before "you could not get plank enough . . . to make a coffin, unless you hauled it from Tampa."[7] A month after the mill opened, Fort Meade was authorized to have its first post office, and Lanier was designated postmaster.[8]

Lanier did not rest with these accomplishments. In September 1859 he obtained title to 160 acres of land centered on the Peace River bridge. The tract extended as far to the west as modern Hendry Street south of Broadway, and on part of this land, he planted orange trees. At his home near the bridge and just to the north of the Tampa–Fort Meade road, Lanier and his wife operated what amounted to an inn. One traveler noted in a Tampa newspaper: "Reader, did you ever stop at [Lanier's] house? If you have not called on him yet, I presume you will soon. I believe every body else stops there, as we did, to save his bill. For the Maj. does not charge anybody, I am told."[9]

Increasing population and activity led to an educational revival in late 1858 or early 1859. Francis C. M. Boggess again served as teacher. In the little time allowed by a three-month term, he instructed pupils such as Serena Willingham "[in] her letters, to spell, read, and to 'figger.' "[10] The Hillsborough county commission in December 1859 officially approved of the school and appointed a board consisting of Boggess, Edward T. Kendrick, and John Rufus Durrance to supervise it.[11]

The Hillsborough commission also recognized growth near modern Homeland by establishing a school district centered on "Levi Pearce's Mill," with Pearce, John L. Skipper, and John McAuley as trustees. The mill, established at the time only a short while, was located on Peace River near "Flat Ford" and offered settlers the opportunity to grind their corn into meal. Early in 1860 the commission made access to the mill relatively easy. It authorized Joseph Howell, Pearce, and Owen R. Blount to build a road from the Tampa–Fort Meade road where it crossed the present Hillsborough-Polk county line (at Howell's home east of Plant City) to Pearce's mill "via Flat Ford on Peas Creek."[12]

During the period 1858–1860 no churches were formally organized at Fort Meade or Homeland. In October 1860, however, Methodist families established near Homeland (on what became known as Campground Branch) a "Camp meeting" that became an annual tradition for over twenty-five years. An "arbor," as well as tents for accommodations, was erected "of such material as will last for many years." The meeting proved a huge success as "40 to 50 persons professed conversion during its progress." Of the gathering one visitor noted, "We have traveled a little in our life, and have been associated with hospitable people, but we defy the world to produce a more whole-souled community than the Peace Creek country boasts."[13]

Thus by late 1860 the area was well on its way to a more "civilized" environment. Schools had been organized, a store opened, mills erected, groves planted, roads laid out, religious institutions initiated, and population increased. In addition, two doctors lived nearby (Gilbert L. Key and James D. Smith) as well as a blacksmith (Thomas Kinney), a wheelwright (Joseph Dawson), a millwright (C. Q. Crawford), a carpenter (J. C. Frasier), and a seamstress (Harriet Farrell). Growth and prosperity seemingly lay right on the doorstep. Other events far removed from the town, however, would soon lead to its almost total destruction.[14]

Secession

The national crisis of 1860 and the election of Abraham Lincoln as president seemed a remote drama to most Fort Meade pioneers, who were concentrating on establishing themselves on a raw frontier only two years removed from Indian war. Lincoln was not even on the Florida ballot, and when election day rolled around, only fifty-two men voted at Fort Meade—thirty-eight of them casting ballots for the most prominent states' rights candidate, Kentucky's John C. Breckenridge. Fourteen men, though, opted for the more moderate pro-Union candidate, John Bell of Tennessee. Numerous individuals, including Francis A. Hendry, William McCullough, John L. Skipper, and Frank Boggess, publicly opposed secession.[15]

Despite their remote location and the antisecession sentiment among community leaders, some residents were very much interested in the slavery issue. Polk County's tax roll for 1861, the county's first year of existence, lists eleven area men with slaveholdings. These individuals owned forty-three men, women, and children, almost 30 percent of the county's total. Thirty-six slaves were possessed by five men: Francis M. Durrance (four); Francis A. Hendry (eight); John I. Hooker (seven); Louis Lanier (nine); and John C. Oats (eight). Total county slaveholdings were valued at about $81,000, while all the county's cattle amounted to only about half again as much. With a few exceptions, outside the circle of slaveholding families and their relations most area pioneer families had little personal connection with slavery, and when war came, they did not rush to join either side in the fighting.[16]

A convention meeting at Tallahassee authorized Florida's secession from the Union on January 10, 1861. At the time no viable military units existed in south Florida, although militia companies had been in the process of organization for about one year. Perhaps angered at the slow pace of militia organization, a group of young men met at Fort Meade the first week of March 1861, as President Lincoln was being inaugurated, and formed a "Company of Mounted Minute Men" promptly named the "Hickory Boys." Streaty Parker was elected captain, and John R. Durrance and Zachariah Seward were designated, respectively, first and second lieutenant. Whether the Hickory Boys entered active service is open to question, although on July 14, 1861, a company detachment under Lieutenant Durrance's command occupied the fort. The occupation lasted only until August 27, but the fact that it occurred suggested the site's future strategic importance.[17]

When the "Hickory Boys" withdrew from Fort Meade, the immediacy of Civil War faded, and the community returned to its normal pursuits. Circumstances over time became more straitened and sacrifices more necessary as communications were disrupted and the Union blockade of Florida's ports shut off the importation of dry goods, medicines, equipment, and other necessities. Occasionally shortages were relieved by the successful exploits of blockade runners such as James McKay and Robert Johnson. Perhaps George W. Hendry best described life during the war's opening years. "Without a dollar to begin with, the eventful period opened upon Polk, as elsewhere, nothing to see, nothing to buy with," he wrote. "Other sections had the advantage of boat or railroad facilities—could garden and sell, but not so with Polk. It was 'root hog or die,' and it seemed that it was 'die hog if you do root.' But our climate was mild, our soil productive, and the inhabitants healthy; being a range country, too, afforded us beef; raised the 'tater, pease, rice, corn, vegetables, sugar-cane; grazed our horses, hunted our scattering beeves, and we lived."[18]

Distance from wartime hostilities during 1861–1863 by no means meant that Fort Meade life was uneventful. Although many area men were released from the Confederate draft by an exemption for cattlemen, others early on volunteered for service or, beginning in late 1862, were swept up by Confederate agents "scouring the woods, looking after deserters and conscripts."[19] A number of the volunteers served with Company E of the Seventh Florida Infantry, known as the "South Florida Bull Dogs," and fought in many of the war's major engagements. Soon enough word of tragedy began to make its way back home. The first such news may have been of the death of D. J. Crum, who succumbed to pneumonia at Columbus, Georgia, only three months after his enlistment. Then came the death of Levi Pearce's boy, James T. Pearce, and in January 1863 of Edward T. Kendrick at Knoxville. Bennett Whidden was luckier. Wounded at Chickamauga and

Future Fort Meade resident, James Alfred Stephens, uniformed as a private in the Seventh Florida Infantry, CSA, 1833–1895. (Courtesy of the Florida State Archives)

again at Murfreesboro, he was captured and held as a prisoner of war. William A. Hilliard, who was interned with Whidden at Camp Chase, Ohio, lost an eye to smallpox while awaiting parole.[20]

Tragedy struck close to home as well. On January 2, 1862, John I. Hooker died from causes unknown. At the time his wife, Cuthbert, was pregnant with their third child—a son, John Jackson Hooker, born February 12. Twelve months later smallpox swept the river valley, and before it had run its virulent course Mariah Godwin, wife of Solomon; Perlina Hollingsworth, wife of Stephen; Francis B. Oats, wife of John; and others, including pioneer John Green, were dead.[21]

Although fear and death became frequent visitors, Fort Meade thrived to a certain extent. The area benefited from the arrival of several new families, such as that of James T. Wilson, seeking proximity to relatives and the protection of a remote location. The cattle trade also prospered. By September 1862 Francis A. Hendry and his associates were concentrating herds at the town preparatory to driving them to Confederate purchasing centers in north Florida and south Georgia. During the period June–September 1862 alone, Hendry's group received in excess of $50,000 in Confederate currency for their efforts.[22]

Some local men also were assisting Jacob Summerlin and James McKay in running cattle through the Union naval blockade for sale at Havana, Cuba. As the blockade became more effective, fewer cattle and more cotton passed through Fort Meade on their way to the island. Just such a cargo creaked and rattled through town in December 1862 on its way to the mouth of Peace River. The wagon train of mules and oxen bore 175 bales of cotton destined for the ship of blockade runner Robert Johnson. Johnson, after a perilous journey, sold his cargo in Havana and returned to Peace River with medicines, drugs, and surgical instruments desperately needed in the midst of the smallpox epidemic.[23]

The Fort's Destruction

During the fall of 1863 Confederate beef-gathering activities at Fort Meade intensified with the appointment of James McKay as south Florida's Confederate commissary agent. Assisted by F. A. Hendry,

Louis Lanier, and others, McKay sought to regularize beef supply operations while preserving the bulk of local herds for sale in Cuba after the war's end. By late in the year he was supplying three-fourths of the beef going to Confederate armies from the state, but the success of McKay's efforts proved short-lived. On February 17, 1864, the Confederate Congress drastically revised its conscription law, eliminating the draft exemptions for cattlemen. The change unleashed squads of conscription agents determined to force all suddenly eligible "cow hunters" into Confederate service, and many individuals were forced to choose sides. Substantial numbers of them living at and below Fort Meade opted to join the Union army.[24]

By late 1863 some area men had already approached Union officials at Charlotte Harbor. To use their potential for recruiting fellow south Floridians and for disrupting the cattle trade, they were formed in December into the Florida Rangers. In January 1864 the Rangers were reorganized as the Second Florida Cavalry, placed under the command of Tampan Henry A. Crane, and sent to occupy the former army post at Fort Myers. McKay and other Confederate officials reacted in alarm to the Second Florida Cavalry's presence, even though the unit possessed fewer than fifty men. McKay's forces skirmished with the Union soldiers on several occasions. In February 1864 the Confederates were encouraged when the state's heralded Confederate cavalry leader John J. Dickison was ordered to Fort Meade to spearhead an attack on Fort Myers. Dickison was recalled before reaching the town, however, and in the meantime the draft law was changed.

Five days after the new draft law's approval, Fort Meade resident William McCullough, wounded during the 1849 Indian attack at Chokonikla and again at the Tillis place in 1856, walked into Fort Myers and was commissioned as first lieutenant in the Second Florida Cavalry. Sixteen days later he was joined by fellow townsman William McClenithan, and with McClenithan came Peace River political leader James D. Green, who resided at Fort Green in modern Hardee County. McClenithan and Green brought with them some valuable news. "They informed me that since the arrival of Troops to this Post," Crane notified his superiors, "no cattle had been driven, but small scouting parties had been watching us, fearing an attack on Ft. Meade. That since the battle near Lake City [the Battle of Olustee], & great loss of

Nancy Whidden McCullough, 1830–1908, and William McCullough, 1821–1890. This illustration is believed to be a photograph retouched with paint, taken after the Civil War. (In possession of the author, courtesy of Colleen Uhl)

provisions the Confederates were compelled to have cattle, and had stored supplies for that purpose at that point. (Ft. Meade) That the forces or most of them had been ordered to Gainesville." Crane continued, "I felt an irresistible desire to destroy their supplies & Capt Green offered to accompany any command I might detach for that service."[25]

On March 21, 1864, Green and fifty Union recruits attacked the Willoughby Tillis homestead south of Fort Meade, where a large part of the area's Confederate supplies were stored. "[They] came to our house and to Thomas Underhill's," recalled J. D. Tillis, "took Thomas Underhill a prisoner and killed him. They took all his horses and wagons—

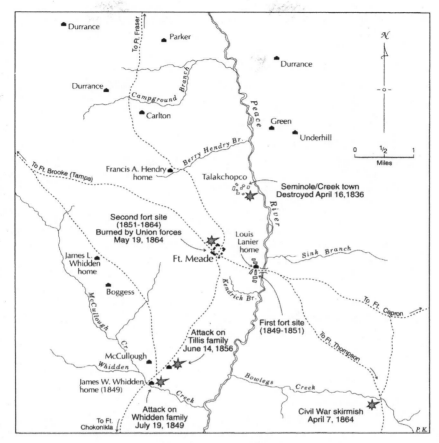

Fort Meade Area, c. 1850s–1860s

loaded up with provisions, corn, fodder and meat—took the Negro men and all firearms and went back to Fort Myers."[26] A Union officer provided additional detail: "Destroyed 1000 Pds Bacon, 75 to 100 Bush corn—400 Belgian Rifle Cartridges—2 Contrabands [slaves] man & woman 12 Horses & 2 Mules—8 Stand small arms—1–2 horse wagon—2 Guerilla spies (now in prison) & shot one notorious scoundrel named *Underhill* in a Skirmish—Procured 26 recruits."[27]

So pleased was Crane with the raid's results that he ordered Green and McCullough to return to Fort Meade. Dated April 2, a portion of their orders read:

> On your arrival at Bowleg's Creek, detach Sergt. Brannon with 5 men,—Corpl Arnold with 3 men & Corpl Hay with 3 men for the capture of Dr Key, Boggess, & others, while your force takes possession of the Cabbage Hammock on the left.
>
> Here you will receive reinforcements & await the arrival of your parties, *after placing a guard at the bridge near Laniers'.—Remember, I have pledged my word and honor, that your flag shall wave over the Hill by Sunrise, on Thursday, the 7th inst & it must be done.*
>
> Your force ought to count over 100 men at this place & it is expected *you will be able to subdue all opposition.* "*Wiggins*" will point out the Indian goods or stores, (if not removed), which must be secured, as it is confederate property, together with all horse & contrabands at the place. See that no runners leave. Put up the papers (marked Ft. Meade) in conspicuous places, securely by pasting. If Capt John is there secure him, and state, that the Indians want *'Their goods' at Ft. Myers, & no more.* Let your whole energies be exerted to Capture (or kill if necessary)—*Tillis, Parker, Lanier, Henry* [Hendry], Summerlin, *Durrance*, Tillman, Boggess, & Seward, as these are the leaders of the Guerillas—this being done, *South Florida is ours. Your wants must be supplied by the enemy.*[28]

The Union forces were within fifteen miles of their target when they were spotted by Confederate pickets. James McKay, Jr., commanding area Rebel forces, massed his men astride the road to Fort Meade as it passed over Bowlegs Creek. There, on April 7, 1864, Union and Confederate forces met in combat. The battle was brief. When the smoke had cleared, Confederate James Lanier was found dead, and Henry A. Prine lay wounded. The Rebels withdrew toward the fort. Rather than press after them, the Union forces crossed Peace River and again occupied the Tillis homestead. "They then . . . burned our home and all that we had," remembered J. D. Tillis.[29] "The detachment sent to Fort Meade . . . ," reported Crane, "had a fight with the Rebs & drove them from the place on Thursday last destroying all their Stores complete, & killing a leading Guerilla named 'Lanier' & wounding several others with horses &c, without any loss whatever." The Union forces returned to Fort Myers without achieving their goal.[30] But they would be back.

Buoyed by the actions near Fort Meade and by recruits gained as a result of those actions, the Second Florida Cavalry became ever more emboldened. Reinforced by three companies of the Second Regiment, United States Colored Troops (USCT), the volunteers attacked and briefly occupied Tampa on May 6, 1864. At the time, James McKay, Jr., with Tampa's garrison of twenty men, was at Fort Meade preparing for the first cattle drive of the year. Alerted to the Union action, he and a force of thirty-five sped to the scene, but the Union men withdrew from the town with their mission accomplished before McKay ordered an attack. One week after their withdrawal from Tampa, five officers with 100 men of the Second Florida Cavalry and 107 black troopers of the Second USCT again set out from Fort Myers for Fort Meade.[31] Their goal was to relieve "distressed families" of Union men who had been rounded up and sequestered at the Peace River town as well as to "secure as many Beef Cattle as posable." The report of Captain Jonathan W. Childs, then commanding at Fort Myers, details the results:

> The troops crossed the Caloosahatchee River at this point [Fort Myers], on the morning of the 14" inst. and immediately took up the line of march. Their carts with Forage & Rations proceeded by the way of Fort Thompson, and joined the command at Prairie Creek. The Enemy discovered our approach when within twenty-five miles of Fort Mead on the 18" inst. Arriving within six miles, we captured two of his pickets and learned that he had ambuscaded the road in the swamp between Bowlegs Creek and Pease Creek. Camping here for the night the march was resumed early on the morning of the 19" inst. avoiding the ambuscade by crossing Pease Creek below the mouth of Bowlegs Creek. Captain Green with fifty (50) men went in advance and took possession of the Fort without meeting with any resistance. About an hour afterwards the Enemy showed himself about sixty strong mounted. A skirmish line was thrown out and he soon disappeared. Considerable Forage and Provisions were captured.—having sufficiently rested the Command and destroyed the Barracks, the march was resumed. I recrossed Pease Creek fifty miles below Fort Mead at "Tic's Ford," We captured seven (7) prisoners of War, obtained sixteen (16) recruits, brought off about seventy (70) women and children who were almost in a state of starvation, and drove from that portion of the country over one thousand Beef cattle which were left on the south side of the Caloosahatchee river about

twenty miles above this Post, where the grazing is much better than about Fort Myers. . . . Arriving at Fort Myers on the 27" inst. having been absent fourteen days and traveled a distance, as estimated, of two hundred and ten (210) miles. The men returned in good spirits, and there was no straggling throughout the march.[32]

A *New York Herald* correspondent learned additional details of the assault from Henry Crane:

> Captain Crane, commanding at Fort Meyers, has arrived here. He tells a good story, illustrative of the value of time. When he landed at Fort Meade he found a solitary sentinel marching back and forth, with a chip hat on his head, a dingy blouse on his back and a double barrelled shotgun across his shoulder. This sentinel marched up and down while Captain Crane and his men were busily removing the stores and doing other things usual on such occasions.
>
> At length the sentinel looked that way, and called out, "I say, fellows, who in hell are you?" Captain Crane, with the brevity of a soldier, replied with the one word, "Yanks." "Are you genwyne Yanks?" was the response. "We are." was the rejoinder. The rebel sentinel passed up and down a few times more, and then called out, "I say, fellows, will you allow a fellow to come up to you?" Captain Crane replied that he might. Upon which he laid down his two barrelled gun and went to where the Union men stood, when he again addressed Captain Crane—"Will you allow a fellow to take arms with you?" The answer was in the affirmative; upon which the rebel expressed himself in this manner:—"Well, I reckon my time with old Jeff. [Davis] is out this day; and, as I don't like to waste time, I will enlist with you." And enlisted he was on the instant. Captain Crane says he has not a better soldier in his corps.[33]

Aftermath

Union forces burned Fort Meade on May 19, 1864, and the legacy of its destruction was fear and apprehension. The transfer of Francis A. Hendry's Confederate "cow cavalry" force to Alafia in mid-June further heightened tensions, and as late as October, those emotions remained close to the surface.[34] Illustrative of the situation is the following letter from a Methodist minister written shortly after the close of the annual Campground Branch "camp meeting":

> I have just closed the Peace Creek camp meeting—the best camp meeting that I ever had the privilege of attending. For the first two days we felt discouraged and uneasy—discouraged, because our [Presiding Elder] Bro. Acton, did not come, for some cause unknown to the writer—uneasy, because we felt ourselves exposed to the raiders.
>
> But we were greatly relieved in this respect. On Thursday evening, the vigilant Capt. Hendry, with his command, arrived—pitched their tents, and put out a strong picket guard around the encampment; and from that time the meeting went on harmoniously.[35]

As the camp meeting closed, Hendry and other "cow cavalry" leaders had begun to reassert Confederate authority north of the Caloosahatchee River, an accomplishment permitted by a change in focus of Union activities to the Brooksville and Cedar Key areas. By the cattle driving season's end in January 1865, the Confederates felt strong enough to mount a direct assault on Fort Myers. Edward J. Hilliard, who participated in the disappointing venture, recalled the experience:

> Capt. F. A. Hendry's company was at this time stationed at the "Old Camp Ground" on Campground Branch, between Fort Meade and Bartow.
>
> It was decided to attempt the capture of Fort Myers. Capt. Hendry furnishing me a horse I went with [him] on this expedition.
>
> Two other companies under Major [William] Footman from a station north of here joined Capt. Hendry making a pretty good battalion. We packed up with rations for several days for ourselves and horses and we understood the wagon train would follow us with provisions.
>
> We went on our line of march for Fort Myers. When we got near Fort Thompson on the Caloosahatchee where we were to cross the river we were halted and formed in line and Major Footman made a speech to us telling us that he was going to take Ft. Myers with a charge under night cover. He gave each of us a white strip of cloth to tie around the right arm so we could know each other in the night. He said if there was a man in the command that was not willing to go into the fight to step out and he would give him a pass back to the rear. One man stepped out and said he had a family to look out for and he did not want to be killed.

We then took up our march to Fort Thompson, crossed the river and got to what was called Mile Creek, night came on and about this time it began to rain and rained all night and that being a low, flat country, the water rose up about a foot deep all over the face of the earth. We could not tell where the road was, much less travel; so the night raid was all up for that night. Next morning we took up our line of march for Fort Myers. Pretty soon we spied a bunch of beef cattle in care of two men from Fort Myers and one colored man. Our advance guard captured one of the men and the other outran us to Punta Rassa. The negro would not surrender and was killed by the guard.

By this time we were at Billy's Branch and captured the guard there. We were then in sight of the fort and they still did not know we were in the neighborhood until our commander under a flag of truce sent in a demand to the fort to surrender. This the commander of the fort refused to do and we filed out to the left and around the fort and had some picket fighting. By this time their men had got into their trenches and were ready for business.

Night came on and we killed and roasted some beef which we ate for supper. That night we took up our line of march back to Fort Meade and our wagon train never came to us, making it just one week without one mouthful of bread. When we got to Fort Meade the good women met us with full baskets of good grub. . . .

Francis C. M. Boggess, 1833–1902. (Courtesy of Florida State Archives)

After the war was over I talked with some of the soldiers who were in Fort Myers and they told me that if we had made the charge on them that night, we surely would have taken them, for they were having a big ball and half of them did not know where their guns were.[36]

Most of the exhausted south Florida supporters of the Union and of the Confederacy welcomed the war's end in April and May 1865. Frank Boggess learned of the peace at Brooksville, where most cow cavalrymen had been sent following the Fort Myers attack. While returning to his home near the burned-out ruin of the military post at Fort Meade, he stopped off just north of town at Francis A. Hendry's residence. Seeing his old friend, Hendry stepped out on the porch and inquired of the latest news. Boggess responded that Robert E. Lee had surrendered his Confederate army at Appomattox, Virginia. His relief evident, Hendry could only exclaim, "Thank God it is over with one way or the other."[37]

THE DECADE of the 1860s opened at Fort Meade with the promise of growth and prosperity for the new town. After four years of Civil War many of her native sons were dead, others had become enemies, and the heart of the settlement lay in ashes. And sad to say for the struggling community that had been so beset by violence and destruction, before things got better they were going to get worse.

4

"A flourishing and growing little village"

Cattle and a Town Reborn

A SAD SIGHT greeted veterans as they made their way home to Fort Meade and Homeland in the months after the Civil War's end. The fort's principal buildings had been destroyed, victims of Union torches on May 19, 1864. The Tillis homestead lay in ashes, and likely Thomas Underhill's was also gutted. The Peace River bridge remained, but Louis Lanier's store, closed from wartime shortages, stood shuttered. Likewise, the post office was gone, transferred by the Confederate government in 1862 to the barely populated county seat of Bartow. And Lanier's steam sawmill no longer sang its "iron whistle" through the town's streets, perhaps dismantled during the war or else also a casualty of Union occupiers.[1]

Gone too were many leaders who had provided the village with energy and promise. John I. Hooker and Edward T. Kendrick were dead. By early 1866 Lanier had disposed of his property to son-in-law Francis A. Hendry and had relocated to Fort Ogden to pursue the cattle business. Teacher Frank Boggess had already made the same move. Soon the community also lost John L. Skipper, John C. Oats, Francis M. Durrance, and John R. Durrance to other locations. Union veteran William McCullough's family did not return at all, preferring to live in the more hospitable clime of Clark County, Missouri. Other Union veterans such as William McClenithan moved south into modern Hardee and DeSoto counties, where many of their fellow soldiers were situated.[2]

Many individuals who moved away had been slaveholders. Of the five men with the largest number of bondsmen in 1861, only F. A.

Hendry remained six years later. Some members of the town's slave population had been captured and freed by Union troops. Others apparently left the area when notified of their freedom. Few, if any, freedmen remained at Fort Meade, and perhaps only Rachel Davis and her children—former slaves of John Parker—still lived at Homeland.[3]

To complicate Fort Meade's postwar problems, the cattle business rested in the doldrums. Tens of thousands of beeves ranged to the east and south of Peace River, but owners were stifled in gaining access to reliable markets. Just prior to the war, trade had been opened with Cuba, and as soon as possible after the peace, James McKay and Jacob Summerlin attempted to revive the business. Their efforts were slow in coming to fruition, however, and not until 1867 were modest but significant numbers of cattle shipped.[4]

As if other problems were not grave enough, the area was revisited by a wave of violence similar to that experienced after the Billy Bowlegs War. "From many parts of the South," recorded George W. Hendry, "men who were fleeing from justice sought seclusion from the main thoroughfares of public travel and to escape identity came to South Florida. Most of these people came to Polk county and to Fort Meade. They soon got to killing each other." Just as in 1858, the community members acted on their own to restore law and order with a Regulator organization. At Fort Meade, remembered Hendry, "One

John Parker, 1818–1881.
(In possession of the author, courtesy of Kyle S. VanLandingham)

man was shot and badly wounded, but made his escape by the assistance of some of the antiregulars. Others were thrashed, while some got very pointed orders to leave the country and they left and were right glad of the chance."[5]

To cap off the wave of ill fortune, in October 1867 Mother Nature turned a violent face on all of south Florida, saturating the peninsula with weeks of rain. A newspaper reported the ensuing disaster. "The flat woods and swamps are under water," its editor declared, "wharves, bridges and causeways washed away, many farms hidden and crops drowned and general ruin staring some of the proprietors."[6] At Fort Meade the river bridge was swept away, not to be replaced until December 1871. Roads to the west were swamped, and the Six Mile Creek Bridge near Tampa was destroyed, rendering travel there by wagon impossible during any period of high water. Farmers lost for over one year the only market for their crops.[7]

The Wire Road

In the months prior to the floods of October 1867, one event occurred that whispered the possibility of a turnaround in Fort Meade's fortunes and had substantial impact upon how the town would develop. The agent of change was the International Ocean Telegraph Company (IOTC).

Fort Meade after the Civil War still lay within an isolated frontier. "Not a railroad Depot nearer than 150 miles," explained a resident, "not a wharf nearer than 35 miles, and not a stream in whose waters floats a common scow."[8] The situation was so extreme that when military authorities worried in 1868 about a possible outbreak of violence by Indians, freedmen, and renegade whites, they considered garrisoning a line of posts as far south as Bartow—everything below that point was considered to lie beyond the pale.[9]

Not everyone thought Fort Meade and the Peace River valley lay beyond the pale, though. Former Union general William F. "Baldy" Smith and his associates determined in the winter of 1867 that the area was ideal as a route for a proposed telegraph link from New York to Cuba. Consequently their International Ocean Telegraph Company crews worked feverishly from April to June 1867 to construct a line from Lake City to Punta Rassa, from where the cable ran underwater to Key West and Havana. In Polk County the wire wound around Wire Lake near the site of modern Lakeland, passed through Bartow and present-day Homeland, and came to a turning point at Fort Meade. At the town it darted east across the river bridge before again turning south for Punta Rassa. By early June residents able to afford the service could communicate with the great northern metropolises. Three months later cattlemen could arrange their affairs directly with agents and buyers in Havana.

Fort Meade's barrier of remoteness was cracked by the IOTC, but the company did more than give residents a way to communicate with the outside world. For one thing it opened there a testing and maintenance station that provided steady jobs with dependable paydays. More important, the company built a road.

Since 1851 roads running to and from the town had focused upon the second fort. The main north-south and east-west arteries met near the center of the area bounded today by Orange and Cleveland avenues on the east and west and First and Third streets northeast on the south and north. The IOTC, though, required a road running alongside the telegraph wire so as to afford access for maintenance purposes. Accordingly the company constructed a new, straight-line road running south-southeast from Homeland to the vicinity of what is now Palmetto Avenue and Ninth Street Northwest. From that point its route and the telegraph wire ran southeast to about where Oak Avenue crosses East Broadway. It then turned and followed a more or less easterly course to the bridge. The road was known throughout its length as "the Wire Road." The Fort Meade portion, which passed through what was then raw land from present-day Oak Avenue to the river, was first called "Wire Street," then "Main Street," then "Broad Street," and finally "Broadway."[10] As will be seen, all town streets came to be platted from the path of Wire Street, and in the years after 1867 along that street there developed the heart of the town's business district.

Catering to the Cattle Business

Within the period from 1869 to 1871 Fort Meade's fortunes and prospects happily reversed themselves in a dramatic manner. The change's cause is easy to pinpoint. It was cattle.

Sluggish beef sales on the Cuban market had frustrated south Florida owners from 1865 through 1868. In 1869, though, excitement began to build that a major upsurge in Cuban sales was imminent, and at the same time, new markets for Florida beef opened at Savannah and New York. The real breakthrough came in 1870, when over 7,000 head were shipped to Cuba, a figure that doubled the following year and remained high through the decade. These sales in turn generated something that was scarce, if not impossible to find, on the south Florida frontier—cold, hard cash. The cash came in the form of gold Spanish doubloons.[11]

Ben Bradley reminisced, with some exaggeration, about the Cuban cattle trade and those gold doubloons:

Why we used to drive our cattle from Fort Meade down to Punta Rassa, sell them to the Spaniards for shipment to Cuba, take our pay in Spanish doubloons, pour the gold into empty oat sacks, throw the sacks over the backs of some led ponies we carried for that purpose and hit the trail back to Fort Meade. Coming back, when we would get tired, we would stop, throw the gold sack under a tree, go to sleep and wake up the next morning to find the sacks untouched. . . .

A man did not think nothing at all of leaving a couple of oat sacks full of Spanish doubloons under a tree if his pony went lame and ride on home, get a fresh pony and come back a week or two later, pick up his gold and go on with it, and nary a doubloon was missing, although people were passing to and fro on that trail every day and knew what was in those sacks under that tree.

Why, when a man wanted to borrow some money, he went to a neighbor's house and told him he wanted five hundred dollars. The man never got out of his chair on the back porch, but just pointed out an oak 'way back in the garden and told him to go out there and take what he wanted out of the box. Sometimes the fellow would holler back that he did not have time to count it, whereupon the man sitting on the back porch said, "Take the box with you, take out what you want and bring the box back when you are coming by this way again." Nobody knew what a note was and as for a mortgage, that word was not even in the language of Polk county folk.[12]

The flow of doubloons into south Florida, or, as in 1869, the potential for it, lured to Fort Meade men intent upon earning a share of that gold through trade. The first merchants known to have located following the Civil War were two friends from Dupont, Georgia, Sherod E. Roberts and Cornelius B. Lightsey. Opening their store in late 1869 on Wire Street's south side just west of what is now the intersection of East Broadway and Washington Avenue, the partners offered "heavy and light dry goods, boots and shoes, hats and clothing, saddlery, crockery-ware, tin-ware, wood-ware, and hardware, and at all times the best of family flour, corn, tobacco, coffee, and all other groceries."[13]

Within a year as the cattle business boomed, Lightsey & Roberts gained competition from J. C. Rockner & Company. The store's proprietor, Julius C. Rockner, had married Cuthbert Lanier Hooker, widow of John I. Hooker. After the war Rockner moved to Fort Ogden, but in 1869, he disposed of his cattle to F. A. Hendry and returned to Fort Meade. He advertised that at his store, located on the south side of Wire Street opposite the present-day intersection of Polk Avenue and East Broadway, "We propose to sell our Goods as cheap as the same Goods can be bought at in Tampa. Our stock is extensive and we flatter ourselves that the selection can not be beaten in this part of Florida."[14]

The new spirit of enterprise did not stop with Roberts, Lightsey, and Rockner. In February 1869, F. A. Hendry established a "tannery and shoe shop" near town. Although Hendry moved to Fort Myers the following year, a tannery business continued in operation under Frederick N. Varn. Located on Sink Branch east of Peace River, Varn's operation proved a great success and within a few years was "turning out weekly 400 pairs of shoes and boots, with an equal proportion of harness and saddlery and other work, besides shipping a large amount of leather."[15]

With the newfound prosperity came an influx of settlers who added increasing vitality to the community. Important among them was cattleman William H. Willingham, who arrived late in 1869 and purchased from F. A. Hendry the original 160-acre Lanier homestead, as

Ulysses A. Lightsey, 1860–1928, and Cornelius B. Lightsey, 1831–1890 (standing).
(In possession of the author, courtesy of Elizabeth Alexander)

well as additional property just to the east and south of the river crossing. Willingham, through the purchase, controlled the town's river access. Hendry disposed of additional land east of Willingham's tract to
John W. Brandon, who erected a gristmill on the site.[16]

Another property transfer was equally important. In September
1871 Confederate veteran James M. Manley purchased from Cuthbert
Rockner one-half of the John I. Hooker homestead at the site of the

Francis Asbury Hendry, 1833–1917, and Ardeline Ross Lanier Hendry, 1835–1917. (In possession of the author, courtesy of Spessard Stone)

second fort. This tract consisted of eighty acres and covered the area now bounded by Oak and Orange avenues, East Broadway, and Sixth Street Northeast. Soon Manley opened a barroom on Wire Street's north side, possibly between Church and Hendry avenues. He installed there a tenpin alley and employed his brother-in-law Arthur Keen to manage the operation. Manley's investment expanded further in March 1874 when he established a saw- and gristmill powered by "one eight horse steam engine."[17]

Home of William H. Willingham, constructed c. 1869 east of Peace River. (In possession of the author, courtesy of Margaret C. Waldron)

Increasing numbers of residents, coupled with business expansion, led to a revival of several fundamental institutions of town life. Formal schooling, suspended by 1862, was available again not later than 1868. The school was not a "public school" in the normal sense of the term but rather an "independent school" offering three-month terms of instruction upon the payment of fees. Tuition in 1868 ran $9.39 per child per term, and four years later $9.89 sufficed for the same instruction. Tradition suggests that this school stood on the south side of Wire Street in "a little white school house" near J. C. Rockner's store, a location identified as that of the residence now located at 700 East Broadway.[18]

Religious institutions were likewise revived and extended. In 1869 "a few faithful Methodists" began meeting in a local storehouse, most likely that of Lightsey & Roberts. This congregation, the forerunner of the First United Methodist Church, later moved to Wire Street's "little white school house." The Pleasant Grove Church, located two miles east of town, also served area Methodists. At this early date worshipers probably met under an "arbor" rather than in a church building.[19]

By April 1871 Fort Meade presented the picture of "a flourishing and growing little village, beautifully located on the lofty bluff which rises from the right bank of the river, (Pease Creek,) 80 miles from its mouth." Reported teacher Robert LaMartin, "The village is bowered among groves of trees, surrounded with a very fertile and healthy country, and society of the *first order*, and in the centre of the cattle trade, doing three-fourths of the whole business in a radius of 70 miles north, east, and south." Two months later its growth was recognized by the post office's reestablishment. Julius Rockner and his clerk, James W. Jones, presided as the first postmasters. When a new river bridge was constructed that December, the town's citizens had every reason to believe that the problems of the past were behind them and that they finally stood on the threshold of long-sought peace and prosperity.[20]

A Land Title Problem

The progress so evident in 1871 continued into the decade. In 1872 Julius Rockner erected the town's first sawmill in the postwar era, and with it came surveyor, engineer, and millwright John E. Robeson. The same year marked the arrival of Dr. Charles L. Mitchell, a physician and licensed druggist, and also the opening of Eli English's general store. Located in the building "formerly known as the James Manley house" at the northwest corner of present-day Hendry Avenue and First Street Northeast, the store operated until 1874, when English transferred its stock to near modern Wauchula. The community also boasted its first lawyer, Hilliard Jones.[21]

Growth trailed prosperity in its wake. By 1874 the town was being described as "flourishing, busy, and bustling." Robert LaMartin wrote, "If the sound of the hammer and mallet is a significance of the progressive spirit that pervades its limits, it can freely claim progress. The

James Madison Manley, 1837–1905, Moriah Hancock Manley, 1842–1907, and family, c. 1877. (In possession of the author, courtesy of Tom Manley)

health and water is fine, and society refined and orderly." C. B. Lightsey pointed out that 20,000 head of cattle were bought and shipped annually from the town, a $300,000 business. Fort Meade merchants turned over about $100,000 in merchandise each year in addition and bought and shipped $50,000 in country produce.[22]

The level of commercial activity during 1873–1874 compelled the first attempts at town planning, subdivision, and development. Attention was first directed at the half of the Hooker homestead that remained the property of Hooker's widow, Cuthbert Rockner. Deeds executed in January 1873 hint that Cuthbert and her husband Julius had already settled upon a scheme for the subdivision of their land, but not until January 1874 was "A Portion of the Plat of the Town of Fort Meade" laid out by county surveyor William B. Varn. As platted, the subdivision comprised six blocks of approximately four acres each lying between Orange and Hendry avenues, East Broadway, and Third

Street Northeast. Streets were not named on the plat, and an undivided strip lay between the northern tier of three blocks and Third Street Northeast. At the time of the survey, C. L. Mitchell, Hilliard Jones, and Philip Dzialynski owned lots. Additional parcels were soon sold to Madison C. Summerlin and William H. Willingham.[23]

The Rockners' subdivision plat disclosed an interesting anomaly in the location of Wire Street, the present East Broadway. The road ran 118 feet north of the actual survey line dividing the north and south halves of the southeastern quarter of Section 27, Township 31 South, Range 25 East. As a result both sides of the town's main street were owned by the Rockners and those who obtained title from them. Three block-long lots of a depth of 118 feet were accordingly platted south of Wire Street. The central lot, upon which stood Rockner's store, was listed as the property of Philip Dzialynski, a Bartow merchant who made a short-lived attempt at local commerce before moving on to assume Jacob Summerlin's Orlando store. Dzialynski later returned to Fort Meade, however, and acted as a driving force behind its future development.[24]

Philip Dzialynski, 1833–1896. (In possession of the author, courtesy of Perry Coleman)

Demand for town lots prompted a second attempt at subdivision. Sherod E. Roberts had claimed eighty acres immediately east of the Rockners' land, and in October 1874 he filed a subdivision plat prepared by S. J. Stallings. Roberts Addition, as it was called, covered the area bounded by Hendry Avenue, East Broadway, and the line of Wanamaker Avenue, and it extended as far north as the midway point between Fourth and Fifth streets northeast. Roberts's land also extended 118 feet south of Wire Street from present-day Hendry Avenue to Washington Avenue. Notations on the plat indicate that by October lots had already been committed to Willingham, Lightsey, Stallings, Robert McKinney, and Wesley Brandon. Willingham, Roberts, and Lightsey owned the frontage north of Wire Street, and the lots to the south were held, from west to east, by Rockner, Ephraim L. Harrison, William W. Willingham, and James C. Wilson.[25]

In two respects Roberts's subdivision went beyond the Rockner attempt. First, Roberts dedicated Lot 1 of Block 7 as a "Grave Yard" and deeded the property to the "Town of Fort Meade" with the qualification that "title to said described premises [is] to rest in the Mayor and common Council Men of the said Town, as soon as the said shall become incorporated." The donation formed the basis of Evergreen Cemetery. Second, Roberts either attempted to name the streets running east and west through his subdivision or else surveyor Stallings recorded names already in use. East Broadway was, of course, labeled "Wire Street or Road," while First Street Northeast was "Cemetery Street" and a short street to the north was "Peace Creek Street." These are Fort Meade's earliest known street names.[26]

Throughout 1874 and 1875, Fort Meade thrived, although its business community entered a transition period. In 1875 the Lightsey & Roberts partnership dissolved to give Roberts time for politics (he had just been elected state representative) and to allow both men to pursue cattle interests. The store was continued, perhaps after a short interval, by Lightsey's son-in-law Richard C. Langford. A new store named Owen H. Dishong & Company opened just east of the old Lightsey & Roberts place south of Wire Street. Dishong remained only a year or so before moving to near modern Arcadia, where he operated a ferry. One final change occurred in March 1876, when Philip and Mary Dzialynski returned, and "Dzialynski & Company" replaced Julius C. Rockner's store.[27]

Despite the national economic depression that followed the Panic of 1873, only one major setback is known to have occurred to local businessmen and investors during 1874 and 1875. That incident foretold, however, a problem that continued to daunt the town for another decade. As has been seen, Fort Meade's remote situation made travel and market access extremely difficult. For years it had been thought that the problem's solution lay in opening Peace River to navigation by the removal of rocks and snags. To that end the Florida legislature offered a huge land grant and additional concessions to any person or company accomplishing the work, an achievement to be proved by running a steamboat downriver from Fort Meade to Charlotte Harbor. In December 1874 a group of men from the vicinity organized "The Peace Creek Navigation Company" to secure the grant. What, if any, work the company performed in clearing the river is unclear, but in August and September 1875, under the superintendence of Rockner and John E. Robeson, it constructed a steamboat on the town's riverbank. Measuring about forty feet in length, with a beam of fourteen feet, the vessel was designed to draw not over twelve inches of water.

Although many at the time felt "the success of the [steamboat] enterprise is doubtful," an expectant crowd of from one to two dozen citizens climbed aboard the little vessel for her first trial run. Problems immediately surfaced with the steam engines, though, and the boat was poled a short distance upstream from the bridge to test its ability to float and maneuver. The vessel was then turned downstream, the steam engines were cranked into gear, and the vessel's paddlewheels propelled her to the south. Unfortunately, only 300 to 400 yards into the voyage the machinery failed and the boat drifted onto a snag. Investors, seeing their dreams dissolve, leapt overboard to push the vessel off the obstruction and to the riverbank. Months later the powerless boat was poled downriver to Charlotte Harbor. It never returned to its original home.[28]

Despite the navigation company's setback, the community continued to enjoy its cattle trade and prosperity. The increasingly sophisticated town could pride itself not only on its own lodge of the "Masonic Fraternity" but also on a second church.[29] By 1873 circuit preacher

Jeremiah M. Hayman was regularly visiting to minister to Baptist families. In 1874 the Baptists were formally organized under the patronage of cattleman Solomon Godwin. With a membership of between twelve and nineteen persons, the congregation met through the decade but did not survive Godwin's July 1880 death by more than a year or two.[30]

Fort Meade's improved status and prospects led community leaders in 1874 to consider its incorporation. Sentiment ran so strongly in favor by the summer of 1876 that a formal decision to incorporate was taken, but then a problem cropped up. John I. Hooker had paid for his 160 acres at Fort Meade on October 24, 1857. Sherod Roberts no doubt had done the same shortly after filing his 80-acre claim. In 1874 the land had been subdivided and much of it sold. Those tracts included all of the town's business district and many of her residences. In making final arrangements preparatory to incorporation, however, it was discovered that neither original owner had secured title to the land. Inquiries revealed that title still rested in the United States government and that no definite date could be given for its transfer. In the meantime ownership of the land remained in limbo, and not until 1881 was the impasse resolved.[31]

Complicating a troubling situation was what one local man called a "train of murderous events."[32] The killings began on December 6, 1875, at James Manley's barroom. Angered by long-standing conflicts, attorney Hilliard Jones had been slandering Julius Rockner as "a ———— d—n flat-headed Dutchman" and stating that he intended to kill the man. On December 6, Jones's feelings had relaxed enough for the two men to enjoy a game of tenpins at Manley's. As they were settling up accounts with the proprietor, Rockner turned suddenly to Jones, yelled "You threatened to take my life," drew his pistol, and shot the lawyer in the head. Jones died instantly. Within three months a new attorney, Stephen M. Sparkman, who had recently married Rockner's stepdaughter, arrived to fill the vacancy.[33]

The chain of violence continued. A short while later Arthur Keen shot Sam Sherrod in circumstances that may have been related to the Jones killing. Since Keen was still operating Manley's bar, the incident likely occurred at or near the saloon. In April 1876 Rockner and Keen were both indicted for murder, tried, and found "not guilty."[34] An uneasy truce then held for the remainder of 1876 and into 1877. On July

23, though, Rockner himself became a target as he was gunned down from ambush by cattleman William W. Willingham, son of William H. Willingham. Philip Dzialynski reported the incident:

> On Monday morning [Rockner], in company with other men, was returning to Fort Meade from a point below Peace Creek, where they had been to herd and start off a bunch of beef cattle, when, about 3 miles from Fort Meade, he was shot. The shooting took place at about 10 A.M. The assassin had concealed himself near the road, and was not over ten paces from his victim when he fired the fatal shot. The gun was charged with a load of buckshot, and the whole load entered the side and three of the shot entered the heart.
>
> Mr. Fred Varn was riding by the side of Rockener, and they two were a little in advance of the main party, when the shooting occurred. Rockener's horse ran some thirty yards when his rider fell off and immediately expired. Mr. Varn having dismounted and reached him just before his last gasp. A man was seen running, by one of the party, from the place of the assassin's concealment, but he did not recognize him, and was unable to give any definite description of him. With the exception of Mr. Varn who remained with the murdered man, all who were along left in a hurry—some going to Fort Meade, and others in various directions, and no effort was made to pursue or capture the murderer. Since this murder we are informed that a deadly feud existed between Rockener and another party living in the vicinity of Fort Meade. . . .
>
> Whatever else one thing is certain, in his death Polk county has lost a citizen of enterprise whose place it will be hard to fill.[35]

Willingham was eventually tried for Rockner's murder. To "a perfect roar of cheers for the jury," he was acquitted.[36]

F ORT MEADE and its vicinity prospered mightily from 1870 to 1877. Sustained by the stable and lucrative cattle trade, the community became a mercantile center and a mecca for cattlemen and their families. With prosperity the town grew and began to develop, while nurturing the institutions necessary to community life. As it was about to seek recognition of its new status, however, it was beset by problems of land ownership and a legacy of frontier violence. Leading citizens killed and were killed, and—as the town looked to its future—what had once seemed so clear had suddenly become cloudy.

5

Waiting for the Train

THE FIVE-YEAR PERIOD encompassing 1877–1881 witnessed slow, steady progress at Fort Meade as well as at Homeland's rural settlement. No great leaps forward were taken, nor were any insurmountable disasters endured. There were trials, and there were unmet needs, but overall there was progress. A pioneer citizen, pen-named "Veteran," returned to Fort Meade in August 1881 after seven years' absence. He left a written snapshot of the visit that offers a unique glimpse of the community:

> We left Manatee [modern Hardee] and entered Polk county. This portion is sparsely settled, but has some new settlement. We crossed Bowlegs creek on the bridge, which is in a dilapidated condition. Four miles [further] we arrived at the crossing of Peace creek. . . .
>
> We were surprised at finding no bridge at the ford, and had to hallow for the ferryman to put us across. Here we found a want of enterprise, and surely a great drawback to the nice village of Fort Meade. I had been familiar with Fort Meade and the surroundings, but could not recognize one familiar object. The trees planted by Capt. Louis Lanier looked like stately oaks, hanging full of oranges. In the business part of the village fine houses and orange groves were all that could be seen, having in a few years replaced the oaks and pine thickets.
>
> Ft. Meade has a population of 200, two religious organizations (Baptist and Methodist), with good memberships, a school of 40 scholars, three stores, a drug store, a tan yard, one saddlebag and shoe shop, one doctor (who makes up the deficiency in his practice by planting orange

groves and raising babies), a dentist, post-office, telegraph office and four operators, two boarding houses. . . .

I met Capt. [Louis] Lanier and enjoyed his hospitality; also Major Phil. Dzialynski. I found my old friend Jack [Robeson] busy as a bee, and talked over old times, oranges and railroads with Capt. [C. B.] Lightsey and John Skipper. . . . Capt. Lightsey is completing a fine house of eight rooms, and anticipates, when he catches his bird, opening a hotel.

Fort Meade is one solid orange grove. In one mile square there are 2,000 bearing trees, and 18,000 not bearing—being [9] not bearing to 1 bearing. The land in the vicinity is all in the hands of private individuals, and is selling from $5 to $100 an acre. Here are guavas in abundance. Grapes are also attracting a good deal of attention. I met Rev. Mr. [S. W.] Carson, who brought in some fine scuppernongs, and has cuttings for sale at 50¢, each.

Fort Meade has good society and hospitable and intelligent people. . . . All the people . . . now require to rapidly advance is a sawmill, and transportation. These will make the place one of the most prosperous in the state, being in the center of the most fertile lands in Florida. Our friend, R. C. Langford, arrived from Orlando, and reports the railroad coming. . . .

Old Will [William H. Willingham] lives on the east side—has a fine place, good orange grove, and no changes are perceptible in him.[1]

Business Affairs

"Veteran" may have found no perceptible changes in "Old Will," but certainly he found them all about town. During his seven years' absence, two particularly striking transformations had occurred. The town's main street and business community had expanded and grown more diverse, and orange groves were popping up everywhere.

We last looked at Wire Street in 1876, and things there had changed indeed by 1881. The leading merchant, Philip Dzialynski, had formed a partnership in 1878 with Dr. Charles L. Mitchell, and Dzialynski, Mitchell, & Company offered residents and cattlemen all varieties of dry goods and groceries. This partnership and the expansion it permitted were made necessary by competition beginning that year from Hooker & Snodgrass, composed of James N. Hooker and Cyrus Adams Snodgrass (a Pensacola merchant). Located on Wire Street's south side west of and opposite Church Avenue, Hooker & Snodgrass prospered. Within a year Howard Acree Snodgrass purchased his father's interest and, in turn, was bought out by Hooker in 1882. J. N. Hooker & Company then remained a town fixture until the 1890s.[2]

Other facets of commercial life had also changed. Richard C. Langford, who was engaged in the dry goods business in 1876 and remained so until about 1880, had superseded James Manley as a saloon proprietor. Arthur Keen had left Manley's employ and by 1878 had become a grocer. Joseph Stallings had also operated a grocery until his July 1880 death. That year the vocation so essential to any community, that of village blacksmith, was pursued by William Peters.[3] While developer Sherod Roberts was pursuing the cattle business, his son William A. Roberts in 1877 opened up a drugstore on the site of the old Lightsey & Roberts store. When Roberts fell ill in 1879, his clerk Victor L. Tillis continued to run "the county drugstore."[4] Charles L. Mitchell served as town physician, and in 1877 his efforts were aided by the arrival of the area's first resident dentist, Dr. Seabren G. Hayman. Attorney Stephen M. Sparkman opted to seek his greater fortune at Tampa in August 1879, and not later than 1882, Charles C. Wilson had arrived to fill the professional gap.[5]

With Sparkman's 1879 departure, Fort Meade was left with a large, comfortable, and unoccupied home on Church Avenue's east side north of East Broadway. Teacher John Snoddy, needing money to supplement his meager salary, leased the home and opened what he called "the first hotel proper in the county." According to Snoddy, "Here my moss mattress accommodations and sumptuous bill of fare, consisting exclusively of [hayti] potatoes, palmetto cabbage and catfish, gained for my house great notoriety as a place of resort."[6] The boardinghouse operated only about one year before the teacher moved to Bartow. His departure may have been speeded by the 1881 opening of the Philip Dzialynski home, "one of the roomiest, most commodious and best finished residences in Polk county," to paying guests.[7]

Throughout 1877–1881 Fred N. Varn continued to operate his celebrated tanyard and shoe and leather shop. C. L. Mitchell by 1881, in addition to other activities, developed "Sunnyside Nursery," which would become a south Florida institution. Somehow Mitchell also found time to serve as postmaster, and assisting him with his postal duties was one of Florida's legendary figures, James Mitchell "Acre-foot" Johnson. From 1877 to 1884 Johnson, said to have been six feet seven and one-half inches tall, carried the mail on foot first once, then twice, a week down the Wire Road to Fort Ogden. Legend insists that he gave up the job in 1884 when the government refused to let him carry passengers.[8]

The postal service offered residents one method of communication, and the telegraph provided another. From the summer of 1867 Fort Meade had been the site of an International Ocean Telegraph Company maintenance depot, but beginning in 1878, it was graced with two telegraph lines. If the telegraph wire did not run through your community, you did not have modern communications. With only one wire running through south Florida and no railroad of any kind, many communities, even those on the coast, remained isolated. One such place was Tampa.

The 1860s and 1870s had been unkind to Tampa. It had been bombed and captured by Union forces; been ravaged by yellow fever; seen the cattle business move off to the south; and at times almost become depopulated. For a while it had even ceased to be incorporated. By early 1877, though, some citizens had begun seeing a little light on the horizon. The village had its port, and as the local newspaper reported that March, "Tampa enjoys the prospect of a railroad within five years."[9] This stir of optimism helped generate a determination by town leaders to break Tampa's isolation. The method chosen was the construction of a private telegraph line to a juncture with the IOTC line somewhere in the interior.[10]

News of Tampa's desire for a telegraphic connection was met with enthusiasm at Fort Meade. Sensing possibilities for profit as well as advantages for the town, local businessmen proposed in June 1877 that they subscribe "one third of the amount of money necessary to construct the line from Tampa to that place."[11] At Tampa the proposal was accepted. Within two months the Tampa & Fort Meade Telegraph Company had been incorporated, Philip Dzialynski had been elected its vice president, and James T. Wilson and Fred N. Varn were serving on its board of directors.[12] Construction of the line was undertaken in December 1877 under Sherod Roberts's superintendence. By January 5, 1878, it stretched to within a mile of Tampa, but its operation was delayed first by the nonarrival of a battery and then by foul-weather damage. Despite the problems, Tampa's editor could report on May 25, "Telegraphic communication between Tampa and Fort Meade was opened on the 15th inst., which imparts new life and vigor to the facility of business in the two places."[13] When a message was sent from Tampa in early June asking someone "to gather the local news," Fort Meade operator William A. Roberts quickly and positively responded. " 'Dzialynski and Mitchell," he wired, "are selling the cheapest goods that have ever been sold in Florida.' MITCHELL."[14]

The Temperance Cause

Fort Meade had two telegraph lines by 1881, but one thing that it did not have was a saloon. Whiskey had been easily available since the military outpost days, and during the 1870s Manley's "bar-room" had been a prominent fixture on Wire Street. Even on the frontier, however, the temperance cause was gaining strength. In late 1877 that trend resulted in the creation by the Reverend S. W. Carson and some thirty others of a lodge of the "Good Templars," an organization founded in 1851 dedicated to "temperance, peace, and brotherhood with emphasis on personal abstinence from intoxicating drink."[15]

The Good Templars' work spurred complaints about "ungodly habits" centered on the town's "grog shop." One man defended the community by remarking, "As to the 'grog shops' there is but one here, and but for the patronage of the country people its proprietor could not pay his license, for there is not an habitual drunkard living in Ft. Meade."[16] The temperance campaign continued, and as residents slept early on Sunday morning, March 27, 1881, R. C. Langford's "bar-room and fixtures" were consumed by fire. Noting a loss of $1,900, local reports labeled the blaze as "evidently the work of an incendiary."[17]

The saloon's destruction did not prompt the arsonist's arrest. Rather, community leaders organized by Philip Dzialynski blocked the bar's reopening. "Our town is now without a liquor shop," one citizen declared in August, "and the probability is that it will remain so for some time, for I think that nearly every person owning land in and around the place has signed a paper drawn up in the form of an agreement to never sell or rent any person a house or land on which to build one, who intends to deal in liquor."[18] When an entrepreneur raised funds for such a purpose one year later, the money was stolen from the post office. A Bartow editor commented, "No clue has yet been found to the robbery of the Ft. Meade post office and the robbery is accidentally of a fund the fate of which causes little regret. It was being sent off for the liquors to start a bar-room, and this crime saves for the time being the injury the town was threatened with. We do not sanction any sort of crime, but we are glad it was not the funds of some poor man seeking to enter a homestead, or to pursue a more honorable calling than liquor selling."[19]

Entertainment, Excitement, and Tragedy

Throughout the final years of the 1870s and early 1880s, Fort Meade remained the most populous town in Polk County and, for that matter, in all of peninsular Florida south of Tampa. In 1877 one writer described the village as "quite a lively place."[20] Two years later a correspondent called it "quite a handsome place," adding that "nature has done much for it."[21] In 1881 a visitor declared with certainty that the town's progress "must be onward and upward."[22]

With the community's increasing size and prominence, residents enjoyed a more diverse civic and social life. Daily routine could be disrupted by anything from cattle drives down Wire Street to the irregular visits of Indian families seeking to avail themselves of Dr. Mitchell's medical skills. More spectacular were events such as the attempt by "Hub" Williams, the "Robin Hood of South Florida," to rob Dzialynski, Mitchell, & Company in October 1878, during which Morgan Snow wounded the outlaw in a shootout. On the more civilized side, the Fort Meade Lyceum offered literary pleasures, and the town was entertained by its first "Fort Meade String Band." Fish fries, dances, and Peace River swimming parties were all the rage. Reflecting a diversity of heritage, residents celebrated on October 31, 1877, the area's first Jewish wedding—that of Philip Dzialynski's daughter, Jennie, to Louis Herzog of Baltimore.[23]

One traditional community event was revived to everyone's pleasure. In 1878 a public invitation was issued to a huge "4th of July Barbecue," the first such celebration at the town since the Civil War. "On the 3d the town was full of arrivals," reported an onlooker, "but it was the morning of the 4th that the stream began to pour in from every quarter. Buggies, wagons, horses, ox-teams and mules came in one extended procession." A pavilion was erected under the oaks on the west bank of Peace River, seats were provided, and tables 200 feet long were piled high with food. Speeches and singing followed the eating. One remarkable moment occurred soon thereafter. "At the close came more singing," disclosed the onlooker, "and—a pistol shot had a startling effect upon the gathering, especially when some shouted 'the Indians are coming'. . . , and now came a weird troupe of mounted figures dressed in most fantastic costumes. They came up in procession and filed around the pavilion, and a representative of the fatherland (German) [Philip Dzialynski] ascended the steps and delivered an oration on 'The fort of Ghuly' in true Teutonic style, eliciting a large amount of laughter." The day's success ensured its continuation as an annual event.[24]

As at any town Fort Meade's busy life and entertainments were occasionally dampened by the private sorrows of its families. Particularly when tragedies affected children the pain was borne throughout the community. Illustrative of these important, though very personal, events were two incidents occurring in 1879. On May 6, this report was published:

> A singular instance of the verification of a dream occurred in Polk county some days ago. A young daughter of Mr. Henry Hill dreamed one night that she had been burned to death. The *Tampa Guardian* says the next morning she went with her brother into the cornfield to keep the birds from the planted corn. As it was cold they built a fire, and while standing around it the clothes of the young girl caught on fire. Her little brother tried to extinguish the flames, but could not. The poor child's clothing burnt nearly off, and she died the next day.[25]

Two months later a second newspaper related a similarly sad incident:

> Mr. Henry Dampier, living 4½ miles from Ft. Meade, was killed last Monday two weeks ago by the falling of a tree. It seems that Mr. Dam-

pier was in the woods felling a tree for board timber and just as the tree was about to fall, he noticed one of his small children in danger from the falling tree. He ran towards the child and told it to "run," and, although the child was saved, the falling tree struck Mr. Dampier on the head, laying open his skull.[26]

Bethel

As Fort Meade grew, so too did the farm community at modern Homeland. "The improvements that have been made in the last five years can but please the most sanguine," wrote one native in 1880. He added, "Within the sound of a horn's blow where I am now writing, there are twenty or more [citrus] groves, and preparations are being made for more. These are well cared for and promise a rich reward."[27] Prominent among the men tending those groves were James T. Wilson and James B. Crum. Their ranks were joined in 1881 by Henry L. Mitchell, C. L. Mitchell, and Philip Dzialynski when John Parker deeded them his 600-acre homestead. The three partners established on the land "an orange grove of considerable size" that came to be "considered one of the most valuable places in Polk County."[28]

Remaining a rural community, the Homeland area possessed no business district or mercantile houses by 1881. It had, however, fostered two very important institutions of community life—a church and a school.

Homeland since 1860 had been the site of the "Camp Ground" at which, each October, Methodist and other families gathered for revival and socializing. In 1875, Joseph L. and Elizabeth Durrance donated five acres of land nearby "for a place of Divine worship for the use of the ministry and membership of the M. E. Church, South." A board of trustees consisting of W. T. Carpenter, James T. Wilson, and James B. Crum erected "a crude wooden structure having no glass windows and no lights except candles." The building may have been a humble one, but to area families its presence meant so much that they began calling their community after it—and for the next decade modern Homeland was known as "Bethel." The structure was the first erected for church purposes at either Fort Meade or Homeland.[29]

A school had existed for Bethel-area children before the Civil War. Records and accounts do little more than hint that it was continued in the postwar period. By 1879, though, a resident could publicly assert, "We have one of the best schools taught here, that is to be found outside the cities in the State."[30] A visitor the following month described Bethel Academy. "Near Bethel Church stands the new school house," he commented, "the existence of which is due to the untiring efforts of Mr. [John] Snoddy. It is large, well ventilated and beautifully situated. Upon entering it, one is favorably impressed to find it so well furnished. Among the most striking objects that meet the eyes of an observer, are some of the large blank blackboards, covered with richly colored maps drawn with great precision by the pupils. Passing from them the next objects of interest are tiers of well constructed seats and desks, occupied by well dressed girls and boys."[31]

Teacher Snoddy recalled the humble beginnings of Bethel Academy. "In the spring of 1878," he wrote, "I put in my appearance in the locality where Homeland now stands, a stranger and a tramp in 'shabby genteel,' more shabby than genteel, however, I wanted a school, the citizens suspicioned I was a 'bad egg,' and did everything in their power to send me on, but at last I started a school of five little A, B, C splats in a board shanty." He continued, "In less than four months my success was so great as a teacher that I found myself at the head of a school of some sixty pupils in a large new school house."[32] In late 1879 Snoddy relocated to Fort Meade, and the following summer the schoolhouse was moved "one mile north from where it was" and reopened by Daniel C. Kantz. Thereafter, it continued to educate Bethel's children and developed into an institution well respected for the many teachers whose education began there.[33]

A final and important aspect of developing life at Bethel during the 1870s was the arrival of a number of black families. Most freedmen had left the vicinity within a short time after the Civil War's conclusion, and in 1880 only a few blacks were living at Fort Meade. Bob Williams and Henry Wells were working at the Peace River ferry, and Tillie Baine was serving as a nurse for C. L. Mitchell's children. Present also were the family of Jennie Tillis, Stephen Hagan, Christine Tillis, and Susan Tillis with her infant son, James.[34]

While Fort Meade's black population remained small, Bethel's black community was becoming much more well established. Rachel Davis's family (including her sons Samuel, Corrie, and Lloyd, who would become prominent cattlemen) was likely present soon after the war. A. C. Robinson and his family arrived from Sneads, Florida, in or just prior to 1870, and by 1873, Charles McLeod was on the scene. Within two years Jack Vaughn had married Margaret McLeod and settled. He was followed in 1878 by Moses Allen, who married Eliza Davis. By 1880, Lewis Honors, Charles Glover, Charles Harden, Mary Jones, Mary Holomon, and the Charity Williams family also resided in the area. From these beginnings grew a community of prosperous farmers and

Hattie Honors Davis, b. 1875, wife of Corrie Davis and child of early Homeland resident Lewis Honors. (In possession of the author, courtesy of Vernice Williams)

Mack Vaughn, born c. 1872, standing in front of his father Jack Vaughn's homestead at Homeland. (In possession of the author, courtesy of Vernice Williams)

cattlemen whose children and grandchildren would become leaders in teaching and other professions and whose descendants continue the same tradition to this day.[35]

A Problem of Transportation

The prosperity of Wire Street merchants and professionals and cattlemen whose pockets were filled with gold doubloons did not benefit the area's largest block of residents—farmers and their families. Separated by a wide economic gulf from their more prosperous fellow citizens, many farmers struggled to keep themselves and their loved ones clothed and fed. George W. Hendry made the point in December 1879 when he wrote, "The cattle business has been the only paying pursuit in South Florida, and at this very time it affords nearly all the money that passes the hands of the farmer, the blacksmith, the merchant, the doctor and lawyer, as well as the fruit-growers of South Florida."[36]

Work as hard as he might, the farmer at Fort Meade or Homeland could not get ahead, because, even if he had a bumper crop, he had no feasible way to get his produce to any desirable market. A local man in August 1877 explained the impact of that fact on area farm families. "Shut out, or rather shut in from the ordinary scenes of busy life," he wrote, "we hear hump and heave, curse and swear, and encounter more ills and inconveniences than are incidental to human life ordinarily. In this discouraging situation the overplus of produce made in this prolific year is such in many cases as the 'cow will not eat,' and is left to lie and rot by the tons, and return to its mother earth on the very spot that gave it life." Despairingly he added, "To submit to a condition that disinherits us of the convenience of life and live an age in the rear of modern progress is chafing to the sensitive part of our nature and is not in harmony with the innate dispositions of our being."[37]

Fort Meade's farmers, at least, did not suffer from the problems inherent in a "one crop" agricultural system. Corn, cotton, rice, peas, potatoes, sugarcane, grapes, tomatoes, okra, guavas, bananas, watermelons, limes, lemons, and many other crops were raised, but the growth industry involved oranges. That fruit could travel somewhat better than other crops and, consequently, could be hauled by ox teams to seaports or railroads with less spoilage. Unfortunately it took cash or a substantial amount of credit to get involved in orange production on any serious scale, and in the absence of a single bank in interior south Florida, only cattlemen, merchants, and professionals had those resources. Consequently, as orange groves spread throughout the area west of Peace River and then east across the stream into "the Deadening" and on toward the Ridge and the Kissimmee River valley, the average farmer and his family found themselves, once again, bypassed by prosperity.[38]

As if farm problems were not bad enough, in 1878 and 1879 the forces of nature combined to lash south Florida unmercifully. Throughout the winter and spring of 1878 rain poured onto range and farmlands. After a short respite the waters returned from September 7 to

10 in the form of the "Great Hurricane of 1878." George W. Hendry waited out the treacherous winds and waters at Fort Meade and then wrote a graphic account describing the horrors he had witnessed:

In the forenoon of the 7th ult. the sun had illumined the earth and sky with its lucid rays, but the firmament was dotted with scattering clouds. Ere the sun had reached its meridian height, showers of rain came thick and rapid, the clouds lowering and musky, while their sombre glory brought with them no omen of good for us. The increasing terror of their passing shrouded the earth in gloom, and warned us of the approaching crisis. By the time the sun had bid adieu to the far west, darkness veiled the earth while madness and fury controlled the elements above.

The scene was terrific and sublime as the nightly orb with its lurid dimness added a grandeur solemn and fearful. All night long the wind came steady and direct from a little N. of E. the clouds emptying a deluge of rain in torrents. Day light brought with it no abatement, the 8th being the holy Sabbath was sacredly kept indoors by the wiley pioneers of Polk.

For about sixty hours the clouds, the rain and wind were an unchangeable feature and possessed an unabating firmness. Not until the afternoon of the 10th were signs favorable for its cessation. Fences were blown down, and in many instances swept away by the mighty deluge of water. Fields on low land and others bordering water courses were submerged while the rails mingled with the floating logs and brush, drifted to a better resting place. The earth around wells of water melted, enveloping curbs, forming a basin in which the frogs congregated to quaintly chirp their happy jubilee.

Boulders of rock and clay tumbled from our chimneys, embedding our hearth-stones, while just outside lay our chimneys a mass of ruins. Cane, potatoes, pea and rice crops were exposed to the roving stock, though the damage from that cause is nothing to compare with that of the wind and rain. The orange trees laden with their golden fruit are riddled, the earth around strewn with leaves and fragments of limbs, while nearer by lie heaps of the fruit punctured by hundreds of thorns. At least half the orange crop is lost.

Cattle being poor many were chilled through and died long before the storm ceased. The damage to stock is serious, but more to cattle as perhaps one-sixth have died and will die from the cause of wind and rain.

Roads are rendered impassable, bridges all swept away and the earth so miry makes traveling much, impossible. The extent of damages cannot be correctly estimated at present, but this we know that 1878 has been one of the most disastrous years in South Florida than any known to its oldest settlers.[39]

During the Great Hurricane of 1878 Peace River rose so high at Fort Meade that its waters lapped the insulators on telegraph poles strung alongside the bridge. The bridge, itself, was swept away when the floodwater "rose even above the railing on it."[40] And Mother Nature was not finished yet. Early in 1879 tornadoes visited the area, leaving widespread destruction in their paths. February brought drought that lasted for months, and to cap everything else off, a "heavy frost" in April destroyed the scattered remaining crops.[41] Facing their losses and with nowhere else to go, Fort Meade's farmers could only begin to rebuild what they had lost and patiently wait for better days. They knew that, until the sound of an approaching train promised easy transportation, they and their families would remain stalled on the road to progress and prosperity.

From 1877 to 1881 Fort Meade grew and prospered as the cattle industry thrived and the development of orange groves promised future rich returns. The community and particularly its farmers, however, continued to be hamstrung by a lack of any reliable form of transportation. By the end of the period, though, some local residents were coming to believe that the trains' whistles were not far distant and that there was money to be made before the rails arrived.

6

"Seeking homes in a summer clime"

Room for All

W INDS OF CHANGE swirled around south Florida in the summer of 1881 as if a mighty storm was about to set upon the land. Stirred by these winds a pulse of energy and excitement built throughout the still remote peninsula. Over the next five years it intensified as the dynamism of investment, large-scale development, and the coming of the railroads began to remake the face and future of the land and its inhabitants. The realization of dreams suddenly seemed within the grasp of every dreamer, and the region's future loomed brighter and ever so much more golden.

The Disston Land Sale

The spark that ignited the flames of dynamism was struck in June 1881, when the Florida state government, its finances precarious, grasped at a financial straw held by Hamilton Disston. A Philadelphia businessman, Disston agreed to take off the state's hands 4 million acres of public lands, mostly in south Florida. In return, the state would receive $1 million, a figure that assigned the land a value of only twenty-five cents an acre. Since Disston did not have $1 million available, he disposed of half his purchase to British businessman Sir Edward J. Reed for $600,000. In case Disston's remaining 2 million acres proved insufficient for his purposes, he also bargained with the state to receive one-half of any acreage he could drain and reclaim.[1]

The heart of Disston's early efforts was a plan to drain the Everglades and open up the Kissimmee River–Lake Okeechobee–Caloosahatchee River system to navigation. Not one to stand idle, the developer hurried his plans into execution, and by late September 1881 his first floating dredge was being hauled up the Caloosahatchee River. Soon the dredge had been joined by three others, and within three years Disston had claimed to have drained over 2 million acres of wetlands.[2]

While the Disston efforts were remaking south Florida to the east and south, their impact was also felt at Fort Meade. His Florida Land and Improvement Company held 102,000 acres in Polk County and an additional 370,000 acres in old Manatee (all of present Hardee, DeSoto, Highlands, Charlotte, Glades, Sarasota, and Manatee counties). Disposal of the lands required a local agent, and to find him the developer looked to the area's oldest and largest town. At Fort Meade Disston found physician, businessman, and real estate dealer Charles L. Mitchell. By the summer of 1882 Mitchell had opened his headquarters at the town and was advertising far and wide "this rare opportunity of securing desirable locations for Orange Groves and other semi-tropical fruits at nominal prices." Mitchell's ads mentioned as well his Sunnyside Nursery, from which he promised to "supply all varieties of Trees, Plants, and Seeds." The entrepreneur added, "I plant Orange Groves, enter lands, pay taxes and attend to all other business for nonresidents."[3]

As the Disston empire was being organized, other developmental influences were combining to make their own impact felt. Premier among these was the likelihood that two, and perhaps three, railroads were about to provide Fort Meade with desperately needed transportation links.

The Jacksonville, Tampa, & Key West Railway (later a part of the South Florida Railroad) originated in meetings held between Tampa, Fort Meade, and Bartow area businessmen in late 1877 and early 1878. Original plans, devised in part by Alexander S. Johnston of Homeland and George W. Hendry and Philip Dzialynski of Fort Meade, called for a link between Tampa, the two Peace River communities, and the St. Johns River. Funding and other problems frustrated its backers, but by October 1882 Henry L. Mitchell, C. L. Mitchell's brother, could report,

"The company has cash subscribed, from parties who are amply able to pay it, sufficient to build 135 miles of the road; that is, from Jacksonville to Palatka, on the northern end, and from Tampa to Medora, Bartow and Ft. Meade on the southern end."[4] At the same time the Florida Southern Railway, organized in 1879 to construct and operate a line from Lake City to Charlotte Harbor, was slowly extending its rail south of Gainesville. Backers planned for the line to run to Fort Meade, where it would cross Peace River.[5]

Buoyed by promised rail links and anxious to profit from Disston's development of the Kissimmee River valley, Fort Meade businessmen also determined to build their own rail line connecting the Florida Southern's proposed Fort Meade river crossing with Keystone (the present-day Frostproof area) and the Kissimmee River. The efforts paid off on December 9, 1882, when the Fort Meade, Keystone & Walk-in-the-Water Railroad Company was incorporated at Jacksonville. "When this road is completed," noted one account, "the journey can be made from Jacksonville to Fort Meade inside of thirty-six hours."[6]

New Arrivals Galore

Publicity from Disston land sales and railroad speculations drew considerable attention to Fort Meade and vicinity. In January 1883 William Thompson, a resident since 1878, wrote, "The large number of strangers visiting this place in the past few weeks is satisfying evidence that, notwithstanding the limited means of transportation, many of those leaving the North and West, seeking homes in a summer clime are finding their way here." He continued, "It is astonishing the number of letters received weekly by Dr. C. L. Mitchell, Disston's enterprising land agent. They come from every state and territory in the Union—from England, Ireland, Wales and Germany—all seeking information; and while it may be true that some are written through curiosity, the majority are in earnest. Let them come; there is room for all, and good people are welcome."[7]

And come they did. Between 1881 and 1885 scores of families cast their lot with the Fort Meade area. Among these settlers were many who, in the years to come, would play vital roles in creating a thriving society on the raw south Florida frontier. While some newcomers shared the Deep South roots of most of the area's population, the greater number hailed from the North and Midwest. Numbered among the arrivals were: in 1881, E. R. Childers of Alabama; in 1882, Dr. M. O. Arnold (IA), James Benedict (PA), W. B. Gardner (MS), and W. P. Sheretz (IL); in 1883, T. W. Anderson (GA), J. W. Boyd (KY), J. W. Henderson (IA), W. T. Hyres (IL), W. H. Lewis (FL), C. F. Marsh (IA), B. F. Perry (AL), J. W. Powell (IA), G. W. Rudisill (IA), G. F. Sater (IA), W. L. Thompson (KS), Winfield S. Thompson (KS), Edward and James Van Hook (IN), V. B. Webster, and F. A. Whitehead (NY & DL); in 1884, Albion H. Adams (MD), Jeff Marchman (GA), A. J. McKillop (GA), Thomas J. Minor (MO), Early Mitchell (GA), and Max Reif (Germany, NY, and FL); and in 1885, W. G. Ball (FL), Arthur B. Canter (MO), Sterling Canter (MO), E. Alonzo Cordery (NJ), H. A. Gardiner (NY), Varnum P. Simmons (RI), E. J. Stinsman (MN), James S. Wade (MO), and Dr. William L. Weems (MO).[8]

One newcomer sat at his Fort Meade desk in the autumn of 1883 to explain what attracted many of these families. "Capital and labor," began Winfield S. Thompson,

> have too long endeavored to convert the bleak prairies and dismal forests of the West into profitable farms and happy homes. Western farmers have learned by sad experience that it does not pay to raise twenty cent corn or three cent pork, and are heartily tired of working hard to furnish railroads the material for enriching the controlling corporations at the expense of honest toil. Add to this the severity of recent winters, and the prevalence of tornadoes and disastrous storms throughout the North and West, and it is not at all surprising that many have turned their faces toward our sunland, while many more are eagerly scanning the southern horizon to catch some word of encouragement, that they may come also.[9]

The transition from North and Midwest to "our sunland" was not always easy for new settlers. Even getting directions could present a considerable problem as explained by the following article which appeared in an 1886 edition of Fort Meade's first newspaper, the *Pioneer*:

> A "sand scrub" in Florida is a sand bank or hill where, on account of the poverty of the soil, the trees and scrubs grow very low and "scrubby."

These spots are sometimes of but a few acres in extent, and again they cover several hundred acres. The immigrant is generally puzzled to know what a "sand scrub" is. An Iowa man showed his knowledge of the Florida terms in the following manner:

Landing at Lakeland several years ago, when that place was the terminus of the South Florida railroad, he attempted to reach Bartow, fifteen miles distant, in the good old-fashioned, though very popular way—on foot. He had just come from a place of firm footing, and ere he reached his destination he fully realized that Florida sand was a "hard road to travel." Weary, and no doubt somewhat disgusted, he approached a cabin by the roadside and meekly asked the inmate, a woman, to direct him on his way. The lady kindly told him to proceed in the direction he was going about a mile, when he would come to a "sand scrub," and there he should take a left-hand road and follow that till it passed a bay head on one side and a big "permeter patch" on the other, and to go on till he came to a "gallberry flat" where he would strike the main road leading out through a "grass pond" into the "flat woods." Here he would find a boy, "boarding off" corn, and he could tell him better than she could.

The Hawkeye bowed gracefully and, with a far away look in his eye, ambled on his now mysterious way, revolving on his perplexed cranium the meaning of all this. Having gone, as he thought, about a mile, he began to look for something, he knew not what. Presently he met a small boy whom he accosted: "Say, bub, are you a 'sand scrub?' " "No," answered the youth, "I'm a cracker." The boy soon enlightened the traveler's bewildered understanding by directing his attention to a "sand scrub" just ahead. Our friend found his way to Bartow, and is now, we believe, a resident of Polk county, and familiar with the terms that so perplexed him on his first Florida journey.[10]

Potential settlers, from wherever they hailed, were not the only ones snapping up land near Fort Meade. Leading politicians, including governors William D. Bloxham and Edward A. Perry and State Superintendent of Public Instruction E. K. Foster, purchased orange grove sites. Seth French, an Orange County state senator, bought substantial acreage, as did state land agent, surveyor, and speculator Marcellus A. Williams of Jacksonville and Connecticut investor Edward M. Brown. Eager to assist prospective buyers—in addition to C. L. Mitchell—were J. E. Robeson and his Garden of Eden Land Agency, J. W. Boyd and the Fort Meade Land Agency, and George W. Hendry and the Keystone Land Agency.[11]

Charles L. Mitchell, 1848–1900 (left), and John Evans "Jack" Robeson, 1847–1898 (right). (In possession of the author, courtesy of Joan Wilson Balega)

Expansion

Flurries of land sales, announcements of railroads a-building, and the arrival of new settlers all had immediate and visible impacts. Since 1874 the village's only subdivided areas had been those of the original "Varn's Survey" and "Roberts' Addition." In terms of modern streets, the area was encompassed by a line beginning on Orange Avenue 118 feet south of East Broadway and running north to a line somewhat short of Third Street Northeast, then eastward to Hendry Avenue, northward to the line of Fourth Street Northeast, eastward to the line of Wanamaker Avenue, southward to 118 feet south of East Broadway, and back to the beginning on Orange Avenue.

In 1883, things began to change. On January 6 James M. Manley sold to Lewis W. Hooker his eighty acres lying west of Varn's Survey, a tract that included the site of the second fort and that had originally been a part of the homestead of Lewis's father, John I. Hooker. Within three months Hooker and Fernandina D. Robeson, wife of J. E. Robeson and daughter of Sherod E. Roberts, had subdivided the tract, as well as some additional land owned by them, as "Hooker and Robeson's Addition." Covering the area within the line of East Broadway, Charleston Avenue, Third Street Northeast, Oak Avenue, Sixth Street Northeast, and Orange Avenue, and including the usual strip south of East Broadway, the "Addition" more than doubled the town's subdivided land.[12]

Hooker and Robeson's Addition was only the beginning of new development. Soon C. L. Mitchell opened up, for the first time, residential lots south of East Broadway. "Mitchell's Addition" comprised 160 acres and lay to the west of Oak Avenue, running to Charleston Avenue between Sixth and Ninth streets southeast and all the way to Sand Mountain Road between Third and Sixth streets. The subdivision lay so far from 1883's "downtown" that some considered it "a survey for a new village" and called the area "New Fort Meade." Regardless, by April 1 Mitchell had sold sixteen lots.[13]

The success of these subdivisions encouraged more of the same in 1884 and 1885. It also paved the way for further subdivision of most of the business district along Wire Street, which by then was known as "Main Street." Important to this process was an 1884 resurvey of Varn's Survey that became known as "Seth French's Addition" and that extended the subdivision to Sixth Street Northeast between Orange and Church avenues. Philip Dzialynski the same year opened up the 200-acre Dzialynski's Addition near the modern business district west of Charleston Avenue, an area so distant from "Fort Meade" that the twenty-acre center of today's downtown was left as an orange grove named "Hard Bargain." In 1885 "Mrs. C. W. Rockner's Addition" filled in the 120-acre gap south of East Broadway between Charleston Avenue, Third Street Southeast, Oak Avenue, Sixth Street Southeast, and Orange Avenue. Mitchell and French, with the aptly named "Mitchell and French's Addition," did the same for the rectangle of Charleston Avenue, Ninth Street Northeast, Oak Avenue, and Third Street Northeast.[14]

In the manner described, the streets and subdivisions of Fort Meade were laid out essentially as they remain today. But for every family settling in town, several chose to live "in the country" where they could farm. This fact gave birth in 1883 and 1884 to the community's first "suburb" apart from the community at Homeland. Known as "Fairview," the rural settlement stretched eastward through "The Deadening" from Peace River to "The Ridge." Some families, such as T. C. Keller's, had lived in the area for a decade or more. The tide of new settlers beginning in 1883, however, created a sense of community that led, by late 1884, to the erection of a schoolhouse. To the area came the families of James M. Manley, H. A. Gardiner, E. J. Hilliard, William Raulerson, Winfield S. Thompson, W. L. Thompson, and others. James and Edward Van Hook settled at "Lookout Hill" on the Ridge and promptly dubbed their "suburb" of Fairview "Fairview Highlands."[15]

Homeland

The increasing numbers of settlers were also reflected in the faces of new arrivals at Bethel. Thomas W. Anderson particularly attracted newcomers from his hometown of Newnan, Georgia. "We have not the Everglades filled with Indians, alligators, insects &c," Anderson informed Newnan's residents, "but a high, dry, beautiful and healthy country, a section that will in a few years, when this erroneous impression is removed, become the most densely populated of any portion of the United States." Anderson brought from Newnan by wagon in 1884 the families of Martin B. Swearingen, Leroy W. Scroggins, A. J. McKillop, and M. C. Puckett, as well as two black families, those of Early Mitchell and Jeff Marchman. Homeland's black community was further enhanced by the arrival not later than 1885 of the Tom Walden, J. L. Robinson, and Emma Hendry families.[16]

The Bethel community had grown to such an extent by the summer of 1885 that, on behalf of his fellow residents, James T. Hancock, Jr., applied for approval of a post office to serve the area. While listing the proposed site as "Bethel," he entered on the blank after the words "proposed office to be called" the single word "Homeland."[17] Legend has it that the name was suggested "by a young Irish peddler, named McCormick, who came to the settlement from Georgia." One reporter explained, "The beauty of the place so reminded him of his native Ireland that he called it Homeland and the name was immediately adopted."[18] More than mere coincidence is likely, however, in the fact that, in the spring of 1885, Jacksonville *Florida Times-Union* reporter Sherman Adams published a descriptive book on Polk County. Sherman's title, of course, was *Homeland*.[19]

Appearances About Town

Celebrating growth and development, Fort Meade in 1882 built a sanctuary worthy of its enhanced status. Since the community remained predominantly Methodist, it naturally erected a Methodist church. Lumber was ordered in the summer of 1881, but not until April of the following year had progress reached the point of painting. Dedication occurred on May 7, 1882, when proud residents inaugurated the house of worship with ceremonies led by the Reverend Charles E. Pelot. In June Methodist ladies held a "Grand Church Festival" to raise funds for finishing touches, as well as for a bell and organ, and were pleased to realize $635. The festival funds permitted installation of lamps, purchase of a bell, and a reduction of the church debt. The 700-pound bell arrived in October and was installed in time to ring out the birth in January 1883 of the Fort Meade Methodist Circuit. The final seal of approval came that May when the Tampa District Conference met at the new sanctuary in a "pleasant and successful district conference," a meeting made more enjoyable by the hospitality of the Reverend and Mrs. Pelot at their leased parsonage, the former S. M. Sparkman home.[20]

Methodist Episcopal Church, South, erected in 1881–1882.
(Courtesy of the Florida State Archives)

The Methodist church was located on the northwest corner of Church Avenue and Third Street Northeast. "It is a neat, comfortable building," recorded C. E. Pelot, "seating about four hundred persons." He added, "This church reflects great credit on . . . the village of Fort Meade, who have built at a cost of $1,200, without assistance from abroad, save $75 from Bartow."[21] The church did more than reflect credit upon the town, it also dominated its skyline. "On entering the village," wrote George W. Hendry, "the spire of a large Methodist Church is seen far above the tallest trees, giving variety to the scenery altogether attractive."[22] The church had its problems, though. "Jack Frost must be a very devotional youth," declared the *Pioneer* in January 1886, "for if he likes one place around here any better than another it is the inside of the church. He had undisturbed possession there all of last Sunday. Next winter, we think that all new churches as well as the old ones will have stoves; even those which, like ours, are 'below the frost line.' "[23]

As Methodist ladies were preparing to use the proceeds of their "Grand Church Festival," sixteen of their fellow townsmen, led by James N. Hooker, acted to improve the town in a different manner. These men applied to the county commission "for a public road commencing at the west end of the business street in Fort Meade, thence down the west side of Peace creek, crossing it at Snow's, on the shoals, thence down the east side of the creek to the line dividing Polk and Manatee counties." Permission obtained, what became known as Orange Avenue, and its extension Mt. Pisgah Road, were opened and became a principal route of access to and from the south.[24]

Travel from the south was eased by the opening of Orange Avenue, but access from the east continued to be a problem. The Peace River bridge had washed away during the Great Hurricane of 1878 and had been replaced by a private ferry owned by William H. Willingham and operated by his son-in-law William McLaughlin. The ferry, according to the 1879 county grand jury, "is very inconvenient to parties who live on either side of Peace Creek, and besides it is very expensive, and in some instances we know of parties who live on one side of the creek who have farms on the other side and have to pay heavy taxes at this ferry to visit and work their farms."[25] These problems were overcome in 1883 when a sturdy wagon bridge was erected at the previous bridge's site by C. B. Lightsey, presumably to the delight of farmers and the community as a whole.[26]

A growing community needed accommodations for prospective settlers, traveling salesmen, politicians, and newly arrived families. Until 1883, though, only boardinghouses were available, specifically those operated by the Philip Dzialynski and Robert McKinney families. That situation promised to change for the better in November 1883 when Sanford's Seth French announced his intention of erecting "a commodious hotel."[27] Over four months on a site on the northeast corner of Orange Avenue and East Broadway, workmen raised the "French House." By May 1884 local ladies were presenting there "grand entertainments" featuring "a representation of Mrs. Jarley's Wax Works, one of the most laughable of all comicalities."[28] For eighteen months the establishment prospered under manager J. L. Bettis. "The rooms

Peace River bridge, built in 1883, as seen from the east looking toward town.
(In possession of the author, courtesy of Vernon Peeples)

are pleasant and the table attractive," a visitor reported, "while the quality of the cooking, etc., is of exceptional excellence."[29] In October 1885 the French House was sold. Renamed "the Fort Meade Hotel," it thereafter came under Mrs. A. J. Bulloch's management.[30]

The French House stood on the north side of "Main Street" at the western end of what was then the business district. Within months of its opening, it drew competition from newcomer Albion H. Adams, who erected his "Adams House" at the opposite end of the street. Located amid a four-acre orange grove on the north side of East Broadway west of Washington Avenue, the hotel enjoyed the advantage of proximity to "the beautiful live oaks and delightful scenery that adorn the river's banks." According to one observer it was "a very pleasant and convenient stopping place."[31]

Between the hotels, that is to say along present-day East Broadway between Orange and Washington avenues, lay the town business district. Located primarily on the south side of "Main Street," a number

Fort Meade Hotel, as it appeared about 1900 (From Polk County, Florida, 1901)

of establishments remained in business or were opened from 1882 to 1885. For instance, Fort Meade's dry goods, grocery, and general merchandise stores continued to cater to cattlemen and their needs as well as to townspeople and farmers. J. N. Hooker & Company maintained a strong business, although Hooker moved his family to Bartow in 1884. The Dzialynski, Mitchell & Company partnership operated for several years after its formation in 1878. It was succeeded by the sole proprietorship of Philip Dzialynski, which, apparently, remained in operation until 1885. Arthur Keen's customers continued to patronize his grocery.[32]

New dry goods and general merchandise stores made their appearance as well. C. C. Wilson opened a store in 1883 and stayed in business for a year or two with the help of assistants Ulysses A. Lightsey and Monroe Scott. E. E. Skipper likewise briefly kept a general establishment. More longlasting was the partnership of F. F. "Tobe" Hendry and James G. Carter, whose "Hendry & Carter" store did an "immense business" until 1888 "on the corner opposite the post office."[33] By 1885 W. M. Ball of Tallahassee had joined other merchants with Ball & Company, as also had Max and Louis Reif with Reif Brothers store. The same year L. W. Johnson operated a meat market.[34]

Dry goods and grocery stores were not the only new businesses. The town's first millinery store, that of Mrs. Edna Hayman, opened in 1883, as did its first barbershop, that of J. C. Munroe. Philip Dzialynski operated a livery stable east of the French House; C. C. Wilson, T. L. Wilson, and W. S. Atkins hung out their shingles for law practices; G. F. Sater did a gun repair business at his home north of town; and Dr. M. O. Arnold settled into the medical practice he had begun the previous year. In 1884 J. Hill & Co. opened a brickyard two miles south of town; the Wilson & McKinney livery stable under F. B. McKinney superseded the Dzialynski operation; and V. B. Webster developed his Seminole Nursery.[35]

The occupations of new—and some old—settlers by 1885 vividly illustrate the area's continuing land boom economy. Working as painters and contractors were James Wynn, George W. Black, E. F. Durrance, W. M. Acree, E. S. Rhoden, and William Smith. Real estate salesmen included F. A. Whitehead, E. E. Skipper, R. C. Langford, J. E. Robeson, Dr. M. O. Arnold, J. F. Black, J. A. Edwards, Philip Dzialynski, E. R. Childers, and George W. Hendry. Three new physicians, Drs. C. F. Marsh, William L. Weems, and James Thompson also had appeared to take up Dr. Arnold's slack. Even the brickyard, bought in 1885 by J. A. Nyland, was prospering in an area with no brick buildings.[36]

Incorporation

In January 1884 mogul Henry Plant's South Florida Railroad crews—composed primarily of black workers—drove the final spikes in his Kissimmee-to-Tampa line, incidentally prompting creation of the towns of Lakeland, Auburndale, Lake Alfred, and Haines City. Through the ensuing year Plant's men toiled to construct a spur line to Bartow, a project realized by the arrival of the town's first passenger train on January 8, 1885. On the same line, fifteen miles to the north of Bartow, was born the town of Winter Haven.[37]

As trains ran a few miles to the north, Fort Meade's residents remained far from the locomotives and their shrill whistles. Disappointed time and again by promises of rail transportation, many settlers had developed a certain cynicism. As one man put it in the spring of 1882, "Hurrah for the railroad! It will get here after a short time. I hear they have begun work with one overseer and one hand."[38] Even the dream of the Fort Meade, Keystone & Walk-in-the-Water Railroad had collapsed, apparently a casualty of insufficient funding.

Despite disappointments Fort Meade had grown, but the area's population explosion had come at Lakeland and the other new railroad towns, as well as at the county seat of Bartow. On July 1, 1882, Bartow had become the first incorporated town in Polk County, and by March of 1884 it was said to be "a larger place than Ft. Meade."[39] The railroad's arrival had accelerated Bartow's growth and widened the population gap between it and Fort Meade. Transportation was a key advantage for Bartow, but Fort Meade's former prominence and its earlier attempts at development hurt as well. The *Pioneer* explained the problem this way:

> People come here daily to locate, but comparatively few are purchasing land in the village. Why is it? They all, to a man, admit that it is one of the most desirable points they have seen, but they go elsewhere to locate, and why is it? This is a grave question, and one we can answer. A stranger arriving here, at first conceives that he is in a pleasant country village, which has a flattering promise for the future; and, not until he prices a town lot, does he realize that he is in a great city. Disgusted at what he terms an extortion, he seeks a home in some other part, where, though it is not so desirable, he can buy property in the bounds of reason.[40]

Shorn of its role as the area's largest and leading community, Fort Meade still was not without its prospects. The railroad was indeed on its way, and the town remained a beautiful and enticing location surrounded by fertile farmlands—a rarity in sandy peninsular Florida. New settlers continued to arrive, and Main Street merchants rang up good business month after month. And so, in December 1884, local leaders acted upon a decade-old dream of incorporating the town.

The incorporation process began on December 8 when a committee chaired by V. B. Webster, with Ulysses A. Lightsey as secretary, posted notices of an election to be held at Philip Dzialynski's store on January 10, 1885, "for the purpose of electing municipal officers for the town of Fort Meade, Fla."[41] At the election twenty-five qualified voters unanimously agreed to incorporate a sixteen-square-mile area "Extending Two (2) miles East and Two (2) miles North Two (2) miles West and Two (2) Miles South from the Section corner post designating the N.E. corner of Section 34 and the SW corner of Section 26, Township 31 S of Range 25 E." Under the supervision of inspectors R. C. Langford, F. F. Hendry, and J. M. Mullen, A. J. French was elected mayor. A board of aldermen was selected composed of C. L. Mitchell, Philip Dzialynski, C. B. Lightsey, V. B. Webster, and F. A. Whitehead. C. R. Jones was named town marshal, and Charles L. Fries was tapped as town clerk. A second election was held on March 10. R. C. Langford received all but one of the eighteen votes cast for assessor, as also did J. G. Carter for an aldermanic seat left vacant by C. L. Mitchell's appointment as state commissioner of lands and immigration. When all the results were filed with the circuit court clerk on March 16, Fort Meade for the first time became an incorporated town.[42]

The spirit of civic pride evidenced by incorporation was quickly mirrored in other actions. In July 1885 Frank Q. Crawford purchased the printing plant of the short-lived *Bartow Express* and within a matter of a week or two had published the first edition of the Fort Meade *Pioneer*. Assisting Crawford were J. F. Marsh as assistant editor and P. A. "Pete" Ruhl, compositor. Reviewing the *Pioneer's* first issue, a Tallahassee newspaper observed, "The paper is well edited and handsomely printed, and its advertising columns prove Fort Meade to be a place of extensive and active business."[43]

That summer assistant editor Marsh must have been a very busy man. A teacher by profession, he not only was helping put out the newspaper but also was overseeing construction of a new school. Erected on the southeast corner of First Street Southeast and Oak Avenue, the building was a vast improvement over the town's former "little white schoolhouse." Designed by Marsh as a two-story structure, it permitted older and younger pupils to be separated for the first time. This "fine academy" was not a public school, however. Rather, it was owned by Philip Dzialynski, C. B. Lightsey, and R. C. Langford who had provided funds and lumber for its construction. Tuition at the academy ran about $14.50 per pupil, and on opening day August 31, twenty-one scholars were enrolled in its first class.[44]

Other municipal facilities and services were also inaugurated. Possibly in conjunction with the school construction, the town opened a

Fort Meade school, 1885, with John F. Marsh (standing at far left) and Lula Marsh Childers (next right). (Courtesy of the Florida State Archives)

public library with H. D. Hester, a partner in the Sunnyside Nursery, as its secretary. The village's first "town hall," described as "a two story frame building, with market on the ground floor," was constructed as well. It stood on the north side of East Broadway about midway between Hendry Avenue and the Adams House.[45]

The new town council likely also took steps in 1885 to regularize the names of the community's streets. North-south routes for the most part carried the same names as at present, although they were called "streets" rather than "avenues." Charleston Avenue, then known as Hooker Street, was an exception, and Oak Avenue was called Francis Street. Usage of "Broad Street," in lieu of "Main Street," also became common after 1885. The east-west streets, then as now, were primarily known by numerical designations. Until well into the twentieth century, however, modern Ninth Street Northeast was labeled Seventh

Street, with six parallel streets numbered Sixth through First streets to the north. To the south of Ninth Street Northeast, streets carried progressively higher numerical designations, with the exception of Second Street Northeast, which was known as "Lemon Street," and, of course, the town's main thoroughfare, "Broad Street."[46]

From 1882 to 1885 Fort Meade grew and prospered, although not as much as towns to the north that received the blessing of rail transportation a little earlier. No longer the premier town of interior south Florida, Fort Meade still looked to the future in eager anticipation, fortified by new and increasingly strong civic institutions. When the railroad finally arrived, that eager anticipation would be richly rewarded—at least for a while.

7

"The promise of a grand future at no remote period"

The British Are Coming

I<small>F THE QUALITY</small> and excitement of life reached a peak at Fort Meade during the nineteenth century, that point fell within the period beginning in 1886 and extending through the decade's end. Although the town may have experienced more prosperous or challenging years, it did not enjoy ones any more lively, interesting, or important in terms of their longlasting cultural impact. Community members felt the electricity in the air. "Fort Meade is a good place for one to live," remarked a townsman on December 27, 1886, "and has the promise of a grand future at no remote period." He added, "We have every advantage that town, county, or township claim in Florida. Good water, good health, good land, good people. And it would make a mean man good."[1]

Trains at Skippertown

The period had not begun auspiciously. The railroad finally arrived, but the train went somewhere else. Residents had assumed that the Florida Southern Railroad, when it finally got to town, would bisect the village on the way to its Peace River crossing. Questions about the certainty of the assumption should have arisen when, early in August 1885, the *Palatka News* authoritatively announced, "The course of the road cannot be exactly determined beyond Fort Meade."[2] The matter soon became clear when crews cleared and graded a roadbed paralleling the river a mile or two west of town. Not only would there be no

---

river crossing at Fort Meade, but the rails would run no closer than a mile from the Broad Street business district.[3]

Taken aback by the railroad's actions, citizens nonetheless prepared at Christmas 1885 to celebrate the arrival of the first train. The Florida Southern had constructed a "siding" due west of the business district, and there during the last week of 1885 or the first week of 1886 the railroad era arrived at long last. All was not as it appeared, however. On January 10, almost as an omen, a hard freeze attacked the area, bringing subfreezing temperatures for three successive days. On the second day a document was filed with the circuit court clerk registering a "Plat of the town of Fort Meade." This innocent-sounding document represented a calculated attempt by real estate dealers James N. Hooker, E. E. Skipper, and F. A. Whitehead to capitalize on the railroad's arrival by re-creating Fort Meade along its tracks and upon land owned by the speculators. The new "town" lay south of modern Ninth Street Southwest between Charleston Avenue and Sand Mountain Road. It encompassed eighty-one city blocks. A railroad depot dominated the business district.[4]

The Florida Southern confirmed its complicity in the developers' scheme. In short order it broke up the first siding and relocated its depot at the new town, soon called Skippertown. The Fort Meade *Pioneer* reported, "The company has located a depot two miles southwest of here, where there has been a town built (on paper,) and we do not think we are unreasonable when we say that an old established and incorporated town ought to be recognized before these wild cat towns." Editor F. Q. Crawford thundered, "The wild cat speculations are of no benefit to originators or to their neighbors, and will prove but froth in the future. The attempt to move the town is an injustice to the citizens that have bought in good faith, and must certainly fail. With a depot two miles from us we are no better off than with one at Bartow, and our merchants ought not to patronize it."[5]

For a month or two in the winter of 1886 railroad matters simmered. In early April the town granted the Florida Southern a fifty-foot right-of-way along Brown Street and within the next month offered the railroad $1,000 in cash and 400 additional acres of land for a depot "within the corporate limits of the town, near the Sunnyside Nurseries."[6] According to a report, the railroad promised to respond "some time soon," and it was as good as its word. "The Florida Southern Railroad Company has made . . . an offer to take up their present track west of town and run the line through the centre of the place, and to build a first-class depot wherever the citizens may elect, in consideration of $25,000," related the *Pioneer* during the last week of May. "We propose in this matter, under the circumstances to let the people who have the bills to pay do the talking, and we will await the development of events." New editor Robert Greenwood concluded, "It is claimed by those best posted that the money can easily be raised, if, after a thorough canvass of the matter, the people decide that it is the best thing to do."[7]

Community leaders had been doing some talking and not just with the Florida Southern Railroad. Most residents realized that, if a second railroad passed through the town and located a depot within it, the Florida Southern would be forced to abandon Skippertown and relocate its facilities. To bring about that desirable result, as well as to forge a long-sought east-west link from Tampa to the Atlantic coast, a "large and enthusiastic meeting" was held in early June "for the purpose of considering the feasibility of building a road from Plant City." Four thousand dollars in stock was subscribed, and one report declared, "The building of the road is almost an assured fact."[8] Quickly the idea took on an even larger life. Millionaire developer Hamilton Disston became involved, and on June 24 the Fort Meade & Plant City Railroad was incorporated to build a rail line "from Plant City via Fort Meade to Lake Worth." C. C. Wilson was named secretary of the road, and J. E. Robeson was designated its treasurer. J. F. Black and M. G. Darbishire were appointed engineers and ordered "to locate the line at once."[9]

The Fort Meade & Plant City Railroad was launched with great expectations, but its progress suffered a major blow in mid-September 1886, when President John B. Simmons succumbed to a heart attack. Yet the following April a Fort Meade man could write, "The Plant City and Fort Meade railroad will certainly be built during the summer."[10] Simmons's death meant, however, that construction would be delayed and that, in the meantime, Fort Meade would be forced to come to grips with the fact that its train station was located over two miles from town.

*Fort Meade Street Car Line, c. 1895, with W. C. Lightsey seen at center of the car.
(Courtesy of the Florida State Archives)*

At that point, someone had a good idea. "Fort Meade has organized a street railway company," noted a nearby newspaper on November 27.[11] Specifically, the Fort Meade Street Railroad Company was organized to provide a rail link for mule-drawn cars between the Florida Southern Railroad depot at Skippertown and the business district on Broad Street. Under President and General Manager J. A. Edwards, Secretary C. C. Wilson, and Treasurer J. G. Carter, crews cleared, graded, and laid rails on a line that ran from the depot eastward to South Oak Avenue, then northward to Broad Street where the rails again turned eastward along the north side of the town's main street and ran to a terminus directly in front of the Adams House. Work proceeded quickly, and by late January 1887 reports acknowledged that "Fort Meade's street railway is completed." One small problem occurred during the train's first run. "The first time the conductor pulled out his bell punch to register fares," an account read, "the passengers all did likewise only their's were six shooters. The conductor has skipped."[12]

Meanwhile, Skippertown's prospects dimmed. James N. Hooker opened a store near the depot, but it was ignored by most residents. Soon Hooker shifted his business back to its old downtown location. The depot remained for the time being, as did a citrus packing house operated by Hooker. A few local merchants also built warehouses at the site. When the conductor punched the first ticket on the Fort Meade street railroad in January 1887, however, the sun had already set on Skippertown.

A Stroll About Town

Bartow editor B. B. Tatum visited bustling Fort Meade in early 1887. His report offers a glimpse of the town in the exciting months after the coming of the railroad:

> It was our pleasure, last week, to spend a day in our beautiful and enterprising neighbor village, Fort Meade, and we freely confess that we were somewhat surprised at the improvements which have been made there since our last visit. Quite a number of handsome residences had been erected recently, around in various parts of town. These buildings add much to the already easy and aristocratic appearance of the city. . . .
>
> We had time to drop into the sanctum of the Pioneer, where we found the hard-working and genial editor busy over a "proof" of—well, of an article which made him smile a "man's rights" smile. The Pioneer and its editor are doing much for Ft. Meade, and deserve the hearty support of the whole people. We next looked in on Mr. Alex V. French, and found him, assisted by Mr. Fries, very busy getting up a map of the city which will be lithographed very soon, for distribution. It is a neat job and will reflect much credit on the engineers and the city.
>
> Underneath the Pioneer's office Messrs. W. M. Ball & Co., are to be found with a good stock of General merchandise, near this we found the livery stable of Mr. J. A. Hart, next door Dr. W. L. Weems keeps a nice and well selected stock of drugs, chemicals, etc., as well as attending to any calls as a practicing physician. Messrs. Whitehead & Alleyne are doing a lively business in real estate, they have located quite a number of English families, recently, and are still selling them, both improved and unimproved property.
>
> The store of J. N. Hooker & Co. is filled with goods and they seem to

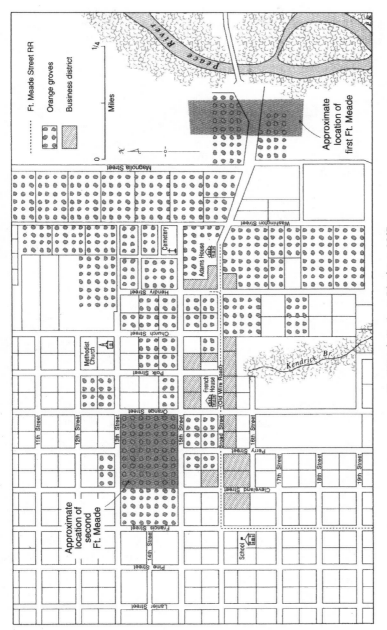

Fort Meade Business District, c. 1887

be doing their share of the business. Reif Bros., carry a big line of general merchandise, and are always in the ring when selling time comes on. These gentlemen keep up with the times in every respect. The law office of C. C. Wilson presented a livelier appearance than any house visited, here we found the amiable and gentlemanly land agent, Mr. A. H. Thompson, who, by his pleasant looks alone, would assure any one that he was at least doing enough to keep him happy.

Mr. C. C. Wilson, the handsome attorney notary public, whose card will be found elsewhere in this issue, is very actively engaged in receiving bonded donations for the purpose of building the Plant City, Ft. Meade and Lake Worth R. R. This road has been long talked of, but Mr. Wilson thinks he will succeed now. He has had lands donated very liberally at Ft. Meade; and in a few days he contemplates an overland trip over the proposed route of the road, for the purpose of seeing what can be obtained of the citizens on the line. . . .

Leaving Mr. Wilson's office, we next called on the druggists, Dzialynski & Co., and found a nice, clean, neat stock, and evidence enough that they can supply their customers with anything needed in their line. Sam. Oppenheimer, formerly of Bartow, is with this firm. Adjoining this store is the office of Dr. C. F. Marsh, who we called to see, but found him out attending some of his patients, we presume. The Post office is a neat, tidy place, and, we have no doubt, is satisfactorily managed by the P. M., Mr. Tobe Hendry. On the same street we noticed a saloon and billiard room, but failed to get the name of the proprietor.

The city barber shop is controlled by J. C. Munroe, a popular, obliging young man and one who thoroughly understands his business. We next visited the establishment of S. N. Weeks & Co., and found these business-like young men in charge of a neat and well displayed stock of dry goods and general merchandise. A millinery store with a fine assortment of new spring hats, trimmings &c., is owned and managed by Mrs. Edna Hayman. Across the street is the store of M. Ottinger, who deals out the groceries extensively.

A beef market comes next, kept by Lightsey & Co. The big store of Hendry and Carter is next in order and we here found business quite lively. These young men have a good, established trade, and are succeeding admirably. The dental office of S. G. Hayman had nearly escaped our memory, but it's there, and when you need a tooth mended he is the man to do it. There are various other enterprises, restaurants, carriage shops, offices of contractors, builders, and perhaps many other places which we might have mentioned had we had time to find them all out.

However, we can't forget the hotels, the Ft. Meade Hotel, under the management of Mrs. A. J. Bulloch, is situated on the main, business street of the city, with street cars passing the door, making it in every way a pleasant and convenient place for the travelling public. The Adams House is situated farther down the same street, with the terminus of the railroad immediately in front of the building. To stop here once, means to stop again. The house needs no further recommendation than its own merits.[13]

Remittance Men

Tatum touched on one of the dynamics changing Fort Meade when he mentioned "Messrs. Whitehead & Alleyne," who had "located quite a number of English families, recently." The *Pioneer* underscored the point when it proclaimed in February 1887, "Fort Meade now has a greater English population than any town in Florida, and they continue to come every week. They have good taste and the best kind of judgement when it comes to selecting a home in Florida."[14] Who were these English families, and what were they doing at Fort Meade?

The tale begins in 1881 when Hamilton Disston consummated his mammoth Florida land purchase. At the time Disston raised cash by selling half his 4,000,000 acres to Englishman Edward J. Reed. Thereafter, Reed and his Florida Land and Mortgage Company launched an extensive advertising campaign aimed at luring Englishmen, as well as Scotsmen and Irishmen, to Florida. Local promoters naturally sought to capitalize on the interest thus created and aggressively pursued schemes for the development of any number of English "colonies."[15]

Four men particularly helped to draw English families to the Fort Meade vicinity. O. M. Crosby used Fort Meade as the railhead for his new town of Avon Park by establishing a free stage line between the two communities. In 1891 he linked them by telephone, the office for which was located in the A. B. Canter and John M. Stansfield drugstore. The other men were Cecil Howard Alleyne and his partners, F. A. Whitehead and E. Alonzo Cordery. Twenty-seven-year-old Alleyne appeared in 1886 after several years spent promoting the English colony of Acton, a community later absorbed by Lakeland. London-born Alleyne first worked with alderman and developer F. A. Whitehead but

Arthur Benjamin Canter, 1860–1945. (Collection of the author)

soon entered into a more enduring relationship with New Jersey native E. Alonzo Cordery, who had arrived in 1885. Every summer Alleyne would travel in England, searching for potential buyers while Cordery took care of the home office. The firm specialized in package deals including land, necessary financing, arrangements for travel, and insurance.[16]

What kind of families did Alleyne, Whitehead, and Cordery manage to attract to Fort Meade? Ernest B. Simmons recalled:

To understand this migration of the Englishmen we must understand the English law of primogeniture. The family estate could not be divided but must pass to the eldest son. The younger sons, in order to secure a

J. M. Stansfield. (From the Tampa Tribune, *January 21, 1900)*

foothold on mother earth, had to emigrate to other lands; so the United States and the over-seas British colonies took these adventurous younger sons. Fort Meade profited by it. These young fellows were supplied with funds from the parental estate and became known as "remittance men." Many of them were of a sporty nature and it was a common sight to see them on horseback, in flat jockey-style saddles with shortened stirrup straps, bobbing up and down as they trotted or galloped along the streets.[17]

Fort Meade had its "remittance men," as well as Englishmen wealthy in their own right. Individuals such as E. F. Lennox Conyngham, A. St. Clair Ford, and G. G. H. D'Aeth brought with them a style of life and a level of affluence previously unknown on the south Florida frontier. From 1886 to the mid-1890s they and their fellow countrymen built and maintained beautiful homes, described by one visitor as "those great square mansions, with wide porticoes and Corinthian columns; [and] pretty little cottages, 'quite over-canopied with lush woodbine' and clematis and roses."[18] As Alleyne's wife explained to a London magazine, their daily lives matched the luxury of their surroundings:

"Modes of life in Florida," Mrs. Alleyne says in her entertaining notes, "are similar to those of India and other tropical countries. You enjoy a canter before breakfast in the early morning, the delicious noon-day siesta in a comfortable hammock or a bamboo chair, the wide shady verandah, and the long, lovely drive about 4 o'clock as an appetizer for the 8 o'clock dinner. Open house is kept, and the house is generally full of visitors, batch after batch following one another throughout the spring. In April or May comes the packing up, and then for the vast ocean, and the whirl and bustle of the London season."[19]

To enhance the relaxed and inviting atmosphere, many of the "English" named their mansions and cottages. Some names reflected a pragmatic outlook, such as engineer M. G. Darbishire's "Bridge End," or the historic nature of the site, as suggested by Alleyne's "The Fort." St. Clair Ford's "The Folly," it is to be hoped, represented only a wry sense of humor on the owner's part. Evan Evans's "Ballyhooly" and M. L. Davis's "Blangwaer" were meant as reminders of home.[20]

For the English as well as for others, social life often centered around sports. Again, from Mrs. Alleyne:

Sports is to be had in abundance at Fort Meade. There is a Jocky Club, a pack of hounds for both deer and foxes, lawn tennis grounds, clay pigeon shooting, etc., while snipe and quail shooting are to be got in the near vicinity, and further away in denser thickets can be found the white tailed deer, and in the swamps the objectionable looking alligator. A few hours journey will bring you to the Gulf of Mexico, where fishing can be indulged in and where you can catch anything in size from the delicious pompana to the Tarpon, par excellence the gamest fish in the South, and perhaps in the world.[21]

One new sport, cricket, had come with the initial wave of English settlers. The first test match of record was held at Acton on December 27, 1886, where, despite the heroic efforts of G. G. H. D'Aeth, Fort Meade lost by "an inning and fifteen runs."[22]

The most important sports event was horseracing, and its focal point was the Fort Meade Jockey Club. The idea grew out of a "knightly tournament" held on May 4, 1887. That event, with a concluding cele-bratory dance at the town hall, proved so enjoyable that, the following

January, interested men organized the jockey club and were advertising throughout the state "a race meeting on the Ft. Meade race course on February 2nd." The notices declared, "Two handsome silver challenge cups will be run for, besides a large sum of subscription and added money."[23]

The first jockey club race enjoyed a huge success. Special trains ran from Bartow and Sanford, and a "big crowd," including "quite a number of ladies," gathered at the course surrounding Three Mile Pond to the east of town. A grandstand had been erected, as well as a tent under which food and refreshments were served. One spectator described the scene. "The brilliant colors of the silk jackets and caps of the riders," he reported, "harmonized well with the elegant costumes of the fair sex and the dark green of the pine woods, surrounding the course."[24]

The 1888 races were so well received that they were repeated each year through 1894. Attendance grew, as did the event's repute. The

Fort Meade Jockey Club race, c. 1889. (Courtesy of the Florida State Archives)

club improved the course, and in 1891 permanent facilities were constructed. "On the south side of the course which is round the three-mile pond at Fairview," noted a local man, "an enclosure has been made inside of which is a very pretty stand capable of seating about seventy-five persons." He continued, "Back of and underneath the stand are the dressing and weighing rooms, and close behind that are the stalls for the competing horses."[25] The following year the course was resodded with "St. Augustine grass" and appeared "smooth as a lawn."[26]

The races were popular, in part, because they afforded some locals an opportunity for getting their hands on a little of the English community's money. "The clever crackers," explained E. B. Simmons, "sold racing ponies to their new English friends. An Englishman, having secured the fastest pony, felt secure to bet on it, but the seller, having that pony's time, managed to find another a little faster to win the next race with." Concluded Simmons, "Thus, the Englishman was separated from his money."[27] Donald B. McKay recalled an incident, however, that suggested the dangers of gambling even with the English:

> E. L. ("Sonny") Lesley owned a fine half-mile horse, one of the first thoroughbreds brought to this section. One afternoon he was matched with a good horse from Fort Meade, owned by an English "remittance" man. Lesley felt confident that his horse could win and had backed him heavily, but a short time before the race was to start a report reached him that his jockey—George Robertson, a professional who had been brought here for the races—had been "fixed." Lesley sent for the jockey, told what he had heard, and said, "Now George, I am sure my horse can win if he is given an honest ride. I will be standing at the finish line, and if he doesn't win I'll empty this .45 into you." The Lesley horse was given a superb ride and won by six lengths. And the gamblers who had "fixed" George recovered their money from him after giving him a beating.[28]

Building a New Life

Not all arriving Europeans were "remittance men." Likely a majority were individuals—many with young families—determined to make a new life for themselves in America. Some who came to stay were well-to-do. Luke B. Flood was such a man. He, his wife Alicia, and their seven children determined to leave Ireland for fear of religious strife. They arrived on the first passenger train to enter the town. Twenty-five-year-old Cyril G. Calhoun Wright arrived the same year from England. A farmer, Wright left his homeland "on account of low prices through foreign competition." He wanted to grow onions, a "most profitable production."[29]

Some arrivals were skilled craftsmen. Robert J. Hodgson, an Englishmen though he had been in the United States for over thirty years, was a blacksmith, plumber, gas fitter, and wagon maker. A. E. Bobbett had perfected his talents as a cabinetmaker, and George Broderick and Dudley Watkins were adept painters. Others were professional men. Charles T. Duce was a physician, and L. B. Flood had experience as a veterinarian.[30]

One of the most remarkable of the Englishmen was an engineer. M. George Darbishire was thirty-two years of age in 1886 when he landed at Fort Meade to "dispose of a bunch of sorry ponies."[31] Liking what he saw, Darbishire—a fellow of the Institute of Civil Engineers at Westminster—remained and was soon employed to lay out the line of the Fort Meade & Plant City Railroad. When that project was delayed, he turned his attention to area geology and topography. During a field trip in the spring of 1887, he discovered "vast beds of phosphate" in Peace River and thereafter brought Atlanta investor G. W. Scott to the area. The result was one of the earliest investments in the local phosphate industry. Later in 1887, when yellow fever broke out at Key West and Tampa, Darbishire offered his services as a consultant. For two years he campaigned for governmental action to clean up urban filth and to require safe sewage practices. In October 1889 he was in Key West, planning that city's first effective sewerage system. On the last day of the month, while returning home to his wife and young son at Fort Meade, he was "overtaken by death" some twenty miles south of Fort Myers. Fort Meade lost a citizen of whom it still can be proud.[32]

Many residents appreciated that the English newcomers had more to contribute than an interest in the ponies. "Some of them," E. B. Simmons wrote, "became shrewd businessmen and they developed bigger stores than Fort Meade had ever known before."[33] Simmons's comments applied to no one more than to R. G. Metcalfe, who settled in 1887 and established himself as a gentleman farmer on an estate west of town at what became Tiger Bay. For a while Metcalfe was best known for his carriage. "Ft. Meade has the 'tandem' of Florida, if not the world," reported one newspaper. "It consists of a two wheel sulky, drawn by horses in single file. Eight of the horses are of a silverish hue, while the remaining two are beautiful bays."[34] In 1889 Metcalfe bought out Philip Dzialynski, purchased a "complete line of general merchandise" at New York, and opened for business with fellow Englishmen W. A. Evans and William H. Francis as his assistants. Within three years he had added furniture to his inventory and employed two additional clerks, Frank Perry and D. E. Ashton. In 1892 he enlarged the store and added a street railway siding at his warehouse. Metcalfe continued in the trade for several years before returning to England about 1895.[35]

Another English firm provided stiff competition for Metcalfe. The partnership, which commenced business in 1889, was composed of Evan Evans and William Beddoes, along with early resident E. J. Hilliard. In 1890 Beddoes retired and returned to England, and Evans bought out Hilliard. Evans combined his operations one year later with those of J. G. Carter, and the firm of Carter, Evans & Company remained a Broad Street fixture until midway through the decade. Also prominent was Stansfield Brothers & Company, a partnership of Charles, Harry, and Thomas Stansfield. Organized in 1889, the firm remained in business until well into the twentieth century. A fourth Stansfield, John M., entered into the drugstore business in 1890 with Arthur B. Canter. A year later Stansfield continued the business as J. M. Stansfield & Company, which he kept in operation until 1895.[36]

Japanese Lanterns and Gayly Lit Streets

The English, Irish, and Scots infused the community with vitality and color and served as a catalyst for the creation of a more cosmopolitan and socially active environment. "Our town is bent on city airs," one man bragged in February 1887, "as the usual bustle of cities can be seen even here in 'this piney woods town.' "[37] Visible reminders of that change were everywhere to be seen. The public library was well patronized, and a new volunteer fire brigade offered protection. The Fort Meade Street Railroad's bell clanged out its warning along Broad Street as it passed pedestrians clad in the latest fashions taking advantage of new board sidewalks, a convenience soon extended to other streets such as Church and Hendry avenues. By the spring of 1888 street lamps had been installed, and the town luxuriated in being "gayly lit up."[38] At decade's close the public streets, at least the north side of Broad Street, boasted a "new clay and rock sidewalk" judged "far superior to the old plank walks."[39]

Through Fort Meade's gayly lit nighttime streets passed a parade of citizens on the way to or from "at-homes," dances, balls, benefits, concerts, parties, and weddings. Typical of these events was Mina Hayman's birthday dance, held June 17, 1889. "Everything was brilliantly lighted up with Japanese lanterns," an enthusiastic attendee recorded. "The dancing room was most artistically decorated with palms, evergreens and lillies. Ice cream, lemonade and cake were served as refreshments, and the party broke up in the 'wee sma' hours, everybody having spent a delightful evening."[40] Many of the functions were held at the town hall, the Fort Meade Academy, "York Hall," "Cooke's Hall," and the "Opera House Hall." Mrs. George W. Black, a talented pianist and singer, was the highlight of numerous affairs.[41]

Some social occasions centered around a newly established church. Only Mr. and Mrs. George W. Black and the family of A. J. Bulloch were present in the Bulloch home on the corner of Washington and Broad streets on September 26, 1886, when Palatka's C. S. Williams held Fort Meade's first Episcopal services. Unexpectedly Mr. and Mrs. James Benedict had not arrived. "We were not present at that memorable first service," Mrs. Benedict later explained, "tidings of Rev. Mr. William's arrival not reaching us till that day noon while the service was in progress! Our ford (over a swollen country stream) was impassable, but by a more distant one above we journeyed through the water-covered woods to town, where we attended the Evening Service, which as the weather cleared, was held in the Methodist Church, and a good sized congregation was present."[42]

At intervals usually of several months' duration, the small Episcopal congregation continued to meet, its numbers slowly enhanced by the arrival of Anglican English settlers. Late in 1887, George S. Fitzhugh was placed in charge of the mission. "A meeting was now called to organize," recorded Fitzhugh's successor J. V. Lee in 1891, "Rev. Mr. Fitzhugh presiding. Opened with prayer. Wm. L. Weems, M.D. chosen Senior Warden, and Mr. James Benedict, Junior Warden; M. L. Flood and Henry Bulloch, Vestry; W. A. Evans, Treasurer; A. W. Grose Secretary; Mrs. Benedict, Ass't Treas." Lee added, "On suggestion of Mr. [R. O.] Baker, name of 'Christ Church' was agreed on. Much interest and enthusiasm."[43]

Under Mrs. Black's watchful eye, Christ Church members undertook a fund-raising drive aimed at construction of a sanctuary. The first event took place at the Fort Meade Academy on December 28, 1887, when Mrs. Black, assisted by Mae Webster, J. W. Laidley, Bert Webster, and R. T. Banks, presented "Offenbach's comic operetta 'The Blind Beggars.' "[44] Within eighteen months sufficient funds had been raised, when added to a $1,000 grant from the Episcopal bishop, to permit construction of a "neo-gothic structure" on the northwest corner of Broad Street and Cleveland Avenue. By decade's end, builder Thomas A. Atkins was well on his way to completion of the church.[45]

Having grown and boasting an increasingly sophisticated manner, the town's appearance and its economy nevertheless remained in some ways exactly as they had for over a decade. "Ft. Meade is an old settled place," remarked a visitor, "and to persons from more sterile points in the North it bears an especial charm. Throughout the town nearly every residence is located in the midst of a bearing orange grove of greater or less extent, while rows of ornamental shade trees line all the streets. . . . the town can hardly be seen for the trees. Ft. Meade is really quite a bustling little city, and it is larger than one would imagine on going through their principal business street, as the trees hide from view all houses except those near by."[46] A Jacksonville reporter commented, "Fort Meade is a perfect gem, the Queen City of the River of Peace, on whose banks it nestles, in the midst of orange groves and flowers of every species, her good people always ready to welcome the coming and to speed the parting guest."[47]

Despite growth the town's summer population at the end of the decade stood at only 267 persons, although almost 1,200 lived in the vicinity.[48] Many of those 1,200 were newcomers, though not of the

English, Irish, or Scot variety, nor were their rural homes safely located on gaily lit streets. Fort Meade still lay near one of the nation's few remaining frontiers, and danger lurked around every corner. J. E. Robeson was abruptly reminded of that fact one winter day in 1887. The *Pioneer* told the story:

> While on his recent trip out to the lake region, one evening, after returning to camp, Mr. Robeson went down to the edge of the lake to quench his thirst, and, finding no cup, he bent over on his hands and knees, to drink like that portion of Israel's hosts that were sent home from the attack on the army of Midian. While in that strained attitude he was surprised by a stunning blow, where his body made a sharp angle, from the tail of a large 'gator, which had been lying near by, hitherto unobserved by him.
>
> The blow overbalancing his center of gravity, sent him headlong ten feet into the lake, followed by the 'gator, which closed in on him with his ugly jaws; but, fortunately, the assailant missed his mark; only getting a hold on Mr. R's coat-tail Being a man of unusual physical strength and served by great excitement, Mr. Robeson managed to tow his unwieldy and uncomfortable appendage to shallow water, where, with the aid of our reporter, his gatorship was dispatched with the use of a heavy ax.[49]

The reporter who rescued Robeson was undoubtedly J. F. Marsh, who in August 1886 had become the *Pioneer*'s editor. Marsh also sought that fall to maintain his position as principal of Fort Meade's school, known as either the Fort Meade High School or the Fort Meade Academy. That action precipitated a crisis at the school and indirectly led to the *Pioneer*'s demise.[50]

Stated briefly, a storm was brewing in Polk County in 1886 over the temperance cause. By June an "energetic" chapter of the Temperance Union had been formed at Fort Meade under the presidency of B. F. Perry and was conducting public meetings "to stop whiskey selling." One of the leading proponents of temperance and prohibition was county school superintendent John Snoddy, a former Fort Meade teacher. One of the voices raised against the movement was that of the *Pioneer* and its then assistant editor J. F. Marsh.[51]

As it happened, funds were being made available through the county school board in 1886 for Fort Meade's first truly "public" school. Teachers would be hired by the school board as a result rather than by the academy's trustees. Accordingly, Marsh submitted a request by twenty-five school "patrons" that he and his sister, Lula B. Marsh, be reemployed "as teachers for the Public School beginning in October, 1886."[52] When the four nonsigning patrons objected to Marsh's appointment, Snoddy seized the opportunity to place the school in the charge of a fellow temperance advocate. To create the appearance of support, he and his allies held a "public meeting" at which a vote was taken as to whether Marsh or Snoddy's man, Winfield S. Thompson, should get the job. Thirteen men turned out for the meeting, and not surprisingly, Thompson got ten of their votes.

Sensing his fate, Marsh withdrew from the contest for school principal in favor of his sister. Through the intervention of school board member James T. Wilson, a compromise was reached by which Thompson was to teach the public school on the Academy's upper floor while Miss Marsh undertook a private school on the lower level. On opening day, Thompson's school drew ten or twelve pupils, the remainder of the town's parents preferring that their children study under Miss Marsh. Ten days later Thompson withdrew, and the schools were combined. Snoddy waited out the year and then attempted to block Miss Marsh's pay.[53]

From the school's opening day in October 1886 to the summer of 1887, the temperance cause grew while editor Marsh's popularity plummeted. In June he was forced to suspend the *Pioneer*, which he transferred to Charlotte Harbor as the *Beacon Light*. Before leaving town, though, Marsh exposed the "school troubles" and demanded that his sister be compensated and otherwise treated fairly. The article received front-page coverage in the Bartow newspaper, where it ran along with a lengthy defense by the school board. If Marsh had hoped to deliver a blow to the temperance forces, he failed. On September 1, 1887, Fort Meade voted almost four to one for prohibition.[54]

Neither Lula Marsh nor W. S. Thompson taught at Fort Meade High School during the school years 1887–88 and 1888–89. Thompson finally became principal in 1889 and kept the job until January 1891, when he died from pneumonia caught in the unheated school. Marsh (by then Mrs. E. R. Childers) returned as an assistant teacher in 1897. The town was without a newspaper from June 1887 until February 7,

1889, when A. L. McFarlane published the first issue of O. M. Crosby's promotional newspaper, the *South Florida Progress*.[55]

Homeland

"Homeland," a visitor noted in July 1888, "is admirably situated, and in its vicinity may be found some of the best orange groves in South Florida." He continued, "Among those which deserve an especial mention is the large grove formerly the property of Judge James T. Wilson, but recently sold to a gentleman from Kansas City for $42,000, and the grove of Mr. J. B. Crum, which is equally as valuable."[56]

The coming of the railroad and the new ease with which farm and citrus crops could be shipped brought settlers and prosperity to Homeland. Recognizing its pressing need for that railroad, the community had reached an accommodation with the Florida Southern by which it gained a depot. The terms required that, after the village was surveyed and platted by T. W. Anderson in April 1886, the railroad would be given every other block. The line erected a depot, and Anderson was named as its first agent. Anderson also opened a store. He was joined in that occupation in the summer of 1887, when James B. Crum built a "first class store." Other businesses also flourished. James Wade commenced a drug and "fancy goods" store; Crum operated a carriage and blacksmith shop; W. B. Lassiter managed the Polk County Nursery and Improvement Company; Mrs. Katie McKillop ran the Homeland Hotel; and Sam Lee and Wiley Scroggins served as builders and contractors.[57]

Homeland also benefited from improvements in educational and religious institutions. Its school continued to be considered "one of the best in the county." In 1887, if not before, a school opened for the community's black residents. Taught in 1887–88 by Ellen Dixon, that school over the next decades provided the training for many distinguished black educators and professionals. In addition Homeland, long known for its Bethel Methodist Church, became a community of churches. The Homeland Baptist Church, organized in 1882, had erected a sanctuary by the end of 1886. In September 1887 a new and larger structure for Bethel Methodist was begun. Finished in 1889, it boasted hand-cut cypress shingles from J. H. and Andrew McKillop and a beautiful pulpit and bookcase from craftsman William Harmon. The year 1887 also saw the organization of the Mount Bunyan Baptist Church. Created through the leadership of G. W. McClendon, the church would provide a religious and social center for generations of Homeland's black Baptists.[58]

THE OPENING OF THE RAILROAD era ushered in a period of progress and change unparalleled in Fort Meade's history. An exciting, colorful atmosphere prevailed as scores of English, Scottish, and Irish families made the town their home and brought to it customs and lifestyles previously unknown in south Florida. Before the highpoint of that dramatic period was reached, however, a discovery was made that by the end of the 1880s was already beginning to bring about an even greater and more longlasting change. The pot of gold at the end of the rainbow had been found in the bed of Peace River, and they called it phosphate.

8

The Phosphate Roller Coaster

"THE PHOSPHATE CRAZE has struck this town in real earnest." With those words written on January 2, 1890, the nineteenth century's last decade opened at Fort Meade.[1] Phosphate had been discovered in the Peace River valley on several occasions during the 1880s. Exploitation had begun only in mid-1888, though, and then principally to the south near Arcadia. In July 1889 the "gold rush" had moved closer to Fort Meade as the DeSoto Phosphate Mining Company purchased thirty-six miles of river frontage below the town and "erected a very complete plant on the river bank where the Florida Southern railroad crosses a mile north of Zolfo." From there "phosphate fever" spread like wildfire.[2] "Some large and valuable deposits have been located in close proximity to [this] town," a local man commented. "Spades and shovels are in good demand."[3]

The phosphate craze having commenced, prospectors literally stumbled over the mineral everywhere they looked. One report declared, "The rocks and beds of the new sidewalks recently constructed, turn out to be nothing else but phosphate."[4] The prospectors included J. E. Robeson, who opened a mine one mile north of the river bridge, as well as a fertilizer factory to complement his phosphate operations. The Fort Meade *South Florida Progress* expressed elation. "The importance of this simple announcement on the progress of the town and district," exulted the publisher, "can scarcely be appreciated at the present time. The business of the town will receive an impetus compared to which a boom, in the general acceptance of the terms, will be a very trifling thing."[5]

Robeson's Fort Meade Fertilizer Company began "grinding phosphate rock" in late March 1890.[6] A few weeks later its operations were described by a resident:

> Some ten minutes' brisk walk in a northeasterly direction from the post-office, through handsome bearing groves and moss covered oaks, brings the saunterer to the Ft. Meade fertilizer works. They are located on a handsome piece of high hammock land but a few yards distant from the run of the famous Peace river. At present only one acre is cleared of the timber which is cut up into suitable length for the furnaces and stacked up to dry in convenient piles around the clearing. On the brow of the hill, some fifty feet apart, are two pits, or rather large ditches, where a score of [black men] are mining the phosphate rock and piling it up on the banks. Another gang of hands conveys this rock in wheelbarrows to a building thirty feet wide and one hundred feet long. Here two hands feed the rock to a Wilson crusher, and after passing through this mill, it is passed on to the Burr stone mill and is then piled up as fine as flour in an allotted space in one corner of the building.
>
> In an adjoining building are located four large kettles, where the potash is boiled down. The large boiler and handsome engine are also located in this part of the building. The different grades and varieties of potash and acids are stored in the main building. The fine-ground phosphate is spread out on the floor of the mixing room where it receives the required amount of potash and acid, and when thoroughly mixed and dried, is placed in sacks, branded and stenciled, and the fertilizer is now ready for the market. The whole process is very simple, but the material turned out will compete with Mapes' best and costs considerable less money. At present these works will turn out only two grades of fertilizer, one an orange tree food and the other a vegetable food.
>
> Charles Parsons, for years connected with a large factory in Boston, is the general manager of the works. . . . A first class cheap fertilizer has been in demand for many years, and the owners of these works, erected at considerable expense, propose to fill this want, and success from the beginning should be their reward.[7]

To permit factory construction and mine expansion, Robeson raised funds from outside investors. To this end he created the Fort Meade

Phosphate, Fertilizer, Land & Improvement Company, capitalized at $50,000. Robeson became its treasurer and general manager. Within a year the company's operations had been linked by a spur track to the Florida Southern Railroad. By that time it had drawn a host of competitors.[8]

Jack Robeson was not the only local promoter and speculator. Cecil Alleyne, Alonzo Cordery, and M. L. Davis knew the surrounding territory, and they soon located prime phosphate lands. For capital they turned to the "remittance men" and English capitalists they had attracted earlier to the area. In October 1890 a group including C. C. Hoyer Miller, Edward Packard, Merrick Shaw, and J. Gardyne agreed to form "the Florida Phosphate Company" with an initial investment of $100,000. Packard was elected president; Miller was designated managing director; Shaw became secretary; and Gardyne was appointed local manager (succeeded by W. S. Warner). The company launched its operations in 1891 five miles west of Homeland at Phosphoria. Near the huge operation "a large saw and planing mill was erected," as well as "quite a village of neat and tasty cottages." It was said of the Florida Phosphate Company, "Only white men are employed; many of them Englishmen," a statement that could not have been made about other area phosphate concerns.[9]

Closer to town the Virginia-Florida Phosphate Company began operations. Started in January 1891, the company was owned by Virginia investors and led by President Paschal Davis. The local general manager was J. W. Wilmott, and its site on Berry Hendry Branch two miles north of Fort Meade was called Wilmott. Not too many years would pass, though, before everyone's name for the area was Pembroke.[10]

Smaller concerns competed with the large companies. E. R. Childers and James Morrison initiated operations in the spring of 1891 near Homeland's Campground Branch. The Homeland Mining and Land Company, composed of Ohio and Kentucky investors, operated in the territory between Kissengen Springs and Peace River. The similarly named Homeland Pebble Phosphate Company, of which T. W. Anderson was treasurer, and Isaac Whitaker's Whitaker Phosphate and Fertilizer Company both mined to the east of Homeland near the river. Whitaker's operation only a short time previously had been James T. Wilson's showplace farm and orange grove.[11]

Mines also sprang up below Fort Meade along Peace River. Owned by the United States Phosphate Company, the Massachusetts Phosphate Company, and the National Peace River Company, these operations gave birth to the community of Acme, located on the railroad four miles south of town. By December 1891 Evans and Carter had opened a general merchandise store in the new village, and a post office had been approved.[12]

Booming Businesses

The phosphate craze launched a business boom. "The general good health and prosperity of Fort Meade at this dull season," a local man wrote in 1890, "go far to prove our advantages over many places in Florida." He added, "Strangers are on our streets daily, some in search of homes, others looking up phosphates, a few in search of pleasure, and all enthusiastic for a boom early this winter. The most incredulous now begin to learn that this phosphate affair is no cunningly devised job to fleece the unsuspecting, but that it is a stubborn reality and means millions for Polk county and Pease creek generally."[13]

To gather some of those millions, members of the English colony in 1889 opened the general mercantile establishments of R. G. Metcalfe & Company; Hilliard, Beddoes, & Evans; and Stansfield Brothers. The next year Lewis W. Hooker followed suit, buying out the firm of J. N. Hooker & Company. F. F. Hendry trailed not too far behind in 1891, as also did the new partnership of Carter, Evans & Company. Arthur Keen maintained his popular grocery, and, by 1892, the circle of Broad Street's mercantile community included Martin Loadholtes's Loadholtes & Company.[14]

From the first day of the 1890s, the town rang with the sounds of commercial and residential construction. The business climate was so lucrative that a bank was finally established. "The bank buildings are receiving the finishing touches now," one resident reported on June 27, 1890, "the safe will be hauled in from the depot to day, and Mr. Parker intends to open the State Bank of Fort Meade on the 1st day of July."[15] A. A. Parker was the bank's first president. W. I. Porter served as cashier until he was succeeded by Englishman Wemyss Jackson.[16]

The "Crawford Place" at 29 North Oak Avenue, similar to many of the residences constructed at Fort Meade during the 1890s. (Courtesy of the Florida State Archives)

Steps were also taken to resolve the Florida Southern Railroad depot dispute. "The indications are," it was said in June 1890, "that Ft. Meade will have a depot within ninety days." The impasse had been broken when developer Edward M. Brown opened up Broad Street through his "Hard Bargain" orange grove and offered to donate "all lands required for sidetracks and depot buildings." A resident explained, "This depot will be three-fourths of a mile from the business center, while the present station is two and one-half miles out of town."[17] The line took its time mulling Brown's offer, and the depot question remained up in the air until the spring of 1891, when the railroad agreed to move its station for an additional $1,000. An agreement was ironed out in July. "Trains are running to the new depot now on the broad gauge track," read an August report. "Every thing comes to those that have patience to wait, even the Florida Southern broad gauge."[18] Days earlier contractor B. F. Perry had extended the

Fort Meade Street Railroad tracks to the new station. The line, as C. G. C. Wright noted, "makes two or three graceful curves and passes just outside a pretty orange grove." Two rows of "Hard Bargain's" trees were removed to permit the passage.[19]

Phosphate mines, new residents, fertilizer and orange crate factories, a bank, prosperous merchants, and a closer depot added up to good financial times. "The two mammoth phosphate plants on each side of town and the orange box factory at the depot," an excited resident wrote in November 1892, "make the whole country around ring with their numerous steam whistles. For a busy town, any one can see Fort Meade is 'in it.' "[20] Business leaders were so "in it" that, early in 1893, they formed the first chamber of commerce or, as it was known, the Fort Meade Board of Trade. The initial meeting was held January 31 in Mayor William Thompson's office. E. Alonzo Cordery was elected president and Wemyss Jackson vice president, while Andrew Laurie, Francis Kempton, J. G. Carter, Thomas R. Dunn, and William A. Evans were named directors. Transportation, public improvements, manufacturing, and statistics committees were organized as well.[21]

Beginnings of a Black Community

The phosphate industry and the business boom attracted hundreds of new residents, and likely, the town doubled or tripled its population from 1889 to 1893. Among the arrivals came the first substantial numbers of blacks to settle in the post–Civil War era. Although a small community of blacks had lived peacefully at Homeland for decades, almost all black men, women, and children had been taken from Fort Meade during the war or else left soon thereafter. Elsewhere in Polk County freedmen had been driven out of their homes in the late 1860s and early 1870s by the threat of vigilante violence. So few returned in the next two decades that, when black railroad crews arrived in 1885, the Fort Meade *Pioneer* could claim, only partly in jest, "that many of the inhabitants have never seen a colored man."[22]

Given the small number of area blacks, relations between the races had been relatively good, a circumstance enhanced by the fact that a number of the black residents were the children of local whites. In the circumstances no instance of a lynching or, with one exception, other racial violence at Fort Meade or Homeland can be found during the nineteenth century, a statement which cannot be made for many other Florida communities. The exception occurred in April 1884, when unknown individuals fired into W. K. Beard's home, which he shared with several helpers, and severely wounded a black man. A public meeting was convened in "outrage," and a reward of $500 was raised "for the capture and proof to convict the guilty parties."[23]

The possibility of racial violence arose in 1887, but some local whites intervened to forestall trouble. The incident occurred when, amid a county prohibition election, Bartow proliquor interests threatened Homeland's black voters. In response, whites led by James T. Wilson and James B. Crum defended their fellow residents. "The good citizens of Homeland," reported a Jacksonville newspaper, "have armed a colony of negroes located near that town, because the negroes have been threatened with a mob from a neighboring town. Besides the guns furnished these inoffensive negroes, they have reserved a few Winchesters for private purposes."[24] On election day Wilson and Crum led Homeland men, including ten black voters, in a public procession to the county seat where they cast their ballots together.[25]

Phosphate attracted blacks to the area beginning about 1889, and many men were employed at J. E. Robeson's mine and fertilizer factory. Absent suitable housing Robeson arranged for the construction nearby of shelter for his hands. This first black community at Fort Meade became known as Villa Park.[26]

The arrival of black laborers did not substantially change the vicinity's race relations patterns. Whites, for instance, happily cheered the jockey, "Brown," at the annual Fort Meade Jockey Club races from 1889 to 1893. Unfortunately Brown's first name was not recorded, although his feats of horsemanship were. He also became one of the town's first black businessmen when in June 1890, much to the delight of children and adults, he opened the community's first "ice cream saloon."[27] Lewis Honors, who was employed by U. A. Lightsey, was well regarded in the community. Paul Young followed in Brown's steps as an entrepreneur. "Paul Young, one of our colored citizens," a correspondent noted in October 1895, "has undertaken to supply the town with fish once a week. He gets the fish from Punta Gorda on ice. In order to suit those who demand fish on a certain day in the week, he gets it in on Friday."[28]

Given the regional rise of legally enforced segregation and the passage of racially motivated "Jim Crow" laws during the late 1880s and 1890s, some contacts between the races continued at Fort Meade on a social as well as a business level. For example, when Masonic Lodge No. 71, F&AM, announced a "good festival" in July 1891, its advertisement specifically noted that "patronage of both white and colored is solicited."[29] Perhaps more illustrative is a story taken from the *South Florida Progress*. "Lewis McSalette [Lewis M. Salette?], in the employ of J. E. Robeson, was married to Mary F. Wilson, both colored," it began. "Mr. Robeson opened his grounds to the wedding party. A large number of guests, both white and colored, assembled to witness the tying of the nuptial knot. Mayor Thompson officiated and afterwards, at request of host and consent of bride and bridegroom, a short, religious service was conducted." Admittedly tensions, of which both races were aware, lay near the surface. "The mayor congratulated Mr. Robeson on the success of an experiment which in the years gone by might have been attended by disorder and would have probably ended in bloodshed," continued the wedding story. "He regarded it as proof that the race question was being gradually solved in a manner that should be highly gratifying to all citizens who valued social order."[30]

For many blacks as well as for many whites, social life revolved around church. Black Baptists at Homeland, led by G. W. McClendon, by 1887 had organized the Mount Bunyan Baptist Church. Five years later McClendon had transferred his ministry and organizational talents to Fort Meade, where his labors helped to create Galilee Baptist Church. "It started on its successful career in 1892," remembered Thomas Sims, "[and] was organized by Rev. D. H. Brown and Rev. G. W. McClendon with six male and female members in the organization." Reflecting in 1916 on the church's beginnings, Sims observed, "There yet remain four of the Charter members, Bro. and Sister Wm. Miles and Bro. and Sister Paul Young." Sims joined the congregation soon after it was formed. "The first revival the church held was in 1892," he reported. "I was converted along with six others." Meeting at first in a "small log house," by 1895 the congregation had moved to its first real church, described as "a small frame structure." Sims concluded, "We have had some of the best ministers in the state serve as pastor."[31]

Black Methodists were also active in the 1890s. One report specifies that St. Paul African Methodist Episcopal Church was organized in 1903, with C. H. Wright as pastor. As early as 1899, however, the South Florida AME Conference appointed J. H. Thomas to a church at Fort Meade, and the origins of St. Paul's may lie in that appointment or may have come at an even earlier date. Similarly, in 1890 Augustus Jackson was designated as preacher for the short-lived AME Fort Meade Circuit. This appointment may suggest a forerunner of "Old Jones Chapel," which stood at Villa Park until its destruction by fire in 1928.[32]

Mrs. Moses (Eliza Davis) Allen, b. 1858. (In possession of the author, courtesy of Vernice Williams)

The black families living at Homeland or Fort Meade by 1895 included those of John Robinson, Jack Vaughn, John Hays, Stephen Hawkins, Henry Wingate, Felix Dixon, J. T. Hollis, Henry Wright, James Alexander, Jeff Marchman, L. Mitchell, G. A. Davis, Charles McLeod, S. J. Davis, Moses Allen, Lloyd Davis, Corrie Davis, William Brewster, Early C. Mitchell, Clem Stafford, Charles Pinkney, James Jones, Jennie Tillis, J. H. Nicholson, Allen Bennett, Darey Johns, Nelson Tillis, Elrich Stephens, Wyatt Young, and Paul Young.[33]

Religious Growth and Diversity

Galilee Baptist Church was not Fort Meade's only new church in the early 1890s, nor were the lives of the established churches uneventful. The white Methodist church prospered. In the spring of 1890, as the phosphate boom was getting under way, William C. Jordan undertook to spruce up the eight-year-old sanctuary. "The Methodist Church," a local man wrote, "has received a coat of paint, inside and out, has been moved some twenty feet north of the street, and will in the near future be enclosed by a neat fence."[34] Three years later church finances permitted construction of a parsonage. Erected by B. F. Perry, the home was ready by July 1893 to welcome E. J. Gates's family. Perry also crafted the church's pulpit and flower stands.[35]

During the early 1890s the English colony was in its heyday, and so, too, was Christ Church. The first services celebrated in its new sanctuary were held January 19, 1890. It was consecrated by Bishop Edwin G. Weed with the assistance of rector Edmund C. Belcher on June 7, 1891. "The belfry of Christ's church is now adorned with a handsome bell," a visitor remarked, "which sends forth its melodious sounds far and wide."[36] In 1897 an onlooker struck by the church's beauty expressed his feelings thus:

Rev. A. Kensey Hall is rector of the Episcopal church which bears the honor of being one of the prettiest in Polk county. This church was erected by the members of 1887, and is elegantly finished on the interior. The chancel and altar are especially attractive and the stained glass windows are very pretty. A handsome new rectory has recently been added

Christ Church (Episcopal), erected 1889. This illustration is believed to be from a promotional postcard printed for Langford Drug Company, West Fort Meade, Florida. (Courtesy of the Florida State Archives)

to the church property, which adds greatly to the beauty of that portion of the city.[37]

Two months prior to Christ Church's consecration, a different denomination held its first services at the town since Father James H. O'Neill celebrated Mass in a "barrack room" at Fort Meade in June 1853. Almost forty years later O. M. Widman, S.J., retraced Father O'Neill's steps to minister to nearly thirty Roman Catholics, many of whom were Italian-born laborers at the Virginia-Florida Phosphate Company mine. Widman's ministrations proved so popular that "a meeting of Catholics and others interested in providing a church for the neighborhood" was held on May 7, 1891, but no permanent mission resulted.[38] Five years later mass continued to be celebrated on an occasional basis and hopes still were being expressed for "a mission-room and later on a church." The mission eventually found a home, but the site was ten miles to the north at Bartow.[39]

Other denominations also organized in the community. Galilee Baptist Church in 1892 was Fort Meade's only Baptist congregation. The same year, however, the white Corinth Primitive Baptist Church was established nearby. W. D. Talley served its members from 1894 to 1899.[40] Mention should be made of another addition. The Church of God began its ministry in Florida near Fort Meade. In the words of a church historian:

> In 1898 the reformation of the Church of God was first brought in the State near Fort Meade, about four and one-half miles north-east of town, known as Pool Branch, holding services in what was then known as the McAuley School Building. About two months later this church was organized holding services in the same building until the erection of a frame church building in the same neighborhood, the latter part of 1898. The latter part of 1899 they established a camp ground in this vicinity, on which a tabernacle was erected.[41]

The End of the Party

The boom began to go bust in 1893. The Panic of 1893 brought about one of the greatest economic depressions in United States history. It occurred at a particularly difficult time for farmers, who were already suffering from poor harvests and low incomes. Because they had lost their farms or were unable to afford to grow crops for the prices paid, farmers had little use for fertilizer. As demand for fertilizer declined, European export markets for phosphates also proved disappointing. Phosphate prices, which had been low since 1891, dropped further in 1894 and 1895. Many companies and their backers were ruined.

The local phosphate industry never collapsed completely. Rather, operations were slowed, some employees were laid off, companies were consolidated, and the value of investments in the industry was depressed—a scenario all too familiar in the modern day. Perhaps the most serious impact was a drastic reduction in the land values, which had been inflated to many times true value. Land that could be sold was marketed at a loss. Bank loans were called, and merchants saw trade reduced.[42]

Apparently the English community especially was hard hit by the depression and phosphate industry problems. Many of its members had invested in the Florida Phosphate Company, and no doubt, many were employed by it. Others had invested in Broad Street commercial houses, and just about everyone who could had bought land. As a result the English began to leave in 1894. By early 1895 the fact was clearly illustrated by the closing of Broad Street's R. G. Metcalfe & Company and of Carter, Evans & Company. The 1894 Fort Meade Jockey Club races proved to be the last run of that colorful reminder of the English presence. Although the races were "well attended" and "a complete success," not enough sponsors remained one year later to justify their continuation.[43]

Fort Meade residents had been confronted again and again during the nineteenth century by disasters and disappointments. Two recent examples—and the town's confident response to them—were fresh in residents' minds as English families packed and, for the last time, departed in 1894 and 1895. And the incidents may have offered some encouragement for those who remained.

First, in November 1892 Fort Meade again lost its newspaper. The *South Florida Progress* had come under the control of Alfred J. Seddon, the Episcopal rector. Seddon, described as "both witty and wise," was a professional journalist who had served in his youth as a European war correspondent for the London *Times*.[44] The *Progress* had begun to rankle some citizens, however. It was reported, for example, that the paper had labeled prominent men as " 'town convicts,' 'green goods men,' and other uncomplimentary insinuations."[45] Seddon, fed up with the hostility he faced, abruptly moved the paper to Bartow. Local businessmen promptly responded. The Board of Trade "unanimously decided to start a newspaper to take the place of the *South Florida Progress* . . . , and a committee was appointed to feel the pulse of the citizens with regard to it."[46] Within five months $2,000 had been raised by selling shares in the Fort Meade Publishing Company, and a new newspaper, the *Fort Meade Pebble*, was born. "The machinery, type, etc. for this is ordered and already on its way here," a resident reported on July 18, 1893. "The paper," he further explained, "will be under the management of Kline O. Varn."[47] When the *Pebble*'s first issue hit the streets on August 1, it served mainly to reemphasize the "can-do" atmosphere in the still booming town.

In 1890 a different kind of problem, this time a real tragedy, had struck the town. For the first time since the Civil War, it was victimized by a major fire. The Jacksonville *Florida Times-Union* of December 11 carried the details:

> The fire was first discovered in Reif Bros.' store at 8:30 p.m., but it had complete possession of the whole of the interior of the building, and a glance showed that it would go in spite of all efforts to save it. The town hall, which was a two-story frame building, with market on the ground floor, was next to Reif Bros.' on the east. Attention was turned to it, but it was soon seen that it, too, was doomed, and the work of saving the books, papers and furniture of the mayor's office was commenced. All the books and papers and most of the furniture was saved.
>
> While this was going on the packing house of E. Evans & Co., which was on the west of Reif Bros., had caught fire, and then the hard fight commenced in earnest. Several hundred people had gathered by this time, and all went to work with a will, but it was a fight against fate; a light wind from the southeast drove the flames fiercely in their faces and they were compelled to retreat, and in a few moments the fire had full sway over the packing house and stable, with the grain house and main store an easy prey. Efforts were then directed toward saving the goods, but action had been delayed too long and only a part of them were rescued.
>
> Canter & Stansfield had also lost all hopes of their drug store, which was a new two-story building, situated on the west side of the street from Evans & Co.'s, and soon willing hands had emptied it of almost the entire stock, except some heavy boxes and barrels which were in the back room.
>
> It was thought at one time that the fire would cross to the south side of Main street and nothing but the stubborn persistency of the heroic citizens kept it back. Lou Reif said that he had only left the store about half an hour, and could give no cause as to the origin of the fire.[48]

Despite the $25,000 loss, town merchants—riding the phosphate boom—quickly recovered. As the Panic of 1893 began to be felt early in 1894, though, another fire struck the business district and rebuild-

Main Street business district before the fire of June 1894, with Aaron Elijah Godwin standing in foreground. (In possession of the author, courtesy of Ben Speight)

ing proved not so easy. "The grocery and hardware store belonging to F. F. Hendry, in the center of town," a resident recorded on January 8, "was discovered on fire before daylight this morning." The report continued, "It was well alight when the alarm was raised. The building and contents soon became a total loss, together with the meat market adjoining on the east side. The fire is supposed to have been caused by rats gnawing matches."[49] Another account added, "The store of Messrs. Carter, Evans & Co. was . . . in great danger, but fortunately after a terrible fight with the fiend was saved."[50]

The strain of economic depression, the departures of increasing numbers of the community's most affluent citizens, and fiery destruction lay heavily upon Fort Meade, and the tensions erupted during elections held in April 1894. Two factions, "the citizens" and "the independents," battled for control of the town's future. In the end, sleight of hand prevailed as all but three ballots were thrown out on technicalities, and longtime mayor William Thompson was ousted by T. J. Minor and his slate of officers and aldermen. Pain was felt, scars were left, and the future looked more unsettled than ever.[51]

After the elections, tragedy returned to the community. Less than one month later Christ Church rector C. E. Butler was found dead by his own hand. "No struggle had taken place," the *Pebble* reported to the shocked community, "and it is generally supposed he took morphine or some other sedative powder just before taking the fatal step." Noted editor Varn, "No note or letter was left, and there is absolutely no clue as to what caused him to take his life."[52]

The train of events continued. In June torrential rains flooded "the whole business portion of the town . . . entirely suspending business," and then a day or two later the terrors of fire for the third time in the decade returned to Broad Street.[53] An observer described the scene:

For the third time in the history of this town it has been visited by a destructive fire. The last time was Thursday morning last, between 2 and 3 o'clock. The large double store, owned by J. G. Carter and rented and stocked by Messrs. Carter, Evans & Co., took fire in the northeast corner, at the back. How the fire came to break out is a mystery at present, but it is supposed to have been the work of some miscreant who had a grudge against some one of the above named gentlemen.

The fire burned rapidly and was discovered by a party of young men returning from a frolic. The alarm was given and everything possible was done to save the goods in that and other stores. Messrs. Carter, Evans & Co. saved only $200 worth, but their books and papers in the safe were found to be uninjured. A little cash, left in the till by accident, has since been picked up in the ashes.

The flames were soon communicated to Stansfield & Co.'s drug store, on the west side. A good deal was saved in this store, but at great risk. Wooden buildings burn so rapidly and fiercely, when once fire gets hold, that it is next to impossible to do anything towards saving goods or fixtures. The fire also soon found its way across the vacant space, where F. F. Hendry's store was burned last January, to the meat market owned by Lightsey & Lewis, on the east side of Carter, Evans & Co.'s, and this also became a smoking ruin in almost as short a time as it takes to write it.

From Stansfield's the fire leaped to Wise Perry's pool room, and it was soon a total loss. The State bank and the Pebble newspaper office were saved, but only by the most strenuous exertions, as they took fire from the heat no less than three times, and everything was taken out that was possible; also all the goods, etc., in R. G. Metcalfe's store, opposite the pool room.

The total loss amounts to nearly $19,000, with only a little over $7,000 insurance. It is reported that Mr. J. G. Carter will erect another large double store on the site of the one just burned, and it is to be hoped that it will be of brick. The town at present presents a very desolate appearance.[54]

To make the desolation even more personal, human tragedy again touched the area in September when fourteen-year-old Willie Durrance was accidentally shot to death by his sister Ella. The story began when Ella was visited by young John Tillis:

> When the young man, John Tillis, went to the house, he laid his pistol which was of the self-acting, hammerless kind, on the water-bucket shelf. Ella saw it, and said:
> "John let me shoot your pistol."
> Willie, who was standing by, echoed his sister's wish by saying:
> "Oh, yes, John; let Ella shoot."
> John agreed, and taking up the weapon, put some cartridges in it and handed it to Ella. While turning around, with the pistol gripped in her hand, she was unconsciously pressing the trigger, her brother being in front of her. Suddenly the pistol was discharged, the ball going through the heart and coming out at his back. The boy, feeling himself shot, ran off to the front porch, where his father and his mother were sitting, and met his father coming to see what was the matter. The boy turned, and, gasping out "Oh, pa!" fell down, and was dead within five minutes.
> The girl is entirely prostrated with grief and remorse, and refuses all food. It is rumored that she asked John to shoot her, as she did not wish to live. Fears are entertained for her reason.[55]

Many Fort Meade residents must have feared for their reason in the late summer of 1894 as they contemplated the terrible losses endured by their community during the past year. At least they could still see and smell the beautiful orange groves that dominated the town. "Lots of groves around here are full of blossoms," it was noted at the time, "giving abundant promise of a second and late orange crop."[56] Whatever else may have happened, the promise of the oranges remained.

THE EXPLOITATION OF PHOSPHATE BEDS in and near Fort Meade beginning in 1890 had led to growth and prosperity during the first years of the decade. By 1894, however, an economic recession held the country in its grip, and the phosphate boom had turned to bust. The English colony was diminished in the wake of these events, and as many of its members prepared to depart, other tragedies struck the town. By the fall of 1894, hopes for the future lay for many residents with the citrus industry. Within months, however, they would discover that their problems were only beginning.

9

"Killing frosts shattered their fond hopes"

The Century's Passing

THE YEAR 1894 was one of pain and dislocation for Fort Meade-area residents. The phosphate boom had been brought to a standstill by national economic depression and weak foreign markets; land values had plummeted; the English colony had begun to drift away; and fire, flood, and personal tragedy had struck relentlessly. The December holiday season helped somewhat to lighten the community's mood, however, and the sounds of saw and hammer echoing from the rebuilding sites of two of the town's major stores—those of F. F. Hendry and J. G. Carter—gave some encouragement for the future. Everywhere around were the thousands of orange trees upon which the town now depended for its economic future.

The Great Freeze of 1895

Four days after the hopeful Christmas of 1894, a cold wave dipped into south Florida, bringing frigid temperatures for a three-day period. Local residents, having feared the worst, found to their relief that the area had been spared the frost's most severe damage. In the following weeks unseasonably warm weather brightened everyone's disposition, and by late January it was reported, "Orange trees are pushing out buds rapidly, and grove owners are looking much more pleasant."[1] In a burst of confidence the State Bank of Fort Meade declared a dividend on its stock, "notwithstanding the late depression."[2] During the first

---

week of February a festive atmosphere emerged in the warm, balmy weather. Homes were painted; the "Bridges quartette" gave "an entertainment"; W. A. Evans held a gala opening for his new store; and many townspeople celebrated W. L. Stephens's marriage to popular Gussie Keen. The only serious controversy swirled around the question of selling cigarettes to minors.[3]

On February 7, 1895, everything changed. That Thursday, frigid weather returned with a vengeance, dropping Fort Meade's nighttime temperature to twenty-five degrees. The next night brought no relief, as the mercury stood but one degree higher. On Saturday, the area endured yet another night of subfreezing weather, with a low of thirty degrees. Sunday saw a slight improvement as temperatures stayed above freezing, but the damage of the Great Freeze of 1895 had already been done.

Damage reports at first were relatively encouraging. "Most vegetables killed," a resident noted, "but at present the orange trees do not appear to be damaged further than the destruction of the young leaves and blossoms which have put out since the last freeze."[4] As late as September optimistic forecasts continued to be issued. "The groves are coming out wonderfully," one man asserted, "and are well on their way to an ultimate recovery."[5]

The sad truth, however, was to the contrary. Irving Keck, surveying the disaster's effects, had seen the truth before the weather warmed. "It is well to look things squarely in the face," he declared. "It is at best a serious disaster, to many it means ruin; to all it means a time of care, anxiety and doubt as to the future."[6] E. E. Durrance, who remembered "only two groves" that were just "slightly damaged," explained the reason. "The 'big freeze' [of December 1894] ruined the oranges that were still on the trees and caused the trees to shed their leaves," he observed. "It turned off warm and rained after the first cold spell, the sap rose and the trees put out new growth. Then in February, 1895, it put the finishing touch on the trees."[7]

The Great Freeze also put the "finishing touch" on the fortunes of many area residents. George W. Hendry noted that it "cleaned out [my] groves and nursery, and left [me] land poor. . . . All values in real estate dropped to about half their former price, and now in [my] old age and decline of life, [I am] drinking the cup of poverty." Hendry

Main Street looking west, c. 1895.
(In possession of the author, courtesy of Walter Crutchfield)

Main Street looking east, c. 1895.
(In possession of the author, courtesy of Walter Crutchfield)

spoke also of his son, merchant F. F. "Tobe" Hendry. "Through fires and freezes, and a combination of causes, reverses came," he explained, "and he lost the bulk of his estate." Wistfully Hendry concluded, "He was recognized at one time as the most successful business man in Fort Meade, and was busy from morning till night."[8]

The freeze's impact was felt almost immediately. The situation was so bad that in March, conveniently, all town records were stolen, permitting suspension of tax collections and affording taxpayers needed relief. By summer the town had declared that "economy is the order of the day." When marshal Belton C. Gardner refused to take a pay cut, he was replaced by John J. Hooker who would. Municipal offices were removed "to the well appointed blacksmith shop of R. J. Hodgson."[9]

The disaster touched individuals more directly and more painfully than it did town government. "Neglected and waste places" could be seen everywhere.[10] Many settlers, their farms and groves ruined, pulled up stakes and moved on. William M. Burdine lost his orange grove at Homeland. After several disappointing years spent attempting to reestablish himself, he moved on to Miami, where his efforts proved more successful, as his department store customers can attest to this day. In June A. H. Adams auctioned off the Adams House furnishings and moved to California. So many followed their examples that, by summer 1895, Fort Meade's population was reduced to only 350 men, women, and children. Bartow, which just over a decade earlier had been the smaller community, boasted almost 2,000.[11]

The Cuban Tobacco Growers Company

In the months following the Great Freeze, few events brought even a little cheer to the demoralized populace. The happy incidents were primarily limited to a single family or to an individual. Interestingly, several had to do with inventions. A. W. J. Best, somewhat ahead of his time, had patented late in 1894 "a wagon to be run by steam," which was "creating a great deal of excitement."[12] A. H. Adams and Lester Haskell followed in Best's footsteps during the next summer. Adams patented an "orange box hoop," from which he hoped to make his fortune. Haskell's ideas were more domestic, leading to his invention of a "portable kitchen."[13]

An event in May 1895, while not a happy occasion, for a time united the community in remembrance of and tribute to the sacrifices of its past. During the 1880s community growth had been fueled by northern and midwestern immigration. A legacy was the establishment about 1894 of a chapter of the Grand Army of the Republic, an organization of Union Civil War veterans. In the spring of 1895 John C. Fremont Post No. 28 called for a community gathering on Memorial Day "to decorate with flowers, the graves of dead heroes." Post Adjutant H. M. Day described the outcome:

> As the affair was the first of the kind in South Florida, so far as known to the writer, there had been considerable anxiety and a good deal of hard work to make it a success; and it was a complete success. Ft. Meade did itself honor by the cordial manner in which its citizens welcomed and aided in the preparations. Without being invidious, special credit is due to Messrs. [J.W.] Powell, [L.W.] Maxwell, and [W.L.] Tireman of the Post, and Capt. [B.F.] Perry and others of our Confederate boys whose names the author does not recall. Also to Mrs. [E.A.] Cordery and Mrs. [George W.] Black for the sweet music which they, with their participation, provided for the occasion, and too the Ft. Meade band.
>
> The place of meeting was lovely, with its magnificent trees, and the platform ornamented with flags and flowers. Harmony, cordiality, and kindly feeling marked the day from beginning to end.
>
> At 10 a.m., a long procession was formed and led by the Post and the soldiers marched with fife and drums to the cemetery, when, according to the Memorial ritual, the graves of the buried soldiers were decorated with beautiful flowers, and the names of about sixty others were reported by the Adjutant as buried in other places. . . .
>
> Returning to the grounds, the programme of recitations, etc., was carried out, interspersed with music by the choir and band. . . . At the beginning of the exercises Commander Powell invited the Confederate boys to take seats with the Post on the platform. One incident is worth mentioning. One "dear old Johnny," as Commander Powell expressed it, came laden with a large box full of lovely flowers and as he poured them out on the platform, the thought of the writer was, "Blessing on his

head," so may it ever be for the future. "The Union forever one and indivisible."[14]

In their time of need residents turned to a man who for a decade had been at the forefront of town development and enterprise, and E. Alonzo Cordery did not disappoint them. Aware that ongoing civil strife had disrupted Cuba's world-famous tobacco industry, Cordery quietly arranged for local soil tests. Samples were sent to a Cuban expert who, after "careful analyses," concluded "that the Fort Meade soil contains the right properties for raising the finest grades of tobacco, [and] that there is present in the soil properties which no other Florida soil possesses, and which are essential to the production of such tobacco as is raised in the famous Vuelto Abajo district of Cuba."[15] Armed with these findings, Cordery contacted several Cuban growers, including Dr. M. A. Abalo, and campaigned to convince them that their fortunes awaited at Fort Meade.

Rumors of Cordery's tobacco plans had run the town's length and breadth when, on October 26, 1895, a "rousing meeting" was held "in the spacious hall adjoining the fertilizer factory of W. A. Evans & Co." Reflecting the crowd's mood, the "Fort Meade silver cornet band" upon Mr. and Mrs. Cordery's entrance struck up "See the Conquering Hero." Rising to address the gathering, Cordery spoke "in his usual eloquent and forcible style, stating the objects in view." The crowd went wild. "The large audience," a report noted, "was fairly carried away by the oratory of the gallant captain, and boiled over with enthusiasm, cheering the speaker to the echo." Within forty minutes after the cheering died, 700 acres of prime land and thirty city lots had been pledged to back the plan. As Cordery left the hall, "the band played the Cuban national air."[16]

With community backing secured, Cordery acted upon his plans. Ten days later he held an "enthusiastic ratification meeting" and announced the formation of the Cuban Tobacco Growers Company with himself as vice president, M. A. Abalo as president, Ricordo Piloto as general manager, and Juan Torralbas as secretary and treasurer.[17] Events then proceeded rapidly. On December 5 a "large crowd" gathered at the depot to welcome the arrival of the first twenty-four Cuban settlers, who were cheered "right lustily."[18] As more settlers arrived, "a monstrous barbecue" was organized to welcome them. Between 800 and 1,000 persons turned out for the event on New Year's Day 1896. On the occasion M. A. Abalo declared "that he already saw signs of success for the enterprise newly started and predicted for its future second to none started in the land of flowers."[19]

January 1896 proved a busy month. First, tobacco seedbeds were set out, a feat accomplished three weeks into the new year. The company was also settling down. "The Cuban Tobacco Growers' Co.," a January 22 report informed residents, "is now installed in the splendid suite of offices in the French block [on the northeast side of the intersection of Broad Street and Orange Avenue]. The rooms have been painted in artistic style by Mr. Thomas A. Blackburn, and have been elegantly furnished."[20] The company also erected a cigar factory. A visitor in early February found it in operation and declared of samples presented to him, "We want no better cigars than those given us."[21]

As winter moved closer to spring, more Cubans settled at the town, and Cordery kept citizens informed of progress made. "We have now fully established a colony of some 60 Cubans near Ft. Meade," he declared, "and expect another colony before many weeks have passed. Five or six of these people are experts and all are of the better class of Cubans—people of refinement and character who are certain to prove an acquisition to any community."[22] The later arrival of ten additional settlers prompted a local man to quip, "If they continue to arrive for a short time longer as they have been for a few weeks past we will soon have Spanish spoken upon our streets as much as we now have English."[23] The "greatly increased" attendance at Fort Meade High School, brought about by the Cuban influx, had already compelled the addition of a second assistant teacher to the school's faculty.[24]

Added numbers of Cubans expert in tobacco and cigar production permitted expansion of company efforts. "The Fort Meade Tobacco Growers Co., commenced setting out tobacco plants last Thursday," proclaimed a March 25 announcement.[25] The company's fields were located just to the west and south of the Peace River bridge, and by mid-April they contained some "100,000 well advanced tobacco plants on seven acres." Nearby the company had erected "a large and well stocked general store, where all sorts of goods suitable to the Cuban trade are kept for sale." Stated M. A. Abalo, "The colonists are delighted with the beautiful and healthy country, are sending their children to the public schools to learn English and adapting themselves with remarkable aptitude to the customs of the country and the hospitable people among whom they have located."[26]

Settlers settled and plants planted, Fort Meade's American and Cuban populations decided to give themselves a party. In April they did just that:

> On the morning of the 25th inst. (Saturday) the Cuban colony here, together with our native citizens, assembled in front of the old Adams House on Main street and formed line under the guidance of Ricordo Piloto, marshal of the day, and took up the line of march to the picnic grounds, just east of Peace river bridge, with banners flying, the Stars and Stripes occupying a conspicuous place, carried by a Cuban, and on either side was displayed the Cuban colors, carried by Americans, all led by the Ft. Meade silver cornet band, and on arrival at the grounds, where extensive arrangements had been made for the comfort and pleasure of the picnicers, national airs and patriotic songs were rendered by seemingly the entire party. . . .
>
> [After numerous addresses] Dr. Abalo then from the stand, in the name of the Cuban colony, thanked the people of Ft. Meade and Polk county for the many kind attentions and courtesies extended to their colony since its arrival here.
>
> Then all repaired to a bountifully spread table of not only nicely barbecued meats and the usual substantials, but many nicest delicacies, with good tea and coffee, and there was an abundance for all and more too. After dinner, music by the band and recitations and vocal music by the young people was the order . . . after which and late in the evening the picnicers bade each other good evening and repaired to their homes, after spending a most enjoyable day.[27]

The tobacco experiment soon attracted statewide and national attention. On May 24 the Jacksonville *Florida Times-Union* ran a front-page story on the town and the industry. The account began, "Fort Meade is conspicuous today as the one place in the state where the growing of Cuban tobacco, by native Cubans and by Cuban methods, has become an established fact." The expected success of the venture had prompted backers to adopt ambitious plans, the article further explained. "Having secured lands and got the first crop well under way," it revealed, "the company will immediately proceed to the erection of a large central curing house in which they will cure, not only their own but also the crops raised by the native farmers. . . . They will also erect waterworks and put in an irrigation plant against next year's crop, when they will be prepared to furnish water to the entire community. They have one cigar factory in operation now, where they make 2,000 cigars daily, all of which are sold in advance. Next year the capacity will be greatly increased."[28]

Almost 5,000 pounds of tobacco were cured from Fort Meade's first crop, and the leaf was said to be "as good as any that was ever grown in Cuba."[29] The venture's practicality established, the company pushed ahead with the additional crops and expanded acreage. "The company . . . have just finished cutting the largest and finest crop of tobacco ever grown in that county," a correspondent recorded the following year. "They cultivated over one hundred acres in fine Cuban seed tobacco the past season, and gathered forty-five thousand pounds of tobacco, which has been pronounced to be fully equal in texture and aroma to the famous Cuban tobacco."[30] The achievement was made possible by a large irrigation system. "They have en route," a resident wrote in February 1897, "127,000 pounds of piping to add to that already laid, 15,040 feet of 6-inch pipe, 13,020 feet of 5-inch pipe, 12,050 feet of 4-inch pipe, and 54,009 feet of 1½ inch. They will erect two more large 25,000 gallon tanks on towers forty feet high and increase their pumping capacity at 20,000 gallons per hour. Their largest plantation consists of 147 acres near the Peace river bridge and the piping is to be laid all over this, with sprays erected fifty feet apart all over the plantation." He concluded, "All are proud of what the Cuban Tobacco Growers company have done here."[31]

Success bred competition, and numerous local men quickly invested independently in the industry. Unequaled by any was A. F. Gartner's and W. A. Evans's "La Cosmopolita" plantation.[32] Begun in October 1896 on forty acres of Virginia-Florida Phosphate Company land just north of town, La Cosmopolita became a showplace within fourteen months. "We had a hurried glance at the extensive tobacco farm at Pembroke the other day," a visitor related in February 1898, "and were surprised at its immensity. There are a large number of houses occupied by the families of the laborers and managers. There are

Americans, Germans, English, Cubans, negroes, and possibly other nationalities and hence the name of 'La Cosmopolita Plantation' is indeed a appropriate one, for certainly no settlement in this county has a more cosmopolitan population." Eighty acres of plants were cultivated by that time, and "a dozen or more" curing houses and a cigar factory were located on the grounds. That February the plantation was visited by United States Secretary of Agriculture James Wilson. "At the house," disclosed one report, "the Secretary was presented with two boxes of elegant cigars, made from and labelled 'from tobacco grown in Polk county, Florida, on La Cosmopolita plantation.' These cigars were to be taken to Washington and opened at the meeting of the cabinet yesterday, where the President and his official family all doubtless enjoyed some of the best smoking they have had for many a day."[33]

Boom Times Return

Tobacco cultivation worked an economic miracle, and the change was apparent immediately. "Business has experienced quite a boom within the past few days," a resident noted as the first Cuban settlers arrived.[34] Two months later a visitor added, "Everything and everybody presents a lively contrast to the situation before the advent of this colony."[35] The *Tampa Tribune* echoed the sentiments in August 1897. "The commercial interests of Fort Meade have nearly doubled in the past twelve months," its account related.[36] A resident summed up the prevailing mood. "The hard times are past and gone in this section," he said, "and the much-wished for prosperity is at hand."[37]

With newfound prosperity Fort Meade began to grow once more. "There are a great many strangers in town looking for land to rent or purchase," a local man wrote in March 1897.[38] By August the corporate limits contained a population of "about 500," a figure not including those living at nearby farms, phosphate mines, tobacco plantations, and turpentine mills.[39] As the total continued to grow, some old faces were seen again. A. H. Adams, F. A. Whitehead, J. G. Carter, and G. W. Hendry all returned in 1896 and 1897. Some longtime residents sank their roots a little deeper as several of the remaining Englishmen, including Henry Shaw, C. G. C. Wright, and James Stansfield, took oaths of American citizenship.[40]

The Broad Street mercantile houses hummed with renewed activity. Businesses such as Stansfield Brothers and M. M. Loadholtes & Company thrived. New grocery, hardware, and dry goods houses were opened to ring up their share of sales, including those of B. B. Bostick, L. H. Johnson, Velasco & Company, and J. W. Earnest & Company. James M. Manley established a meat market; Mrs. Henry Rumohr operated a millinery house; W. F. Noble settled into a partnership in W. L. Stephens's drugstore; John Cordullo moved into his new barbershop; and Max Reif took over James T. Hancock's livery stables. One concern reflected a new fad that "was all the thing."[41] In 1897 W. F. Noble started "a bicycle exchange" in connection with his drugstore, and F. F. Crawford opened a repair shop in which he promised to "keep a full supply of bicycle sundries."[42] Soon everyone had to have his own machine. The fad evidenced a rough side, however. "A number of bicy-

W. L. Stephens's drugstore, 1895, with promoter E. Alonzo Cordery standing at center. (Courtesy of the Florida State Archives)

clists will be called before the Mayor," an April report declared, "to answer the charge of riding on the sidewalks."[43]

Renewed prosperity gave birth to civic improvements. In March 1896 the town council extended the school term to eight months, an unusual commitment to public education for a town so small. Early the following year city fathers continued the paving of Broad Street with phosphate clay, so that by February the approaches from east of the river bridge, as well as Broad Street west to Oak Avenue, had been completed. The Fort Meade Street Railroad tracks also were extended eastward "to the Central curing house of the Cuban Tobacco Growers' company."[44] Excitement may have reached its peak in April 1897 when railroad magnate Henry B. Plant, builder of the exotic Tampa Bay Hotel, arrived for a tour of the tobacco operations. According to one account, Plant "declared that Fort Meade was gifted with one of the most flourishing industries in the United States, and one which was sure to make Fort Meade famous all over the world." The reporter added, "It is rumored that Mr. Plant selected a site for a hotel which he intends to erect here shortly."[45]

From the bust of 1894 and 1895 to the boom of 1897 and 1898, the community was served by the *Fort Meade Pebble*. In July 1895, however, at the depth of the bust, Kline O. Varn resigned as editor. He was replaced temporarily by John Northcutt, and within a couple of months the paper was placed under F. F. Crawford. In May 1896, the *Pebble* was described as "six columns, four pages; democratic, issued every Friday; $1 per annum."[46] Changing economic realities demanded a rethinking of its name after the phosphate bust, and in July the Fort Meade Publishing Company selected a new name, the *Fort Meade Times*. In 1897 the retitled paper was labeled as "a very creditable weekly newspaper . . . doing much for the upbuilding of the town."[47]

Busted Again at Century's End

Had residents not so desperately wanted the tobacco companies to succeed, they likely would have foreseen that, as long as the industry depended on Cuban expertise, it could not last forever—one day the Cubans would want to go home. At the town picnic held April 25,

1896, speaker after speaker, Cuban and American, had spoken of the cause of Cuban independence. The remarks of John Torralbas, Ricordo Piloto, and M. A. Abalo particularly "were very animated in touching on the Cuban cause."[48] The following month the *Florida Times-Union* noted, "Many of the Cubans who work for the Cuban Tobacco Growers' company are anxious to go back and fight for 'Cuba libre,' and it is expected they will soon have a chance." The paper also suggested that four local men—Harry Stansfield, Max Reif, Lewis W. Hooker, and H. H. Taplin—themselves intended to go.[49]

When the Spanish-American War erupted in 1898, the town did send many of its residents to fight. "Fort Meade is largely deserted of its young men," a July 19 letter stated, "several have joined the army, and a number have secured work at Tampa in the different departments of the army stationed there."[50] The war and their absence did not hurt the community, but the peace did. "Promptly upon the freeing of Cuba in 1898," explained Ben W. Johnson, "this Cuban population departed for their own 'Patria' (Country) and Fort Meade was left in what seemed then to be in about as bad condition as possible."[51] Events did not move quite as quickly as Johnson remembered. In February 1899 the Tobacco Growers Company announced its intention to "put in" another crop, and La Cosmopolita was targeted for a "tenfold" increase "for the coming season."[52] The number of Cubans was dwindling, however, and by April 1899 "less than one hundred" remained. The colony's last remnant departed on April 12, citing "the long continued drought in the early part of last year and the killing frosts of this winter and spring [which] resulted in great disaster and shattered to pieces their fond hopes."[53]

Denied Cuban expertise, the tobacco industry collapsed, and the local economy again plunged into depression. "Times were certainly hard," Ben Johnson recalled, "and just about all the work to be had then was with the road overseer working our country roads."[54] Many residents arbitrarily turned their anger on the Cubans, the value of whose expertise, particularly in the curing process, they had so underestimated. "It was freely whispered," E. B. Simmons recorded, "that the Cuban workers purposely spoiled [the tobacco] in curing, so it would not compete in the market with the island-grown leaf."[55]

Through the last year of the nineteenth century, the community's social and economic lifeblood slowly drained away. Only a fortuitous rise in phosphate prices and the opening of a new mine three miles to the west at Tiger Bay prevented a complete collapse. Weather deepened the crisis. Early in 1899, a hard freeze struck the area. On February 13, it snowed. According to one account, "It was indeed a rarity to many who had never seen such a sight."[56] That night and for the next two days, snow turned to bitter cold. Only by chance was the orange crop saved. Four months later fickle nature paid a return visit. "The worst windstorm known to this region," a Lake Buffum man reported on June 6, "visited this place about 1:30 P.M. last Sunday. The surrounding country is strewn with what were majestic pine trees—now bent and twisted logs. Fences were completely wrecked, corn blown to the ground, fruit trees twisted from their roots and fruit wrenched from the trees. Small outbuildings were completely wrecked."[57]

All the while, many area residents were deciding to take their chances elsewhere, a dynamic vividly illustrated by the July departure of Charles L. Mitchell, a man who had done so much to bring the town into being. By the summer of 1900, only 261 residents continued to live within the town limits, a drop of six from the 1890 total. It was as if the phosphate, citrus, and tobacco booms had never occurred.[58]

The nineteenth century had given birth to Fort Meade and had often teased it with visions of growth and prosperity only to blindside it with disaster. The military had created a haven in the south Florida wilderness only to destroy it in a war few residents had wanted. From the cattle industry after the Civil War had flowed a wealth of gold doubloons to build a vibrant mercantile economy, but the cattlemen's desire for open ranges had discouraged settlers. When farmers came, no railroad stood ready to transport their crops. When the railroad finally arrived, its tracks first went elsewhere and drew away the momentum of growth. English colonists created an artificial economy and lifestyle that could not be maintained after their departure. The phosphate industry boom was expected to last forever but barely endured for three years. At the end of the century, hard freezes destroyed citrus and vegetable crops to administer a final economic coup de grace.

With each tease and with each fresh disappointment, the craving for real growth, real success, and real prosperity intensified. Each new opportunity provoked expectations and commitments far beyond those justified by any objective appraisal. By the time E. A. Cordery gave birth to the idea of a Cuban tobacco industry, desperate residents were willing to grasp at any straw and to turn a blind eye to problems while doing so. Too often they had been given a glimpse of the golden ring, only to find that their pockets had been picked while their attention was diverted. Even though the departure of the English colonists and the effects of that experience on the town and the local economy were fresh in everyone's mind, the town was willing to put it all on the line for an industry dependant on Cuban colonists, hoping against hope for the big payoff at last. For the last time in the nineteenth century, the big payoff became the big payout.

Unlike other disappointments in the previous decade, no new opportunities for economic salvation presented themselves at Fort Meade in the several years immediately following the collapse of the tobacco industry. As local depression and hard times settled in, even the town's existence was imperiled. On June 4, 1903, the Florida legislature abolished it as an incorporated municipality. The town had hit rock bottom.[59]

One fact of life in Florida's history has been the cycle of boom and bust. In the first decade of the twentieth century the cycle continued at Fort Meade. By 1907 another boom had set in, and on October 25, 1909, the town was again incorporated. It was a different town, though, centered not on the old business district to the east of Perry Avenue but rather on the railroad with a new business district to the west of Hooker Street or, as it came to be called, Charleston Avenue. The shift of the business district eliminated the need for the Fort Meade Street Railroad, and it became only a memory. "Old town," itself, passed from existence, a victim of the flames that had attempted to destroy it in 1890 and 1894. On August 3, 1909, four buildings were burned at a loss of $5,000. The final stroke was delivered on November 8, 1912. "All the wooden buildings remaining in the business section of the city," a local man reported, "were wiped out by a disastrous fire at an early hour this morning." He continued, "The cause is not known."[60] And so, from causes known and unknown, the nineteenth century ended symbolically at the oldest town in interior south Florida.

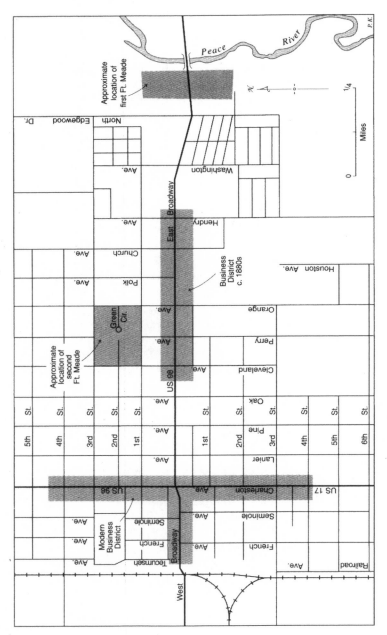

Modern Street Grid of Old Fort Meade Business District and Adjacent Areas

Appendixes

Commanding Officers of the United States Military Post at Fort Meade, Florida

1849–1850
Brevet Lieutenant Colonel Henry Bainbridge, Seventh Infantry
(December 19–June 8)

1850
Captain Israel Vogdes, First Artillery
(June 8–16)
Brevet Lieutenant Colonel Edward J. Steptoe, Third Artillery
(June 16–July 18)
Brevet Major Francis O. Wyse, Third Artillery
(July 18–October 4)
Brevet Major William Austine, Third Artillery
(October 4–November 19)
First Lieutenant Lewis O. Morris, First Artillery
(November 19–December 18)

1850–1851
Brevet Major William H. French, First Artillery
(December 18–October 3)

1851
Brevet Captain Samuel K. Dawson, First Artillery
(October 3–December 18)

1851–1852
Captain Henry D. Grafton, First Artillery
(December 18–March 20)

1852
Captain Henry Swartwout, Second Artillery
(March 20–June 29)
Brevet Captain Samuel K. Dawson, First Artillery
(June 29–October 16)

1852–1853
Brevet Lieutenant Colonel Harvey Brown, Second Artillery
(October 16–January 22)

1853

Second Lieutenant Robert B. Thomas, Second Artillery
(January 22–February 3)
Brevet Colonel Harvey Brown, Second Artillery
(February 3–May 30)
Captain William F. Barry, Second Artillery
(May 30–September 27)
Captain Henry D. Grafton, First Artillery
(September 27–November 29)
Brevet Major William Hays, Second Artillery
(November 29–December 1)

1853–1854

Brevet Major Lewis G. Arnold, Second Artillery
(December 1–November 30)

1857

Brevet Major John B. Scott, Fourth Artillery
(March 13–June 13)
First Lieutenant James J. Dana, Fourth Artillery
(June 13–August 14, 1857)
Brevet Major Thomas Williams, Fourth Artillery
(August 14–September)

Appendix 2

1860 United States Census,
Heads of Households in the Fort Meade Area

(age in parentheses)

#88	Cason, John (30)	#217	Altman, John (32)
#89	English, Eli (29)	#218	Hicks, D. O. (28)
#90	Summerall, Thomas (38)		Sealey, W. S. (30)
#92	Hollingsworth, Stephen (66)	#219	Boggess, F. C. M. (27)
#94	Tillis, Willoughby (39)	#220	Whidden, James L. (33)
#96	McCullough, William (38)	#222	Hendry, Albert J. (25)
	Dawson, Joseph (29)	#223	Martin, L. A. (33)
	White, J. (24)	#224	Low, Allen (46)
#97	Curry, T. J. (26)	#225	Kendrick, Edward T. (40)
#98	Brooker, Margaret (48)		Moore, Joseph (60)
#99	Allen, William (29)	#226	Hooker, John I. (48)
#100	[Carson?], Robert (27)	#228	Crawford, C. Q. (51)
#101	Powell, John (45)	#230	Lanier, Louis (47)
#102	Pearce, J. M. (25)	#231	Waldron, Daniel (24)
#104	Lanier, Mary B. (34)	#232	Hendry, George W. (21)
#105	Key, Gilbert L. (26)	#234	Hendry, Francis A. (27)
#106	Godwin, Solomon (35)		Seward, Zachariah (21)
#107	Carney, William (23)	#235	Seward, Henry S. (51)
#108	McAuley, Robert A. (28)	#236	Singletary, Simpson (39)
#109	McAuley, John (58)	#237	Durrance, Francis M. (51)
#111	Green, John (36)		Frasier, J. C. (25)
#112	Pearce, Levi (54)	#238	Oats, John C. (38)
#114	Hollingsworth, W. R. (35)		Gunter, John B. (24)
#115	Skipper, John L. (35)	#239	Durrance, Jesse H. (30)
	Watson, Alexander (24)	#240	Kinney, Thomas (50)
#116	McKinney, Thomas L. (28)		Tucker, Daniel (30)
#209	Hancock, James T. (22)	#241	Durrance, Joseph L. (43)
#210	Stephens, Isham (23)		Durrance, Joseph (78)
#211	Main, David (57)	#243	Durrance, John R. (37)
#212	Main, Eleanor (50)		Ellis, A. J. (26)
#213	Hancock, Jordan (45)	#244	Durrance, William H. (44)
#214	Whidden, Bennett (32)		Davis, James (117)
#215	Ivey, Francis A. (31)	#246	Smith, James D. (43)
	Willard, Edward (20)	#248	Crum, James B. (35)
#216	Waters, Isaac (50)	#249	Davis, Irvin (39)

1870 United States Census, Heads of Households in the Fort Meade Area

(age in parentheses)

The 1870 census of Polk County tended to be a hit-or-miss affair. Numerous individuals and families known to be in the area were omitted, and many families listed were likely transients. The following heads of households are listed and, likely, were present in the Fort Meade area.

#199	Hilliard, Elias (29)		#238	Whidden, Spicey (35)
#200	McAuley, Robert (34)		#239	Underhill, Matthew (29)
#202	McAuley, John (60)		#240	Underhill, James (29)
#203	Green, Delia (45)		#241	Sullivan, Thomas (35)
#204	Green, Lewis (30)		#242	Lewis, John (55)
#205	Land, Thomas (40)		#243	Lewis, Madison (45)
#206	Rivers, John (30)		#244	Carlton, James (27)
#207	Smith, Lizzie (21)		#245	Langford, William (45)
#208	Hollingsworth, William (40)		#246	Joyce, John (30)
#210	Wallace, William (50)		#247	Peters, Mary (31)
#211	Tison, James (57)		#248	Keller, John (35)
#212	Grandy, William (22)		#249	McDonald, William (22)
#214	Rawles, John (20)		#251	Hicks, James (35)
	Gandy, Green (35)			Childs, J[onathan] W. (37)
#215	Wallace, William (24)		#252	Hicks, Robert (38)
#216	Handy, Madison (31)		#253	Hicks, Reuben (30)
	[William Marion Hendry?]		#254	Brandon, John (55)
#217	Key, Gilbert L. (36)		#255	Carson, Robert (35)
#220	Raulerson, William (34)		#256	Gunter, John (42)
#221	Godwin, Elijah (32)		#257	Collier, William (46)
#222	Godwin, Thomas (50)		#287	Pylant, [Robert N.?] (37)
#223	Godwin, Solomon (45)		#288	Duncan, Lemuel (53)
#224	Guy, Benjamin (45)		#291	Page, Solomon (24)
#225	Willingham, Wm. H. (54)		#292	Crum, James (45)
#226	[Bellamy?], William (35)		#293	Crum, Jane (30)
#227	Walters, John (28)		#294	Mitchell, Robert (33)
#228	Wade, John (28)		#295	Page, Bernice (25)
#229	Wade, James (35)		#296	Wingate, Richard (35)
#231	Prescott, Nelson (35)		#297	Phelps, Eliza (35)
#232	O'Kerr, Muster (26)			Phelps, William (25)
#233	O'Kerr, John D. (21)		#299	Hammond, Martin (21)
#235	McClelland, William (45)		#300	Parker, William (25)
#236	Underhill, William (41)		#301	Johns[t]on, Alex (38)
#237	Underhill, John (38)		#302	Singletary, Simpson (45)

#304	Brown, William (33)	#339	Duncan, James (57)
#305	Pollard, Mary (31)	#340	Duncan, Webster (28)
#306	Wilson, James T. (40)	#341	Waters, Sophia (35)
	Kinney, Thomas (69)	#342	Dultina, Luke (33)
#307	Bloom, William (25)	#343	Hancock, James (36)
#308	Seward, Henry (41)	#344	Arnold, Daniel
#309	Moody, Benjamin (34)	#346	Carwan, Mary (23)
#310	Roberts, Sherod E. (33)	#347	Womack, James (36)
#311	Lightsey, C. B. (36)	#348	Womack, Frank (34)
#312	Chaney, Jacob (22)	#349	Cummings, Mary (30)
#313	Scott, James	#350	Watson, Solomon (47)
#314	Smith, Reuben (46)	#351	Hill, James (47)
#316	Raines, Arlan (24)	#352	Raulerson, James (34)
#317	Hilliard, James (67)	#353	Stephens, Charles (44)
#318	Homely, Oscar (41)	#354	Allen, Hannah (52)
#319	Houze, Monroe (21)	#355	Rice, James (42)
#320	Houze, James (67)	#358	Averra[?], John (27)
#321	Willis, Mary (24)	#359	Crews, Ashberry (37)
#322	Hade, John (35)	#360	Whidden, Bennett (35)
#323	[Moore?], James (34)	#361	Whidden, Elias (26)
#324	Long, Nathan (45)	#362	Collier, James (18)
#326	Long, Lilla (30)	#363	Page, Lucy (36)
#328	Baker, Julius (34)	#364	Durrance, William (59)
#329	Redick, Nancy (45)	#365	Smith, Mary (45)
#330	Altman, William (22)	#366	Campbell, Mary (45)
#331	Tillis, Willoughby (62)	#367	Hill, James (24)
#332	Bloom, James (38)	#368	Eubank, Frank (41)
	Bloom, Daniel (21)	#370	Prince, James (35)
#333	Altman, Ann (38)	#371	Underhill, James (35)
#335	Holloway, Charles (38)	#372	Benton, George (40)
#336	Bryant, Francis (52)	#373	Davis, Matthew (43)
#337	Watts, Solomon (41)	#375	Thomas, Henry (43)
#338	Stephens, William (41)	#559	Robinson, A. C. (50)

Appendix 4

1880 United States Census, Heads of Households in the "Village of Fort Meade"

(age in parentheses)

#284	Manley, James (44)	#293	Rockner, Cuthbert (48)
#285	Monroe, Neill (45)	#294	Hooker, James (31)
#286	Dzialynski, G. I. P. (23)		Tillis, Susan (23)
#287	Langford, Richard (31)	#295	Hayman, Seabren (33)
	Coachman, Walter (16)	#296	Keen, Arthur (32)
	Lightsey, Ulysses (22)	#297	Snodgrass, Howard (22)
#288	Brandon, John (44)	#298	Snoddy, John (46)
#289	McKinney, Robert (60)	#299	Mitchell, Charles (32)
	Tillis, Victor (22)		Boyd, Wesley (24)
#290	Robeson, John (32)	#300	Hart, Barney (26)
#291	Roberts, Sherod (38)	#301	Collins, Joseph (26)
#292	Peters, William (65)	#302	Stallings, Joseph (44)

Fort Meade and Homeland School Trustees

Fort Meade

1855–1856	Alderman Carlton, Francis M. Durrance, James L. Whidden
1859–1860	Edward T. Kendrick, Rufus Durrance, Francis C. M. Boggess
1861	C. Q. Crawford, Louis Lanier, Willoughby Tillis
1891–1892	Richard C. Langford, V. B. Webster, William L. Weems
1894–1895	R. C. Hodgson, John E. Robeson
1895–1896	Luke B. Flood, William Lebo, V. B. Webster
1896–1897	Richard C. Langford, Benjamin F. Perry, V. B. Webster
1897–1898	Richard C. Langford, Benjamin F. Perry, J. W. Powell
1898–1899	Charles L. Mitchell, J. W. Powell, Henry L. Rockner

Homeland

1859–1860	Levi Pearce, John L. Skipper, John McAuley
1861	Robert A. McAuley, John Green, W. R. Hollingsworth

Fort Meade and Homeland School Teachers

Fort Meade

1855	Francis C. M. Boggess
1858–1860	Francis C. M. Boggess
1860	Daniel Waldron
1861	Miss C. A. Tippens, F. J. Seward
1871?–1874?	Robert LaMartin
1878–1879	H. C. Carney
1879–1881	John Snoddy
1881	———— Blackburn
1882	M. L. Menges
1884	Mary E. Webster
1885	Henry Everett
1885–1886	J. F. Marsh, Lula Marsh
1886–1887	W. S. Thompson, Lula Marsh Childers
1887–1888	F. L. Wimberly, William R. Thomas, Annie McCaskey, Mrs. G. W. Black
1888	William R. Thomas, D. F. Wren, Annie McCaskey
1889–1891	W. S. Thompson
1891–1892	———— Richards [Henry Rickards?]
1893–1894	William Meade, Rowena Longmire
1894–1895	S. W. Graham, Pearl Thompson
1895–1896	J. A. Cox
1897	———— Moon, Mrs. J. J. Hooker, Lula Marsh Childers
1898–1899	J. E. Thwaits, Mrs. J. J. Hooker, Mr. W. R. Clayton
1899–1900	O. M. Given, Mrs. J. J. Hooker

Homeland

1860–1861	Alexander Watson
1861–1862	Alfred T. Bulloch

1878–1879	John Snoddy
1880	Daniel C. Kantz
1881	F. M. Wilson
1882	John Calhoun Jordan
1883	J. K. Stuart
1887–1888	Annie Swearingen, Miss _____ Vischer [white school]; Ellen Dixon [black school]
1890	M. L. Menges, Mrs. _____ Lanyham
1891–1894	Cora Lee Bullock
1894	Lucie Bullock [white school]; C. J. McLeod, Supt., Dora Purcell [black school]
1895	Henry Wright, Supt., Dora Purcell [black school]
1896	Dora Purcell [black school]
1898–1899	Mrs. G. R. Longmire [white school]; J. B. Lake [black school]
1899–1900	Mrs. Irene Pennington [white school]; J. B. Lake [black school]

Appendix 7

Fort Meade Town Officers

Mayor

A. J. French (1885–1886); William Thompson (1886–1894); T. J. Minor (1894–1897); William Thompson (1897–1900); Max Reif (1900–1901); T. J. Minor (1901–1902).

City Clerk and Treasurer

Charles L. Fries (1885–1886); S. G. Hayman (1886–1888); J. G. Carter (1888?–1893?); Frank B. Harless (1893–1895?); M. J. O'Connor (1895?–1898); F. F. Crawford (1898–1900?); E. O. Flood (1900?–1902).

Marshal

C. R. Jones (1885–1886?); Stephen L. Griffin (1886?–1890); Frank Perry (1890–1893?); Kit Mahon (1893–1894); T. B. Sherrill (1894–1895); Belton C. Gardner (1895); John J. Hooker (1895–1900?); Herman Gay (1900–1901); P. E. Alfred (1901–1902).

Assessor

Richard C. Langford (1885–1886?); Arthur B. Canter (1889–1891); Ulysses A. Lightsey (1891–1893?); J. E. Robeson (1893?–1895?); M. J. O'Connor (1895?–1898); F. F. Crawford (1898–1900?); E. O. Flood (1900?–1902).

Aldermen

J. G. Carter, Philip Dzialynski, C. B. Lightsey, Charles L. Mitchell, V. B. Webster, and F. A. Whitehead (1885–1886); A. J. Bulloch, Philip Dzialynski, Arthur

Keen, J. E. Robeson, and E. E. Skipper (1886–1887); E. A. Cordery, C. F. Marsh, B. F. Perry, J. E. Robeson, and S. N. Weeks (1889–1890); E. A. Cordery, Evan Evans, W. A. Evans, C. E. Jones, and W. H. Lewis (1890–1891); E. A. Cordery, Evan Evans, W. H. Lewis, and James L. Close (1891–1892); E. R. Childers, George Shelby, Jeff Tillis, and B. F. Woods (1893–1894); J. G. Carter, Wemyss Jackson, B. F. Perry, and Max Reif (1894–1895); F. B. Harless and F. F. Hendry (1895–1896); F. B. Harless, F. F. Hendry, Wemyss Jackson, Max Reif, W. L. Stephens, and James Thompson (1897–1898); P. D. Buzzi, F. B. Harless, L. P. Johnson, H. L. Rockner, and J. M. Stansfield (1898–1899); D. E. Ashton, J. O. Densford, and M. M. Loadholtes (1900–1901); D. E. Ashton, M. F. Dampier, J. O. Densford, M. M. Loadholtes, and W. L. Stephens (1901–1902).

Appendix 8

Fort Meade and Homeland Area Ministers

Methodist Episcopal Church, South

1866–1867   Robert A. Carson [Pease Creek Circuit]

1867–1872   William C. Jordan [Bartow Circuit]

1872–1873   S. W. Carson, supernumerary [Bartow Circuit]

1872–1874   William Davies [Bartow Circuit]

1874–1876   William C. Jordan [Bartow Circuit]
[1869–1876: itinerant and lay preachers also included Enoch H. Giles, Robert A. Carson, John W. Carlton, and Jared W. Brandon]

1876–1878   Enoch H. Giles [Bartow Circuit]

1878–1881   George W. Mitchell [Bartow Circuit]

1881–1883   Charles E. Pelot [Bartow Circuit]

1883–1884   Charles E. Pelot [Fort Meade Circuit]
William C. Jordan [Bartow Circuit (Homeland)]

1884–1885   Adam A. Robinson [Fort Meade Circuit]
J. R. Sharpe [Bartow Circuit (Homeland)]

1885–1886   William C. Jordan [Fort Meade Circuit]
T. J. Nixon (1885–1886) and S. B. Carson (1886) [Bartow Circuit (Homeland)]

1886–1889   John R. Taylor [Fort Meade and Homeland]

1889–1891   William C. Jordan [Fort Meade and Homeland]

1891–1894   E. J. Gates [Fort Meade]; William C. Jordan (1891–1893); A. W. J. Best, William C. Jordan, supernumerary (1893–1894) [Homeland]

1894   I. A. Vernon [Fort Meade and Homeland]

1894–1896   A. W. J. Best [Fort Meade and Homeland]

1896–1897   John Dodwell [Fort Meade and Homeland]

1897–1900   George W. Mitchell [Fort Meade and Homeland]

Saint Paul AME Church, Fort Meade

1899	J. H. Thomas
1903	C. H. Wright

Christ Church [Episcopal], Fort Meade

1887–1889	George S. Fitzhugh
1890–1891	J. V. Lee
1891–1892	Edmund C. Belcher
1892	Alfred J. Seddon
1892–1893	J. H. Weddell
1893–1894	W. H. Bates
1894	C. E. Butler
1894–1895	A. B. Dunlap
1896– ?	Kensey Hall

Galilee Baptist Church, Fort Meade

1892	D. H. Brown
1892–1896	G. W. McClendon

Corinth Primitive Baptist Church

1894–99	W. D. Talley

Appendix 9

Fort Meade and Homeland Postmasters

Fort Meade

1860–1862	Louis Lanier
1871	Julius C. Rockner, James W. Jones
1871–1873	Sullivan Lightsey
1873–1884	Charles L. Mitchell
1884–1885	E. E. Skipper
1885–1886	Victor L. Tillis
1886–1887	Richard C. Langford
1887–1888	Frederick F. Hendry
1888–1889	Wemyss Jackson
1889–1893	Alban H. Adams
1893–1897	Henry L. Rockner
1897–1901	John W. Powell

Homeland

1885–1886	James T. Hancock, Jr.
1886–1887	Thomas W. Anderson
1887–1897	Anna S. Anderson
1897–1907	Leroy W. Scroggins

Appendix 10

Registered Voters, September 1896

Precinct 2 [Fort Meade]

Abalo, M. A.
Acree, William M.
Adams, Alban H.
Altman, G. L.
Ashton, D. E.
Atkins, W. S.
Baker, Isaac
Barnes, Milton
Best, Peter
Blackburn, T. A.
Blackburn, W. H.
Blume, D. P.
Blume, Lafayette
Boatwright, R. B.
Bobbett, A. E.
Bone, Thomas
Bowen, W. M.
Bryan, A. B.
Bryan, A. L.
Bryan, Frank
Bryan, T. J.
Bryan, Travis
Buck, A. H.
Canter, Arthur B.
Carlton, A. T.
Carter, J. G.
Childers, E. R.
Collins, F. B.
Collins, Henry N.
Collins, John M.
Collins, Perry
Collins, W. R.
Collins, W. R.
Cook, Jason E.
Cordery, E. A.
Cowart, Perry
Cox, J. A.
Craig, George McC.
Craig, John L.
Crawford, F. F.
Crawford, H. F.
Dampier, W. F.
Davis, D. E.

Davis, E. G.
Davis, Matthew
Davis, Wm. S.
Devineau, A.
Devineau, J. L.
Devineau, V.
Dishong, E. D.
Dobbs, J. E.
Durrance, A. L.
Durrance, David
Durrance, F. M.
Durrance, J. A.
Durrance, J. G.
Durrance, J. H.
Durrance, J. R.
Durrance, Nathan B.
Durrance, T. E.
Durrance, T. J.
Durrance, W. M.
Evans, W. A.
Everett, C. H.
Flood, Luke B.
Francis, W. H.
Gardner, W. B.
Gartner, A. F.
Gay, Hiram
Gillespie, F. C.
Gray, W. T.
Gustofson, John E.
Hancock, H. H.
Hancock, J. T., Sr.
Hancock, J. T., Jr.
Hancock, Robert W.
Hancock, Shade
Harless, Frank B.
Hart, Barney
Hart, Samuel
Haskell, Lester
Hayman, E. M.
Hayman, S. G.
Hendry, F. F.
Herman, H.
Hicks, Jesse

Hilliard, E. J.
Hodgson, R. J.
Hogan, W. H.
Holland, D. H.
Holland, E. E.
Holland, Harris
Holland, J. J.
Holland, W. B.
Holland, Willoughby
Hollingsworth, J. W.
Hooker, J. J.
Howard, Calab
Howell, K. H.
Howell, Wesley
Howze, E. A.
Howze, F. M.
Howze, James W.
Howze, W. D.
Huckeby, J. B.
Hunter, J. H.
Hurst, John I.
Hurst, N. W.
Hurst, W. T.
Hyers, W. T.
Ivey, W. A.
Jackson, Wemyss
Johnson, R. S.
Johnson, W. H.
Jones, Nathan
Jordan, John C.
Jump, H. M.
Justice, Henry
Justice, M. A.
Keen, Arthur
Keen, J. W.
Keller, E. A.
Keller, Luther
Keller, Thomas
Kingsbury, H.
Krause, Ed
Langford, G. R.
Langford, R. C.
Langford, T. B.

Langford, W. R.
Lebo, J. W.
Lewis, W. H.
Lilly, J. G.
Loadholtes, M. M.
Manley, J. W.
Mann, H. D.
Mann, J. A.
Mann, James F.
Marshall, E. E.
Maxwell, L. W.
McAuley, John A.
McAuley, L. L.
McAuley, R. A.
McAuley, Wm. M.
McClelland, Wm.
McLean, David D.
McLean, James W.
McLean, Malcolm
McLeod, C. N.
Merck, D. S.
Miller, W. H.
Minor, T. J.
Mitchell, C. L.
Munroe, J. C.
Nicholson, J. H.
O'Brien, John
O'Connor, M. J.
Parish, J. Henry
Parker, W. H.
Pearce, J. A.
Perry, A. T.
Perry, B. F., Sr.
Pollard, A. J.
Pollard, R. L.
Poole, Banister

Poole, Benj. B.
Poole, George L.
Powell, E. E.
Powell, Henry N.
Powell, J. C.
Powell, J. W.
Powell, Leven
Powell, Samuel F.
Prevatt, E. M.
Reif, Max
Roberts, C. E.
Roberts, J. Q.
Roberts, M. S.
Roberts, N. E. B.
Robeson, J. E.
Robinson, J. L.
Rockner, H. L.
Rowell, Moses
Rowell, Thomas
Rowell, Wm. M.
Rudisill, O. E.
Russell, D. F.
Shanahan, J. E.
Shaw, Henry W.
Shelter, E. M.
Sims, Thomas
Singletary, J.
Smith, J. R.
Smith, John F.
Snow, Morgan
Stansfield, C.
Starling, Thos.
Stephens, W. L.
Stokes, Thomas
Story, H. R.
Sturgis, Wm.
Sutherland, Wm.
Taylor, J. D.

Thompson, A. H.
Thompson, James
Thompson, Wm.
Tillis, C. A.
Tillis, C. C.
Tillis, F. M.
Tillis, J. D.
Tillis, J. S.
Tillis, J. V.
Tillis, John W.
Tillis, Nelson
Tillis, R. C.
Tillis, W. W.
Tireman, W. L.
Tyler, J. R.
Varn, F. N.
Varn, George H.
Varn, K. O.
Vogler, A. W.
Vogler, F. L.
Wade, James
Wade, Thomas
Walker, Matthew
Watson, J. B.
Webster, Virgil B.
Weems, Wm. L.
Whidden, B.
Whidden, J. L.
Whitfield, Wm.
Wilson, James
Wilson, John
Wilson, Joseph
Winegord, G. W.
Woods, Fon
Wright, J. H.
Young, Paul

Precinct 16 [Homeland]

Albritton, H. M.
Albritton, J. L.
Alexander, J. S.
Allen, Moses
Anderson, T. W.
Axlin, W. J.
Barnett, C. E.
Blanks, S. L.
Brooks, Alonzo
Bunch, J. J.
Clement, D. C.
Clement, F. L.

Clement, J. W.
Close, J. L.
Connery, T. A.
Crum, C. F.
Crum, D. W.
Crum, J. B.
Crum, J. D.
Crum, J. M.
Crum, Z. L.
Cummings, John
Davis, C. W.
Davis, Lloyd

Davis, Samuel
Denham, W. T.
Dunn, A. A.
Dunn, F. J.
Durrance, J. W.
Edwards, J. W.
Fuller, M. W.
Gill, A. J.
Goodman, Wm.
Hamilton, V.
Harmon, Wm.
Hays, T. L.

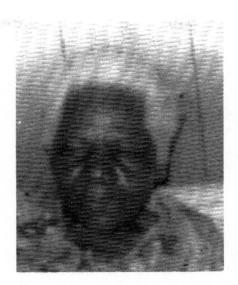

Mrs. James (Ellen Velora) Wright, 1885–1972, daughter of pioneer Homeland settlers Mr. and Mrs. Jack Vaughn and mother of Vernice Williams. (In possession of the author, courtesy of Vernice Williams)

Hollis, Thomas
Humphries, R. H.
Jordan, C. E.
Jordan, W. C.
Lang, B. C.
Langham, J. L.
Lewis, H. W.
Marchman, Jeff
Mayo, B. G.
Mayo, F. M.
Mayo, J. A.
Mayo, M. D. L.
McDaniel, W. W.
McGregor, M. C.
McKillop, A. S.
McKillop, J. H.
McKinney, A. D.

McLane, S. S.
Mereweather, D. B.
Mitchell, Early
Mitchell, James T.
Mitchell, R. B.
Moody, B. F.
Moody, Benjamin
Parker, Thomas H.
Payne, J. H.
Perry, J. T.
Porter, Charles F.
Pylant, R. N.
Saxton, D. E.
Scroggins, Leroy W.
Sheretz, W. P.
Short, A. J.
Short, S. W.

Singletary, E.
Sparkman, J. L.
Taylor, A. T.
Vaughn, Jack
Waters, J. H.
Watson, John
Webster, E. E.
Whidden, W. J.
Wilson, C. L.
Wilson, H. S.
Wilson, J. A.
Wilson, J. E.
Wilson, J. H.
Wilson, L. G.
Wingate, Henry
Wingate, J. H.
Wright, Henry

Source: Bartow Courier-Informant, September 23, 1896.

Notes

Abbreviations

BAC	Bartow *Advance Courier*
BC-I	Bartow *Courier-Informant*
BI	Bartow *Informant*
DN-H	Jacksonville *Daily News-Herald*
DNR	Florida Department of Natural Resources, Tallahassee
Election Returns	Returns of elections, RG 156, series 21, FSA
FHQ	*Florida Historical Quarterly*
FML	*Fort Meade Leader*
FP	Tampa *Florida Peninsular*
FSA	Florida State Archives, Tallahassee
FT-U	Jacksonville *Florida Times-Union*
FT-U&C	Jacksonville *Florida Times-Union and Citizen*
NA	National Archives, Washington, D.C.
PCHG&L	Polk County Historical and Genealogical Library, Bartow
PCN	Bartow *Polk County News*
PCR	Bartow *Polk County Record*
RG	Record Group
SMN	*Savannah Morning News*
ST	Tampa *Sunland Tribune*
WF	Tallahassee *Weekly Floridian*
WPA	Work Projects Administration

Preface

1. Frederick Jackson Turner's essay "The Significance of the Frontier in American History" was first read in July 1893 at the Chicago annual meeting of the American Historical Association. See also Frederick Jackson Turner, *The Frontier in American History*.

2. Stanley Elkins and Eric McKitrick, "A Meaning for Turner's Frontier, Part I: Democracy in the Old Northwest."

3. See, for example, Richard C. Wade, *The Urban Frontier*; Robert R. Dykstra, *The Cattle Towns*; Bradford Luckingham, *The Urban Southwest*; Don Harrison Doyle, *The Social Order of a Frontier Community*; Robert V. Hine, *Community on the American Frontier*; Andrew R. L. Cayton, *The Frontier Repub-*

lic; Kenneth J. Winkle, *The Politics of Community*; Harold L. Platt, *City Building in the New South*; Kathryn Joyce Carr, "Belleville and Galesburg"; Timothy R. Mahoney, *River Towns in the Great West*.

1. Lieutenant Meade's Reward

1. Gibbon, *Address*, 3. Portions of this chapter have appeared in Brown, "Moving a Military Road." For more on George G. Meade's service in Florida during 1849–1850, see Brown, "George Meade, John Pemberton, and A. P. Hill."

2. Cullum, *Biographical Register*, I, 601–608; Meade, *Life and Letters*, I, 201.

3. Brown, *Florida's Peace River Frontier*, 80–84. For more on the Florida Indian Crisis of 1849–1850, see Schene, "Not a Shot Fired"; Covington, "Billy Bowlegs"; and Matthews, *Edge of Wilderness*, 181–203.

4. Brown, *Florida's Peace River Frontier*, 68–80.

5. Ibid., 78–79, 84–89.

6. Survey sketch maps, Florida, 1849, and "Sketch of the road from Chokkonikla to Forts Fraser & Basinger," December 13, 1849, in notebook "General Meade, Appointments—Assignments and Reports, 1835–1865," Meade Papers.

7. "Journal and Surveyor's Notes, 1849–1850," 54–56, Meade Papers; sketch map included with statement of R. C. Langford, Fort Meade, Florida, November 23, 1886, Reports of Site Locations, 1837–1950, Records of the U.S. Postal Service, RG 28, box 103, NA; *United States Congress Serial Set*, "Statistical Report on the Sickness and Mortality in the Army of the United States," 330–31.

8. "Statistical Report on the Sickness and Mortality in the Army of the United States," 330–31; Brown, *Florida's Peace River Frontier*, 1–46, 370.

9. Meade, *Life and Letters*, I, 202; "Sketch of the road from Chokkonikla to Forts Fraser & Basinger" and George Meade to David E. Twiggs, December 13, 1849, Meade Papers.

10. "Sketch of the road from Chokkonikla to Forts Fraser & Basinger."

11. W. W. Mackall to Henry Bainbridge, December 17, 19, 1849, Letters, Reports, and Orders Received and Other Records, Fifth Military Department, box 1 [1848–1849], in RG 393, NA.

12. Mackall to Bainbridge, December 19, 1849, in ibid.

13. George Andrews to A. P. Howe, December 31, 1849, Fifth Mil. Dept. Records, box 1; Post Return, Fort Meade, FL, December 1849, U.S. Army Commands/Returns from United States Military Posts, M–617, roll 763 (hereafter cited as "Fort Meade Post Returns").

14. Brown, *Florida's Peace River Frontier*, 88–90.

15. William H. French to Thomas Childs, December 21, 1850, Letters Sent, Registers of Letters Received, and Letters Received by Headquarters, Troops in Florida, Dept. of Florida, 1850–1858, RG 393, M–1084, roll 2, NA.

16. "Statistical Report on the Sickness and Mortality in the Army of the United States," 331; Fort Meade Post Returns, July–November 1850.

17. French to Childs, December 21, 1850, M–1084, roll 2; Childs to French, December 23, 1850, Post Records: Fort Meade, Florida, Letters Received, June 1850–August 1853, box 1, RG 393, NA.

18. Diary, December 13, 1849–May 15, 1850, entry of January 1, 1850, and A. P. Hill to [Edward Baptist Hill], August 16, 1850, Hill Papers. For more on A. P. Hill's service in Florida, see Brown, "George Meade, John Pemberton, and A. P. Hill."

19. Cullum, *Biographical Register*, I, 676–79; Vandiver, *Mighty Stonewall*, 56–57.

20. Vandiver, *Mighty Stonewall*, 57–63.

21. Hill, "Real Stonewall Jackson," 624–25; Vandiver, *Mighty Stonewall*, 64–65.

22. Thomas J. Jackson to Francis H. Smith, April 22, 1851, Jackson Letters.

23. Vandiver, *Mighty Stonewall*, 67–70; Fort Meade Post Returns, May, October 1851.

24. Samuel K. Dawson to John H. Winder, December 10, 1851, M–1084, roll 2.

25. "Statistical Report on the Sickness and Mortality in the Army of the United States," 331.

26. Harvey Brown to J. M. Brannen, October 17, 1852, Fifth Mil. Dept. Records, box 2.

27. *PCR*, March 7, 1922.

28. *FML*, May 8, 1913.

29. Orders No. 2, Fort Meade, FL, December 2, 1853, Department of Florida, Field Records, Letterbook: Letters Sent and Orders Issued, November 1853–January 1856, 6, RG 393, NA.

30. *FML*, March 8, 1913.

31. *PCR*, March 7, 1922.

32. "Statistical Report on the Sickness and Mortality in the Army of the United States," 333.

33. *PCR*, January 26, 1940; Durrance and Folk, *Lineage*; Poll book, Peas Creek precinct, October 4, 1852, Election Returns; Survey Plat, Township 31 South, Range 25 East, DNR.

34. *PCR*, March 7, 1922; Hendry, *Early History*, n.p.; Stone, "Francis Asbury Hendry."

35. *FML*, May 1, 1913; *PCR*, March 7, 1922.

36. Harvey Brown to Commanding Officer, Troops in Florida, April 2, 1853, M–1084, roll 3; Whidden, "James Whitton Family."

37. *FML*, May 1, 1913.

1. Brown, *Florida's Peace River Frontier*, 106–107.
2. Fort Meade Post Reports, January–November 1854; Lewis G. Arnold to Samuel Cooper, May 18, 1854, Department of Florida, Field Records, Letterbook: Letters Sent and Orders Issued, November 1853–January 1856, 145, RG 393; W. G. Freeman to John Munroe, June 30, 1854, Records of the Adjutant General's Office, Letters Sent, RG 94, M–565, roll 18, NA.
3. Brown, *Florida's Peace River Frontier*, 106.
4. VanLandingham, "John I. Hooker," 8–9; "Report of the Secretary of War," Senate Exec. Doc. 7, 34th Cong., 1st sess., 41; Casey diary, entry of December 4, 1854. John I. Hooker apparently paid an additional $200.18 for the 160 acres of land upon which Fort Meade had been located. Affidavit of Louis Lanier and Francis A. Hendry, October 24, 1857, in John I. Hooker file, Permits for & Final Proofs of Settlement & Occupation of Land under Florida Armed Occupation Act of August 4, 1842, Tampa Office, Records of Bureau of Land Management, RG 49, NA.
5. Hillsborough County Deed Book B, 19.
6. Survey plats, Townships 30, 31, 32 South, Range 25 East, DNR; Ives, "Military Map."
7. Hillsborough County Commission Minute Book A, 65, 74–75.
8. White, *History*, 7; Boggess, *Veteran*, 66.
9. Returns of elections, Hillsborough County, October 1, December 3, 1855, and return of election for justices of the peace, Hillsborough County, 1855, Election Returns, box 7.
10. Covington, *Billy Bowlegs War*, 1–2, 35–36; *PCR*, March 7, 1922.
11. *PCR*, March 7, 1922.
12. Brown, *Florida's Peace River Frontier*, 107–108; Durrance and Folk, *Lineage*, 341.
13. S. L. Sparkman to James E. Broome, January 10, 1856, Correspondence of Gov. James E. Broome, RG 101, series 777, box 2, folder 3, FSA.
14. *FP*, July 17, 1856.
15. *FP*, July 5, 1856; F. M. Durrance and Jesse Carter, June 14, 1856, Durrance Papers; Tillis, "Indian Attack"; Boggess, *Veteran*, 50–55.
16. *ST*, June 23, 1877. See also Brown, *Florida's Peace River Frontier*, 112–15.
17. *Tampa Tribune*, September 26, 1948.
18. Tillis, "Indian Attack," 180–81.
19. Boggess, *Veteran*, 54. Oscen Tustenuggee may have been involved in the death of Willoughby Tillis's brother, Temple Tillis, during the December 18, 1835, Battle of Black Point, which began the Second Seminole War. Willoughby was present at the battle, which was directed by Oscen's relation Osceola. Mahon, "Black Point," 23; Compiled Service Records of Volunteer

Soldiers, McLemore's Mounted Company, Florida Militia, M–1086, roll 47; Livingston, "Willoughby Tillis," 4. See also the 1842 Indian attack upon the family of Willoughby's relation Richard Tillis. *St. Augustine News*, March 5, 1842.

20. *FML*, August 16, 1923.

21. *Savannah Morning News*, November 30, 1877. A similar incident has been told regarding John Henry Hollingsworth. Plowden, *Hardee County*, 13.

22. Covington, *Billy Bowlegs War*, 78–79. One Savannah newspaper reported that, prior to his surrender, Billy Bowlegs visited Fort Meade and told the local residents that he intended to leave Florida. The report is questionable and is not otherwise verified. Bowlegs did have close ties to the Fort Meade area, having spent a good part of his youth at a Bowlegs Creek village. *Savannah Daily Morning News*, March 18, 1858; Brown, *Florida's Peace River Frontier*, 27, 371.

23. *FP*, September 6, 1856.

24. Brown, *Florida's Peace River Frontier*, 115–18; Canova, *Life and Adventures*, 81; Fort Meade Post Returns, March–September 1857.

25. George W. Hazzard to John D. Howland, March 4, 1857, Hazzard Papers.

26. Thomas Williams to Mary H. Williams, August 14, 1857, Williams Family Papers.

27. Thomas A. McParlin to W. H. and Cassandra McParlin, June 7, 1857, McParlin Papers.

28. Williams to Williams, August 15, 1857, Williams Family Papers; *FP*, November 7, 1857.

29. *FP*, June 28, 1856; Livingston, "Benjamin Moody"; VanLandingham, "John I. Hooker"; *FML*, August 14, 1947; *Tampa Tribune*, September 26, 1948 (quoted).

30. Williams to Williams, August 27, 1857, Williams Family Papers.

31. *FP*, September 12, 1857.

32. Williams to Williams, August 14, 1847.

33. McParlin to W. H. and Cassandra McParlin, June 7, 1857.

34. Ibid., September 4, 1857.

35. Thomas H. Williams to Mary H. Williams, August 21, 1857, Williams Family Papers.

36. Dana, "Sketch of the route of the regular and volunteer force on the 3d & 4th March 1857, in the vicinity of 'Hookers Prairie' "; *FP*, March 27, 1858; Brown, *Florida's Peace River Frontier*, 124–25.

3. Civil War

1. Louis Lanier to "Dear Sister," April 30, 1858, Miller Family Papers.
2. *FML*, June 12, 1913.

3. Brown, *Florida's Peace River Frontier*, 126–27.

4. Ibid.; *BC-I*, October 5, 1905.

5. *BC-I*, September 21, 1890.

6. Smith, *Slavery and Plantation Growth*, 26; Manuscript Returns, Eighth U.S. Decennial Census, 1860, Hillsborough County, FL (population and slave schedules).

7. *FP*, February 4, April 14, 1860.

8. Ibid., March 21, 1860.

9. *BI*, September 15, 1881; *FP*, June 9, 1860.

10. *Tampa Tribune*, March 10, 1957.

11. Hillsborough County Commission Minute Book A, 91–93.

12. Ibid., 85, 91–93; *FP*, August 18, 1860.

13. *FP*, October 20, 1860.

14. Manuscript Returns, Eighth U.S. Decennial Census, 1860, Hillsborough County, FL (population schedule).

15. *FP*, October 10, 1860; *FT-U*, April 14, 1893; William McCullough to "My Dear Sir," July 4, 1864, McCullough Papers; VanLandingham, "John Levi Skipper"; Boggess, *Veteran*, 67.

16. 1861 Polk County Tax Roll; "Copy of Statement furnished Gov. John Milton showing the number & value of Slaves, Cattle, Sheep, Swine &c in the State of Florida as taken from the Tax Books on File in this Office, Oct. 13, 1862," Incoming Correspondence, Correspondence of the Comptroller, folder 2, box 3, RG 350, series 554, FSA.

17. Serving in the Hickory Boys at Fort Meade in 1861 were William H. Mansfield, sergeant; Berrien Platt, corporal; John Altman; Jesse Altman; William Brown; William H. Durrance; Jesse H. Durrance; Joseph L. Durrance; George S. Durrance; Francis M. Durrance; Andrew J. Ellis; Edward T. Kendrick; William P. Rodgers; T. [Timothy?] Hollingsworth; Charles H. Scott; Lewellen Williams; and James D. Smith. *FP*, March 9, 1861; Florida Board of State Institutions, *Soldiers of Florida*, 57.

18. Brown, *Florida's Peace River Frontier*, 146–52; Hendry, *Polk County*, 6.

19. *Official Records of the Union and Confederate Navies in the War of the Rebellion*, series 1, XVII, 309. Adult men remaining at Fort Meade in October 1862 included John McAuley, Jesse H. Durrance, Isham Lewis, Thomas L. McKinney, F. M. Durrance, Thomas L. Kinney, John Green, Levi Pearce, Henry S. Seward, D. R. Douglas, W. H. Durrance, J. R. Durrance, Willoughby Tillis, Gilbert L. Key, James B. Crews, J. Davis, Simon P. Smith, J. L. Durrance, Louis Lanier, Benjamin Guy, William Underhill, William H. Willingham, Thomas Griffin, Isaac Waters, J. T. Durrance, Thomas Underhill, and Ashley P. Weeks. Petition of residents of Fort Meade to His Excellency John Milton, October 5, 1862, Governor John Milton Letterbook 1861–1864, 493.

20. Florida Board of State Institutions, *Soldiers of Florida*, 178; Harrison, *Genealogical Records*, 103–108; "Bennett Whidden Family," 4–6.

21. VanLandingham, "John I. Hooker"; Brown, *Florida's Peace River Frontier*, 153.

22. *BC-I*, January 2, 1908; Brown, "Tampa's James McKay," 424.

23. Brown, "Tampa's James McKay," 415–17; Brown, *Florida's Peace River Frontier*, 150–52.

24. Brown, "Tampa's James McKay," 425–28; Brown, *Florida's Peace River Frontier*, 161–62.

25. Brown, *Florida's Peace River Frontier*, 157–63; Henry A. Crane to H. W. Bowers, March 16, 1864, Department and District of Key West, 1861–1868, RG 393, NA (hereafter cited as Key West Letters).

26. Livingston, "Willoughby Tillis," 10.

27. Crane to Bowers, April 12, 1864, Key West Letters.

28. Crane to James D. Green, April 2, 1864, Key West Letters.

29. Brown, *Florida's Peace River Frontier*, 163–64; Livingston, "Willoughby Tillis," 10.

30. Crane to Bowers, April 12, 13, 1864, Key West Letters.

31. Brown, *Florida's Peace River Frontier*, 167–68.

32. Childs to Bowers, May 27, 1864, Key West Letters.

33. *New York Herald*, June 16, 1864.

34. Brown, *Florida's Peace River Frontier*, 169–70.

35. Augusta [GA] *Southern Christian Advocate*, November 3, 1864.

36. *FML*, February 24, 1916.

37. Boggess, *Veteran*, 74.

4. Cattle and a Town Reborn

1. Brown, *Florida's Peace River Frontier*, 145.

2. Polk County Deed Book A, 498; Boggess, *Veteran*, 74; VanLandingham, "John Levi Skipper"; 1867 Polk County Tax Roll; Durrance and Folk, *Lineage*, 38, 293; *Tampa Tribune*, October 22, 1950; Livingston, "William McClenithan."

3. 1867 Polk County Tax Roll; Stone, "Profile of Lloyd Davis," 25.

4. Brown, *Florida's Peace River Frontier*, 197–99.

5. *FML*, June 12, 1913.

6. *Ocala Banner*, quoted in Jacksonville *Florida Union*, October 19, 1867.

7. *FP*, June 27, 1868.

8. *ST*, September 1, 1877.

9. John T. Sprague to Drum, May 31, 1868, Letters Sent by the Department of Florida and Successor Commands, April 18, 1861–January 1869, RG 393, M–1096, roll 2, NA.

10. Brown, "International Ocean Telegraph."

11. Brown, *Florida's Peace River Frontier*, 198–200; Akerman, *Florida Cowman*, 104–17.

12. *BC-I*, April 18, 1912.

13. Durrance, *R & M*, 84–85; 1870 Polk County Tax Roll; Polk County Deed Book B, 336; Stone, "Sherod E. Roberts"; Stone, "Ulysses A. Lightsey"; *FP*, March 15, 1871.

14. *FP*, November 3, 1869, October 19, 1870; VanLandingham, "John I. Hooker"; Polk County Deed Book B, 228–29.

15. *FP*, February 13, 1869; *FML*, January 2, 1919; Eagan, *Sixth Annual Report*, 189–90.

16. Polk County Deed Book B, 73, 83; McKay, *Pioneer Florida*, III, 738–40.

17. James Madison Manley, biographical information; Polk County Deed Book B, 153, 260; White, *Fort Meade*, 6; *SMN*, March 1, 1876.

18. Receipts for tuition at Fort Meade School, August 4, 1868, November 7, 1872, Lewis W. Hooker et al., guardianship, loose packet 18, Polk County Probate Records; *FP*, September 30, 1871; McKay, *Pioneer Florida*, III, 79; Ames, "First United Methodist Church," 1; John E. Brown, historical notes.

19. Ames, "First United Methodist Church," 1; Polk County Deed Book B, 73.

20. *FP*, September 30, December 16, 1871; "Fort Meade, FL," Records of Appointment of Postmasters, 1832–Sept. 30, 1971, M–841, roll 21, NA.

21. *Savannah Morning News*, January 13, 1872; *BC-I*, May 10, 1900; Adams, *Homeland*, 69; Polk County Deed Book B, 163, and Deed Book 41, 153; Stringer, *Watch Wauchula Win*, 7.

22. Hilliard Jones to Dennis Eagan, May 14, 1873, Incoming Correspondence, Internal Improvement Trust Fund, box 15, folder 1873–J; Eagan, *Sixth Annual Report*, 189.

23. Polk County Deed Book B, 247, 275, and Deed Book E, 179.

24. Polk County Deed Book E, 179; Kissimmee *Osceola Sun*, September 18, 1975.

25. Polk County Deed Book B, 274–79.

26. Ibid.

27. 1875 Polk County Tax Roll; *FML*, March 16, 1922; *ST*, March 1, 1879; Polk County Deed Book B, 356, 413–15; *Transcript of Record, State of Florida v. Charlotte Harbor Phosphate Company*, 505–36.

28. Incorporators of the Peace Creek Navigation Company included C. L. Mitchell, C. B. Lightsey, F. A. Hendry, J. C. Rockner, J. E. Robeson, J. C. Nelson, E. L. Harrison, William Smith, Nathan S. Blount, Fred N. Varn, W. M. McAuley, John McAuley, John Skipper, R. C. Langford, William Underhill, S. J. Stallings, W. H. Addison, S. E. Roberts, C. E. Harrison, J. M. Pearce, Jesse H. Durrance, Solomon Godwin, Willoughby Tillis, J. D. Tillis, N. R. Raulerson, W. H. Raulerson, John Parker, Newton Parker, Lewis Parker, B. Hordy, Z. Curry, S. A. Hart, William Raulerson, Isham Lewis, S. M. Chandler, E. E. Mizell, W. W. Chandler, W. J. Carroll, James T. Wilson, G. W. Gant,

W. B. Varn, Peyton S. Pearce, M. G. Fortner, James H. Manley, George R. Langford, David Skipper, Jacob H. Tyre, D. S. Bunch, J. J. Bunch, J. R. Feroux, and R. H. Peeples. Articles of Incorporation of the Peace Creek Navigation Company, December 12, 1874, Old Misc. County Files, Folder: Incorporation, Articles of 1868–1896, Manatee County; *Savannah Morning News*, September 18, 1875; *Transcript of Record*, 525–31.

29. Jacksonville *Florida Union*, July 10, 1876.

30. *Memorial Sketch of the Life and Ministerial Labors of Rev. J. M. Hayman*, 14. See also proceedings of the annual sessions of the South Florida Baptist Association, 1874–1881, Baptist Historical Collection, Stetson University Library, DeLand, FL.

31. Polk County Deed Book E, 178; Tract book, Township 30 South, Range 25 East, DNR.

32. *ST*, September 1, 1877.

33. *Savannah Morning News*, March 1, 1876; *ST*, January 6, 1877.

34. *Savannah Morning News*, March 24, 1876; Polk County Circuit Court Minute Book A, 124–30.

35. *ST*, August 4, 1877.

36. *BI*, June 16, 1883.

5. Waiting for the Train

1. "Veteran" likely was Francis C. M. Boggess. *BI*, September 15, 1881.

2. *ST*, April 20, June 15, 1878, March 29, 1879, February 2, 1882; *FT-U*, February 8, 1890.

3. Manuscript Returns, Tenth U.S. Decennial Census, 1880, Polk County, FL (population schedule); *ST*, May 25, 1878, July 15, 1880.

4. *ST*, January 6, 1877, November 13, 1879; V. L. Tillis to W. D. Bloxham, February 10, 1881, Letters of Resignation and Removals, 1845–1904, RG 150, series 24, box 6, folder 13, FSA.

5. *ST*, August 18, 1877, August 28, 1879; *Makers of America, Florida Edition*, I, 390.

6. 1876 Polk County Tax Roll; *BAC*, March 14, 1888.

7. *BI*, September 22, 1881.

8. *ST*, November 27, 1879; *WF*, November 1, 1879; Plowden, *Hardee County*, 18–19; "Acrefoot Johnson," in DeVane, *DeVane's Early Florida History*, I, n.p.; Brown, *Florida's Peace River Frontier*, 265–66, 273; Stone, "A. B. Canter."

9. Grismer, *Tampa*, 147–69; *ST*, March 17, 1877.

10. *ST*, March 17, 1877.

11. Ibid., June 16, 1877.

12. Ibid., June 30, September 1, 1877.

13. *ST*, December 1, 1877, April 6, May 25, 1878.

14. Ibid., June 8, September 28, 1878.

15. Ibid., January 5, 1878. For more on the growth of the temperance movement in south Florida, see Brown, *Florida's Peace River Frontier*, 301–306.

16. *ST*, May 13, 1880.

17. Ibid., April 2, 1881.

18. *BI*, August 11, 1881; *ST*, October 26, 1882.

19. *BI*, September 16, 1882.

20. *Savannah Morning News*, March 20, 1879; Wells, *Facts*, 23.

21. *Savannah Morning News*, March 20, 1879.

22. *BI*, September 22, 1881.

23. *WF*, September 18, 1877; *ST*, November 24, 1877; October 19, 1878, March 29, 1879; *Savannah Morning News*, April 9, 1879.

24. *ST*, July 13, 1878.

25. *Savannah Morning News*, May 6, 1879.

26. *ST*, July 17, 1879.

27. Ibid., July 15, 1880.

28. Ibid., December 3, 1881.

29. *PCR*, June 2, 1944.

30. *ST*, September 11, 1879.

31. Ibid., October 9, 1879.

32. *BAC*, March 14, 1888.

33. *ST*, July 15, 1880.

34. Manuscript Returns, Tenth U.S. Decennial Census, 1880, Polk County, FL (population schedule); *FT-U*, July 29, 1884; *ST*, November 25, 1880.

35. Vernice Williams interview; Sallie Robinson interview; Stone, "Profile of Lloyd Davis," 25–26; Manuscript Returns, Ninth and Tenth U.S. Decennial Censuses, 1870–1880, Polk County, FL (population schedules); 1870–1880 Polk County Tax Rolls; Polk County Marriage License Book A, 218, 248.

36. *ST*, January 8, 1880.

37. Ibid., September 1, 1877.

38. Wells, *Facts*, 4–5; Hendry, *Polk County*, 5–26. By 1878 George W. Hendry and Fred N. Varn had pushed the citrus-growing frontier to a small lake four miles east of Fort Meade. On its south shore the two men planted a grove of about 400 trees of oranges, limes, and lemons. Since that time the lake has been known, after one of the partners, as Lake Hendry. *ST*, February 26, 1881.

39. *ST*, October 5, 1878.

40. Ibid., September 21, 1878.

41. *WF*, January 7, 1879; St. Augustine *St. Johns Weekly*, May 9, 1879.

6. Room for All

1. Tebeau, *History of Florida*, 278–80; Hanna and Hanna, *Lake Okeechobee*, 97–98. See also Davis, "Disston Land Purchase."

2. Grismer, *Fort Myers*, 105; Hanna and Hanna, *Lake Okeechobee*, 99.

3. Florida Land and Improvement Company, *Disston Lands*, 1–8; Jacksonville *Florida Daily Times*, 1882.

4. Brown, *Florida's Peace River Frontier*, 268–69; *ST*, October 5, 1882.

5. Brown, *Florida's Peace River Frontier*, 268; Treveres, "Map of Polk County."

6. W. B. Brown, C. B. Lightsey, J. N. Hooker, Philip Dzialynski, R. C. Langford, C. C. Wilson, J. W. Wilson, J. E. Robeson, George W. Hendry, Fred N. Varn, and W. S. Atkins were among the investors in the Fort Meade, Keystone & Walk-in-the-Water Railroad Company. *Laws of Florida* (1883), 123; Jacksonville *Florida Daily Times*, December 14, 1882.

7. *BI*, February 3, 1883; *BAC*, March 21, 1888.

8. *FML*, May 1, 1919, September 27, 1917, May 27, 1920, September 13, 1928; *BI*, July 29, 1882, April 28, May 26, October 13, 1883, February 9, 1884; *PCR*, December 10, 1920, October 14, 1921; *FT-U*, October 8, 1890; *Newnan* [GA] *Herald*, October 16, 1883; *BAC*, June 1, 1887, February 29, March 7, 14, 21, 1888; Hetherington, *Polk County*, 279–80; *BC-I*, April 3, 1895, July 16, 1902; *WF*, December 24, 1885; McKay, *Pioneer Florida*, III, 90; *Tampa Tribune*, August 6, 1950; Adams, *Homeland*, 69; Stone, "A. B. Canter."

9. *BI*, September 29, 1883.

10. *Savannah Morning News*, September 19, 1886.

11. *ST*, January 5, 1882; *FT-U*, October 24, 1884, February 3, 1896; Polk County Deed Books B, 514–18, E, 18, 21, G, 164–65; *BI*, June 17, 1882; Hendry, *Polk County*, 48–50.

12. Polk County Deed Books E, 219, I, 217.

13. Ibid., Deed Book F, 4; Hendry, *Polk County*, 35; *BI*, April 7, 1883.

14. Polk County Plat Book 1–A, 8; Polk County Deed Books G, 187, P, 15, L, 302.

15. *FT-U*, October 22, 1884; *BAC*, August 10, 1887, March 21, 1888; *BI*, April 19, 1884; *PCN*, June 19, 1891.

16. *Newnan* [GA] *Herald*, October 16, 1883; *BI*, February 9, 1884; 1885 Florida State Census, Polk County.

17. Reports of Site Locations, 1837–1950, "Homeland, FL," M–1126, NA.

18. *PCR*, June 2, 1944.

19. Adams, *Homeland*.

20. *BI*, June 9, 1881, April 8, May 6, June 17, 1882, February 17, June 2, 1883, May 31, 1884; *ST*, October 12, 1882; *Minutes of the Annual Conferences of the Methodist Episcopal Church South, for the Year 1883*, 5–9.

21. *BI*, June 24, 1882.

22. Hendry, *Polk County*, 34.

23. *WF*, January 28, 1886.

24. *BI*, June 17, 1882.

25. *ST*, May 31, 1879.

26. *BI*, February 3, 1883.

27. *BI*, May 10, November 3, 17, 1883.

28. Polk County Plat Book 1–A, 8; *BI*, May 3, 1884.

29. Adams, *Homeland*, 68.

30. *FT-U*, October 7, 1885; *BAC*, April 13, 1887.

31. *BC-I*, July 16, 1902; Adams, *Homeland*, 67.

32. *FT-U*, April 2, 1899; Polk County Mortgage Book A, 297–99; 1885 Florida State Census, Polk County.

33. *BI*, March 10, 1883; W. S. Thompson to P. W. White, June 4, 1884, Incoming Correspondence, Internal Improvement Trust Fund, box 38, FSA; Adams, *Homeland*, 68; *BAC*, May 23, 1888.

34. *FT-U*, December 31, 1886; 1885 Florida State Census, Polk County.

35. *BI*, February 3, June 16, October 10, 1883, May 17, 1884; Hendry, *Polk County*; *FT-U*, November 26, 1884, May 24, 1896; Adams, *Homeland*, 68.

36. 1885 Florida State Census, Polk County; Adams, *Homeland*, 67–70; *Savannah Morning News*, January 5, 1886.

37. Brown, *Florida's Peace River Frontier*, 272–77.

38. *BI*, March 25, 1882.

39. Ibid., March 8, 1884.

40. *WF*, October 23, 1885.

41. Polk County Mortgage Book A, 297.

42. Ibid., 297–99; *WF*, May 28, 1885.

43. *Fort Myers Press*, July 18, 25, 1885; *BAC*, November 9, 1887; *WF*, July 23, 1885.

44. *FML*, June 3, 1920; Gibson, Hymerling, and Schaill, "Fort Meade"; *Lakeland Ledger*, January 12, 1977; Receipt for Tuition, July 31, 1886, Julius C. Rockner probate records, loose packet 48, Polk County Probate Records; *FT-U*, September 5, 1885.

45. *FT-U*, September 16, 1886, December 11, 1890.

46. "Map of Fort Meade, Fla. [c. 1885]," FSA.

7. The British Are Coming

1. *FT-U*, December 31, 1886.

2. *Palatka News*, quoted in *Fort Myers Press*, August 15, 1885.

3. Brown, *Florida's Peace River Frontier*, 277–78.

4. *FT-U*, December 24, 1885, January 21, 1886; White, *History*, 10; Polk County Deed Book Q, 311–12.

5. White, *History*, 10; Simmons, "Early Days"; Fort Meade *Pioneer*, quoted in *WF*, February 4, 1886.

6. Polk County Deed Book U, 91–93; Plant City *South Florida Courier*, May 15, 1886.

7. *WF*, March 25, 1886; Fort Meade *Pioneer*, quoted in *WF*, June 3, 1886.

8. *WF*, June 24, 1886.

9. *FT-U*, June 25, 1886.

10. *WF*, September 16, 1886; Plant City *South Florida Courier*, April 16, 1887.

11. Plant City *South Florida Courier*, November 27, 1886.

12. J. A. Edwards to E. A. Perry, February 24, 1887, Correspondence of the Secretary of State, Letters of Resignation and Removals, 1845–1904, box 6, folder 13, FSA; White, *History*, 10–11; *BAC*, April 13, 1887; *FT-U*, January 17, 1887.

13. *BAC*, April 13, 1887.

14. Fort Meade *Pioneer*, quoted in *WF*, March 3, 1887.

15. Boehm, "History of Christ Church," 6–7.

16. WPA, "Highlands County," 5–7; *PCN*, February 27, March 13, June 26, 1891; Boehm, "History of Christ Church," 8–9; *BAC*, February 29, 1888; *PCR*, December 10, 1920.

17. Simmons, "Early Days."

18. *PCN*, January 9, 1891.

19. Ibid., June 26, 1891.

20. *BAC*, March 7, 1888; *PCN*, January 16, April 3, June 26, 1891.

21. *PCN*, June 26, 1891.

22. *FT-U*, January 5, 1887.

23. *BAC*, May 11, 1887, January 11, 1888.

24. *FT-U*, January 31, 1888; *BAC*, February 8, 1888.

25. *PCN*, January 30, 1891.

26. *FT-U*, February 1, 1892.

27. Simmons, "Early Days."

28. *Tampa Tribune*, May 9, 1948.

29. *Lakeland Ledger*, January 12, 1977; *BAC*, February 29, 1888.

30. *FT-U*, May 23, 1890, May 24, 1896; Manuscript Returns, Twelfth U.S. Decennial Census, 1900, Polk County, FL (population schedule); *BI*, August 5, 1896; *PCN*, February 27, 1891; Boehm, "History of Christ Church," 12.

31. *BAC*, March 7, 1888.

32. *FT-U*, September 10, 1886, March 2, July 13, August 29, 1888, November 3, 1889; *DN-H*, June 26, 1887.

33. Simmons, "Early Days."

34. *BAC*, July 27, 1887.

35. *FT-U*, October 3, 11, November 19, 1889, January 24, March 16, 1890; *PCN*, November 4, 1892.

36. *FT-U*, October 11, 1889; *PCN*, September 19, 26, 1890, January 9, August 14, 1891; *Tampa Tribune*, August 4, 1897; *FML*, March 23, 1923; *BC-I*, January 30, 1895.

37. *FT-U*, February 11, 1887.

38. *FT-U*, February 1, 1887, April 27, 1888; *FML*, March 2, 1922; White, *History*, 17.

39. *FT-U*, December 21, 1889.

40. Ibid., June 25, 1889.

41. *BAC*, May 30, June 13, 1888; *FT-U*, January 9, 1889.

42. Lee, "Early History of Christ Church," 1.

43. Ibid., 3.

44. *BAC*, December 21, 1887, January 4, 1888.

45. *FT-U*, January 24, 1890; Boehm, "History of Christ Church," 18.

46. *FT-U*, July 13, 1888.

47. Ibid., October 12, 1888.

48. Department of Commerce and Labor, Bureau of the Census, *Thirteenth Census*, 578.

49. Fort Meade *Pioneer*, quoted in *WF*, February 14, 1887.

50. *FT-U*, August 14, 1886.

51. *Tampa Guardian*, June 9, 1886.

52. The school patrons were J. T. Sherritt, H. F. Crawford, John A. Nyland, B. F. Perry, William Thompson, L. B. Flood, J. E. Robeson, Arthur Keen, Philip Dzialynski, Barney Hart, Henry H. Hancock, S. Perry, C. B. Lightsey, S. A. Hart, A. J. Bulloch, M. Ottinger, A. H. Adams, Louis Herzog, Perry Collins, E. M. Hayman, J. M. Armstrong, C. C. Guyer, W. L. Weems, G. A. McClenithan, and Lucinda McKinney. *BAC*, July 13, 1887.

53. Ibid.

54. Ibid., June 22, July 13, September 7, 1887.

55. Gibson, Hymerling, and Schaill, "Fort Meade"; *FML*, March 2, 1922.

56. *FT-U*, July 13, 1888.

57. Polk County, *Polk County*, n.p.; *BAC*, September 14, 1887.

58. *BAC*, September 14, 1887, January 4, 1888; *PCR*, June 2, 1944; "Homeland Baptist Church," and "Mount Bunyan Baptist Church," in Church Records.

8. The Phosphate Roller Coaster

1. *FT-U*, January 4, 1890.

2. Ibid., January 14, 1890.

3. Ibid., January 4, 1890.

4. Ibid., January 11, 1890.

5. Boehm, "History of Christ Church," 24–25; Fort Meade *South Florida Progress*, quoted in *FT-U*, January 30, 1890.

6. *FT-U*, March 26, 1890.

7. Ibid., April 16, 1890.

8. Shrader, *Hidden Treasures*, 51; *FT-U*, October 5, 1890.

9. *PCN*, October 10, 24, 1890, January 9, 16, March 13, 1891; Shrader, *Hidden Treasures*, 49–50.

10. Shrader, *Hidden Treasures*, 50; *PCN*, February 6, March 27, 1891.

11. *FT-U*, December 25, 1888, October 5, 1890; *PCN*, January 30, April 10, 1891; Shrader, *Hidden Treasures*, 48–50.

12. *FT-U*, January 1, 1892.

13. Ibid., September 4, 1890.

14. Ibid., February 8, 1890; *PCN*, April 24, 1891; *Tampa Tribune*, August 4, 1897.

15. *FT-U*, June 30, 1890.

16. *PCN*, January 9, February 20, 1891.

17. *FT-U*, June 30, 1890.

18. *FML*, April 13, 1922; *PCN*, July 10, August 7, 1891.

19. *PCN*, July 31, 1891.

20. Ibid., November 25, 1892.

21. Other members of the Fort Meade Board of Trade in 1893 were J. E. Robeson, John Northcott, Max Reif, W. H. Warren, V. B. Webster, B. F. Perry, R. J. Hodgson, M. J. O'Connor, G. S. Shelby, Alfred Williams, J. M. Stansfield, J. E. Gonzalez, and C. G. C. Wright. *FT-U*, February 2, 1893.

22. Brown, *Florida's Peace River Frontier*, 204–207; Fort Meade *Pioneer*, quoted in *FT-U*, August 12, 1885.

23. Area residents contributing to the reward included C. L. Mitchell, Philip Dzialynski, A. J. French, G. I. P. Dzialynski, E. R. Childers, Alfred Williams, R. C. Langford, J. P. Wilson, E. E. Skipper, C. B. Lightsey, F. A. Whitehead, S. A. Hart, J. E. Robeson, V. B. Webster, S. G. Hayman, S. H. Robeson, S. W. Carson, J. L. Skipper, William M. Brown, J. D. Tillis, U. A. Lightsey, and A. J. Pollard. *WF*, April 22, 1884; Stone, "Profile of Lloyd Davis," 25–26.

24. *FT-U*, August 12, 1887; Vernice Williams, interview.

25. *BAC*, September 7, 1887.

26. *FML*, April 13, 1922.

27. Possibly Brown was the Reverend D. H. Brown who helped found Galilee Baptist Church. *FML*, March 2, 1922; *FT-U*, June 6, 1890, February 8, 1893.

28. *BC-I*, October 2, 1895, October 22, 1902.

29. *PCN*, July 24, 1891.

30. Fort Meade *South Florida Progress* clipping in Pearl Thompson diary.

31. *FML*, January 20, 1916; "Galilee Baptist Church" in Church Records.

32. "St. Paul AME Church" in Church Records; *FT-U&C*, March 11, 1899; *FT-U*, January 28, 1893; AME Conference, Florida, East Florida Conference Minutes, 1891; *FML*, April 5, 1928.

33. 1895 Florida State Census, Polk County.

34. *FT-U*, April 16, 1890.

35. *BC-I*, July 19, 1893; Ames, "First United Methodist Church," 2.

36. *FT-U*, June 11, 1891.

37. *Tampa Tribune*, August 4, 1897.

38. Brown, *Florida's Peace River Frontier*, 335; *PCN*, April 24, May 1, 1891.

39. *FT-U*, February 3, 1896.

40. "Corinth Primitive Baptist Church" in Church Records.

41. "Church of God, Fort Meade" in Church Records.

42. Brown, *Florida's Peace River Frontier*, 316–17.

43. Ibid., 338–39.

44. Simmons, "Early Days"; *FT-U*, June 13, 1893.

45. *PCN*, November 4, 1892.

46. *FT-U*, February 2, 1893.

47. Ibid., July 19, 1893.

48. *FT-U*, December 11, 1890.

49. Ibid., January 9, 1894.

50. *BC-I*, January 17, 1894.

51. *FT-U*, April 7, 1894; *BC-I*, April 11, 1894.

52. *Fort Meade Pebble*, quoted in *BC-I*, May 2, 1894.

53. *FT-U*, June 28, 1894.

54. Ibid., July 2, 1894.

55. Ibid., September 7, 1894.

56. Ibid., June 28, 1894.

9. The Century's Passing

1. Brown, *Florida's Peace River Frontier*, 321–22; *BC-I*, January 30, 1895.

2. *BC-I*, January 30, 1895.

3. Ibid., February 13, 1895.

4. Ibid.

5. Ibid., September 25, 1895.

6. Ibid., February 13, 1895.

7. *Tampa Tribune*, July 10, 1955.

8. Hendry, *Family Record*, 37, 40–41, 43–44.

9. Hetherington, *Polk County*, 78; *BC-I*, September 11, 25, 1895.

10. *BC-I*, March 18, 1896.

11. Frisbie, *Peace River Pioneers*, 63; *BC-I*, June 12, 1895; *FT-U*, September 3, 1896.

12. *FT-U*, November 29, 1894.

13. *BC-I*, June 12, 1895; *FT-U*, August 2, 1895.

14. From 1894 to about 1898 the John C. Fremont Post No. 28, GAR, maintained a "hall" at Fort Meade. Additional members of the post included T. J. Lake, [V. B.?] Webster, ———— Hampton, George C. Scanlin, and W. T. Hyres. *BC-I*, June 5, 1895.

15. Ibid., December 11, 1895.

16. Others active in preparations for the October 26, 1895, meeting were U. A. Lightsey and C. C. Wilson of Bartow, L. B. Robertson and George Rudisill of Bowling Green, Hugh Thompson of Bowlegs Creek, and C. G. C. Wright of Acme. Fort Meade participants included Wemyss Jackson, T. J. Minor, E. D. Dishong, A. W. J. Best, M. J. O'Connor, J. E. Cook, F. B. Harless, W. L. Weems, B. F. Perry, Alpheus Minor, Robert Benedict, J. R. Tyler, E. J. Hilliard, J. W. Powell, V. B. Webster, George McC. Craig, Fred N. Varn, R. J. Hodgson, W. A. Weems, R. A. McAuley, H. M. Shaw, F. F. Hendry, and George L. Broderick. *BC-I*, October 30, 1895.

17. Ibid., November 13, 1895.

18. Ibid., December 11, 1895.

19. Ibid., January 8, 1896.

20. Ibid., January 22, 1896.

21. Ibid., February 5, 1896.

22. Ibid., March 11, 1896.

23. Ibid., March 23, 1896.

24. Ibid., January 22, 1896.

25. Ibid., March 23, 1896.

26. Ibid., April 22, 1896.

27. Ibid., April 29, 1896.

28. *FT-U*, May 24, 1896.

29. Jacksonville *Daily Florida Citizen*, September 20, October 25, 1896.

30. *Tampa Tribune*, August 4, 1897.

31. *FT-U*, February 16, 1897.

32. Included among tobacco growers and investors were Charles Stansfield, Frank H. Huttgreen, John L. Anderson, C. G. C. Wright, James Thompson, Victor Devineau, H. H. Taplin, John W. Gardner, E. M. Hayman, W. M. Sturgis, George McC. Craig, Henry McKenzie, McLeod Boyd, A. W. Grose, Wemyss Jackson, George Broderick, A. B. Canter, Sterling Canter, Fred N. Varn, Henry Rumohr, R. J. Hodgson, E. D. Dishong, and Harris Holland. Jacksonville *Daily Florida Citizen*, September 20, 1896; *Tampa Tribune*, August 4, 1897.

33. *BC-I*, February 16, 1898.

34. Ibid., December 11, 1895.

35. Ibid., February 5, 1896.

36. *Tampa Tribune*, August 4, 1897.

37. *FT-U*, August 20, 1897.

38. Ibid., March 3, 1897.

39. *Tampa Tribune*, August 4, 1897.

40. *BC-I*, April 15, 1896, January 20, September 22, November 3, 1897; *FT-U*, September 3, 1896.

41. *Tampa Tribune*, August 4, 1897; *FT-U*, August 20, October 27, December 6, 1897; *BC-I*, April 28, 1897.

42. *FT-U*, August 20, 1897.

43. Ibid., December 6, 1897, April 7, 1898.

44. *BC-I*, March 18, 1896, January 20, February 3, 1897; *FT-U*, June 4, 1897.

45. *FT-U*, April 8, 1897.

46. *BC-I*, July 17, 1895; *FT-U*, May 24, 1896.

47. Frisbie, *Peace River Pioneers*, 55; *Tampa Tribune*, August 4, 1897.

48. *BC-I*, May 29, 1896.

49. *FT-U*, May 29, 1896.

50. Ibid., July 20, 1898.

51. *FML*, June 8, 1922.

52. *FT-U*, February 4, 1899; *BC-I*, February 1, 1899.

53. *BC-I*, April 19, 1899.

54. *FML*, June 8, 1922.

55. Simmons, "Early Days."

56. *FT-U*, July 8, September 1, 1899; *BC-I*, February 15, 1899.

57. *FT-U*, February 17, June 7, 1899.

58. Pearl Thompson diary, June 24, 1899; Department of Commerce and Labor, Bureau of the Census, *Thirteenth Census*, 578.

59. *Laws of Florida* (1903), 407.

60. *FT-U*, August 4, 1909; *Tampa Tribune*, November 9, 1912.

Bibliography

Manuscripts and Collections

Brown, John E., historical notes and files. Collection of John E. Brown, Fort Meade, FL.

Casey, John Charles, Diaries. United States Military Academy Library, West Point, NY.

Church Records. Questionnaires of the Florida Writers Program, WPA. Florida Collection, Florida State Library, Tallahassee.

Durrance, Francis M., Papers. Transcripts at PCH&GL.

Hazzard, George W., Papers. United States Military Academy Library, West Point, NY.

Hill, Ambrose Powell, Papers. Virginia Historical Society, Richmond.

Jackson, Thomas J., Letters. Virginia Military Institute Archives, Lexington, VA.

McCullough, William and Nancy, Papers. Collection of Colleen Uhl, Bountiful, UT. (Transcripts in collection of the author)

McParlin, Thomas W., Papers. McParlin Family Papers, Maryland Hall of Records, Annapolis.

Manley, James Madison, biographical information. Collection of Tom Manley, Seffner, FL.

Meade, George G., Papers. Historical Society of Pennsylvania, Philadelphia.

Miller, Nancy Ann, Family Papers. Georgia Department of Archives and History, Atlanta.

Milton, Governor John, Letterbook 1861–1864. University of South Florida Special Collections, Tampa.

Thompson, Pearl, Diary, April 7, 1888–August 28, 1900. Collection of Walter Crutchfield, Fort Meade.

Williams, Thomas, Papers. Williams Family Papers, Burton Historical Collection, Detroit Public Library, Detroit, MI.

Public Documents, Public Records, and Maps

Dana, J. J. "Sketch of the route of the regular and volunteer force on the 3d & 4th March 1857, in the Vicinity of Hookers Prairie [1857]." Included in Memoir of Reconnaissances with Maps During the Florida Campaign, M–1090, roll 1, NA.

Department of Commerce and Labor, Bureau of the Census. *Thirteenth Census of the United States Taken in the Year 1910: Abstract of the Census . . . With Supplement for Florida.* Washington, D.C.: United States Government Printing Office, 1913.

Department of the Interior. Records of the Bureau of Land Management. RG 49, NA.

Department of War. Compiled Service Records of Volunteer Soldiers Who Served in Organizations from the State of Florida During the Florida Indian Wars, 1835–1858. RG 1025, M–1086, NA.

———. Records of the Adjutant General's Office. RG 94, NA.

———. Records of U.S. Army Continental Commands, 1821–1920. RG 393, NA.

———. U.S. Army Commands/Returns from United States Military Posts, 1800–1916, Records of the Adjutant General's Office. M–617, NA.

Eagan, Dennis. *Sixth Annual Report of the Commissioner of Lands and Immigration of the State of Florida, for the year ending December 31, 1874.* Tallahassee: State of Florida, 1874.

Florida. Board of State Institutions. *Soldiers of Florida in the Seminole Indian-Civil and Spanish-American Wars.* Tallahassee: State of Florida, 1903.

———. Department of Natural Resources, Survey Plats, Field Notes, and Tract Books.

———. 1895 Florida State Census, Polk County. Available at PCH&GL.

———. Election Returns, 1824–1970, Division of Elections. RG 156, series 21.

———. Florida State Archives. Correspondence of the Comptroller. RG 350, series 554.

———. Internal Improvement Trust Fund. Incoming Correspondence. RG 593, series 914.

———. *Laws of Florida,* 1883, 1903.

———. Office of the Governor. Governors' Correspondence. RG 101.

———. Secretary of State. Incoming Correspondence. RG 150, series 24.

———. State Census, 1885. RG 1020, series 5. Available at PCH&GL.

Hillsborough County. County Commission Minute Book A.

———. Deed Book B.

Ives, J. C. "Military Map of the Peninsula of Florida South of Tampa Bay [1856]." Printed in United States Senate Document 89, 62d Cong., 1st sess.

Manatee County. Old Miscellaneous County Files. Manatee County Historical Records Library, Bradenton.

Official Records of the Union and Confederate Navies in the War of the Rebellion. 30 vols. Washington, D.C.: United States Government Printing Office, 1894–1927.

Polk County. Circuit Court Minute Books.

———. Deed Books. Available on microfilm at FSA.

————. Marriage License Books. Available on microfilm at FSA.

————. Mortgage Books.

————. Plat Books.

————. Probate Records. Available on microfilm at FSA.

————. Tax Rolls, 1861–1870. Available on microfilm at FSA.

Polk County, Board of County Commissioners. *Polk County, Florida, Issued by the County Commissioners*. Bartow: Board of County Commissioners, 1887.

Post Office Department. Records of Appointment of Postmasters, 1832–September 30, 1971. M–841, NA.

————. Records of the United States Postal Service. RG 28, NA.

————. Reports of Site Locations, 1837–1950. M–1126, NA.

Transcript of Record, State of Florida v. Charlotte Harbor Phosphate Company. U.S. Circuit Court of Appeals for the Fifth Circuit. Federal Archives and Records Center, Fort Worth, TX.

Treveres, J. J. "Map of Polk County, Florida." Jacksonville, 1883.

United States Congress Serial Set, Washington, D.C. "Report of the Secretary of War Showing Contracts Made Under Authority of the War Department during the year 1855." Senate Ex. Doc. 7, 34th Cong., 1st sess.

————. "Statistical Report on the Sickness and Mortality in the Army of the United States . . . From January, 1839, to January, 1855." Senate Ex. Doc. 96, 34th Cong., 1st sess.

Work Projects Administration, Writers Program. "Highlands County." Typescript, 1936.

Newspapers and Periodicals

Augusta [GA] *Southern Christian Advocate*, 1864.

Bartow *Advance Courier*, 1887–1888.

Bartow *Courier-Informant*, 1890–1912.

Bartow *Informant*, 1881–1884.

Bartow *Polk County News*, 1891–1892.

Bartow *Polk County Record*, 1920–1922, 1940–1944.

Fort Meade Leader, 1913–1928.

Fort Myers Press, 1885.

Jacksonville *Daily Florida Citizen*, 1896.

Jacksonville *Daily News-Herald*, 1887.

Jacksonville *Florida Daily Times*, 1882.

Jacksonville *Florida Times-Union*, 1884–1899, 1909.

Jacksonville *Florida Times-Union and Citizen*, 1899.

Jacksonville *Florida Union*, 1867, 1876.

Kissimmee *Osceola Sun*, 1975.

Lakeland Ledger, 1961, 1977.

New York Herald, 1864.
Newnan [GA] *Herald,* 1883.
Plant City *South Florida Courier,* 1886.
St. Augustine News, 1842.
St. Augustine *St. Johns Weekly,* 1879.
Savannah Daily Morning News, 1858.
Savannah Morning News, 1872–1886.
Tallahassee *Weekly Floridian,* 1879–1886.
Tampa *Florida Peninsular,* 1855–1861, 1867–71.
Tampa Guardian, 1886.
Tampa *Sunland Tribune,* 1877–1882.
Tampa Tribune, 1896–1897, 1912, 1948–1957.

Secondary Sources

Adams, Sherman. *Homeland: A Description of the Climate, Productions, Resources, Topography, Soil, Opportunities, Attractions, Advantages, Developments and General Characteristics of Polk County, Florida.* Bartow, FL: Tigner, Tatum, 1885.

Akerman, Joe A., Jr. *Florida Cowman: A History of Florida Cattle Raising.* Kissimmee, FL: Florida Cattlemen's Association, 1976.

Ames, Frieda Zander. "First United Methodist Church, East Broadway at Pine, Fort Meade, Florida." Typescript, Fort Meade, n.d.

"The Bennett Whidden Family." *Polk County Historical Quarterly* 12 (March 1986): 4–6.

Boehm, Terry. "The History of Christ Church, Fort Meade, Florida 1886–1895." Typescript, Fort Meade, 1980.

Boggess, Francis C. M. *A Veteran of Four Wars: The Autobiography of F. C. M. Boggess.* Arcadia: Champion Job Rooms, 1900.

Brown, Canter, Jr. *Florida's Peace River Frontier.* Orlando: University of Central Florida Press, 1991.

———. "George Meade, John Pemberton, and A. P. Hill: Army Relationships During the Florida Crisis of 1849–1850." *Tampa Bay History* 13 (Fall/Winter 1991): 5–26.

———. "The International Ocean Telegraph." *Florida Historical Quarterly* 68 (October 1989): 135–59.

———. "Moving a Military Road." *South Florida History Magazine* 2 (Spring 1991): 8–11.

———. "Philip and Morris Dzialynski: Jewish Contributions to the Rebuilding of the South." *American Jewish Archives* 44 (Fall/Winter 1992): 517–39.

———. "Tampa's James McKay and the Frustration of Confederate Cattle-Supply Operations in South Florida." *Florida Historical Quarterly* 70 (April 1992): 409–33.

Canova, Andrew P. *Life and Adventures in South Florida*. Palatka, FL: Southern Sun Publishing House, 1906.

Carr, Kathryn Joyce. "Belleville and Galesburg: Decision-making and Community Political Culture on the Illinois Frontier." Ph.D. dissertation, University of Chicago, 1987.

Cayton, Andrew R. L. *The Frontier Republic: Ideology and Politics in the Ohio Country, 1780–1825*. Kent, OH: Kent State University Press, 1986.

Covington, James W. "Billy Bowlegs, Sam Jones, and the Crisis of 1849." *Florida Historical Quarterly* 68 (January 1990): 299–311.

———. *The Billy Bowlegs War, 1855–1858: The Final Stand of the Seminoles Against the Whites*. Chuluota, FL: Mickler House Publishers, 1982.

Cullum, George W. *Biographical Register of the Officers and Graduates of the United States Military Academy . . . 1802–1890*. 3 vols. Boston: Houghton Mifflin, 1891.

Davis, T. Frederick. "The Disston Land Purchase." *Florida Historical Quarterly* 17 (January 1939): 200–210.

DeVane, Albert. *DeVane's Early Florida History*. 2 vols. Sebring, FL: Sebring Historical Society, 1978–1979.

Doyle, Don Harrison. *The Social Order of a Frontier Community: Jacksonville, Illinois, 1825–70*. Urbana: University of Illinois Press, 1978.

Durrance, Margaret. *R & M: Our Family*. Lakeland, FL: privately printed, 1977–1978.

Durrance, Margaret, and Ann Durrance Folk. *Lineage of Joseph Durrance*. Lakeland, FL: privately printed, 1986.

Dykstra, Robert R. *The Cattle Towns*. New York: Alfred A. Knopf, 1968.

Elkins, Stanley, and Eric McKitrick. "A Meaning for Turner's Frontier, Part I: Democracy in the Old Northwest." *Political Science Quarterly* 69 (September 1954): 321–53.

———. "A Meaning for Turner's Frontier, Part II: The Southwest Frontier and New England." *Political Science Quarterly* 69 (January 1955): 565–602.

Florida Land and Improvement Company. *The Disston Lands of Florida*. Philadelphia: Florida Land and Improvement, 1885.

Frisbie, Louise K. *Peace River Pioneers*. Miami: E. A. Seemann Publishing, 1974.

Gibbon, John. *An Address on the Unveiling of the Statue of Major-General George G. Meade, in Philadelphia, October 18th, 1887*. Philadelphia: Allen, Lane & Scott, 1887.

Gibson, Marcia, Dona Hymerling, and Paula Schaill. "Fort Meade Got Start in Wooden Building." *Lakeland Ledger*, February 5, 1961.

Grismer, Karl H. *The Story of Fort Myers: The History of the Land of the Caloosahatchee and Southwest Florida*. St. Petersburg, FL: St. Petersburg Printing, 1949. Reprint. Fort Myers Beach, FL: Island Press Publishers, 1982.

———. *Tampa: A History of the City of Tampa and the Tampa Bay Region of Florida*. St. Petersburg, FL: St. Petersburg Printing, 1950.

Hanna, A. J., and Kathryn Hanna. *Lake Okeechobee: Wellspring of the Everglades.* New York: Bobbs-Merrill, 1948.

Harrison, Charles E. *Genealogical Records of the Pioneers of Tampa and of Some Who Came After Them.* Tampa, FL: E. W. B. Willey, 1915.

Hendry, Francis A. *Early History of Lee County and Fort Myers.* Privately printed, n.d.

Hendry, George W. *Family Record of Lydia Moody, nee Hendry, nee Carlton of Polk County, Florida.* Jacksonville: n.p., 1900.

————. *Polk County, Florida: Its Lands and Products* Jacksonville, FL: Ashmead Brothers, 1883.

Hetherington, M. F. *History of Polk County, Florida.* St. Augustine, FL: The Record Company, 1928. Reprint. Chuluota, FL: Mickler House, 1971.

Hill, Daniel H. "The Real Stonewall Jackson." *Century Illustrated Monthly Magazine* 47 (November 1893–April 1894): 623–28.

Hine, Robert V. *Community on the American Frontier: Separate But Not Alone.* Norman: University of Oklahoma Press, 1980.

Lee, J. V. "Early History of Christ Church." Fort Meade, 1891. Typescript. (In the author's collection.)

Livingston, Richard M. "Benjamin Moody, 1811–1896." *South Florida Pioneers* 8 (April 1976): 9–11.

————. "William McClenithan, 1817–1892." *South Florida Pioneers* 11 (January 1977): 4–5.

————. "Willoughby Tillis, 1808–1895." *South Florida Pioneers* 39/40 (January–April 1984): 4–11.

Luckingham, Bradford. *The Urban Southwest: A Profile History of Albuquerque, El Paso, Phoenix, Tucson.* El Paso: Texas Western Press, 1982.

McKay, Donald B. *Pioneer Florida.* 3 vols. Tampa, FL: Southern, 1959.

Mahon, John K. "Black Point: First Battle of the Second Seminole War." *Florida Living* (July 1988): 22–25.

Mahoney, Timothy R. *River Towns in the Great West: The Structure of Provincial Urbanization in the American Midwest, 1820–1870.* New York: Cambridge University Press, 1990.

Makers of America, Florida Edition. 4 vols. Atlanta: A. B. Caldwell, 1909.

Matthews, Janet Snyder. *Edge of Wilderness: A Settlement History of Manatee River and Sarasota Bay, 1528–1885.* Tulsa, OK: Caprine Press, 1983.

Meade, George. *The Life and Letters of George Gordon Meade, Major-General United States Army.* 2 vols. New York: Charles Scribners' Sons, 1913.

Memorial Sketch of the Life and Ministerial Labors of Rev. J. M. Hayman. Nashville, TN: Marshall & Bruce, 1901.

Minutes of the Annual Conferences of the Methodist Episcopal Church, South, for the Year 1883. Nashville, TN: Methodist Episcopal Church, South, 1884.

Platt, Harold L. *City Building in the New South: The Growth of Public Services in Houston, Texas, 1830–1910.* Philadelphia: Temple University Press, 1983.

Plowden, Jean. *History of Hardee County.* Wauchula: Florida Advocate, 1929.

Robinson, Sallie. Interview by John E. Brown. Fort Meade, FL, May 20, 1987. Notes in collection of the author.

Schene, Michael G. "Not a Shot Fired: Fort Chokonikla and the 'Indian War' of 1849–1850." *Tequesta* 37 (1977): 19–37.

Shrader, Jay. *Hidden Treasures: The Pebble Phosphates of the Peace River Valley of South Florida*. Bartow, FL: Varn, 1891.

Simmons, Ernest B. "Early Days of Fort Meade, Florida." *Fort Meade Leader*, December 25, 1947.

Smith, Julia Floyd. *Slavery and Plantation Growth in Antebellum Florida, 1821–1860*. Gainesville: University of Florida Press, 1973.

Stone, Spessard. "Francis Asbury Hendry, 1833–1917." *South Florida Pioneers* 33/34 (July–October 1982): 18–23.

———. *John and William, Sons of Robert Hendry*. 2d rev. ed. Bradenton, FL: Genie Plus, 1989.

———. *Lineage of John Carlton*. Wauchula, FL: privately published, 1991.

———. "Profile of A. B. Canter." *Polk County Historical Quarterly* 18 (December 1991): 6.

———. "Profile of Lloyd Davis." *Sunland Tribune* 27 (November 1991): 25–26.

———. "Profile of Sherod E. Roberts." *Polk County Historical Quarterly* 17 (December 1990): 6–7.

———. "Profile of Ulysses A. Lightsey." *Polk County Historical Quarterly* 17 (June 1990): 6–7.

Stringer, Margaret. *Watch Wauchula Win: Facts, Figures and Fun—1886–1930*. Bartow, FL: Bartow Printing, 1979.

Tebeau, Charlton. *A History of Florida*. Coral Gables, FL: University of Miami Press, 1971.

Tillis, James Dallas. "An Indian Attack of 1856 on the Home of Willoughby Tillis." *Florida Historical Quarterly* 8 (April 1930): 179–87.

Turner, Frederick Jackson. *The Frontier in American History*. New York: Henry Holt, 1920.

Vandiver, Frank E. *Mighty Stonewall*. New York: McGraw-Hill, 1957.

VanLandingham, Kyle S. "John I. Hooker, 1822–1862." *South Florida Pioneers* 15/16 (January–April 1978): 8–9.

———. "John Levi Skipper, 1826–1907." *South Florida Pioneers* 12 (April 1977): 24–26.

———. "William Brinton Hooker, 1800–1871." *South Florida Pioneers* 5 (July 1975): 6–12.

Wade, Richard C. *The Urban Frontier: The Rise of Western Cities, 1790–1830*. Cambridge, MA: Harvard University Press, 1959.

Wells, George W. *Facts for Immigrants*. Jacksonville: Press Office, 1877.

Whidden, Mrs. H. P. "The James Whitton Family of Polk County." *Polk County Historical Quarterly* 12 (March 1986): 4–5.

White, Robert M. *History of Fort Meade, Florida.* Longwood, FL: privately printed, 1988.

Williams, Vernice. Interview by the author. Fort Meade, FL, March 8, 1987. Notes in collection of the author.

Winkle, Kenneth J. *The Politics of Community: Migration and Politics in Antebellum Ohio.* New York: Cambridge University Press, 1988.

Index

Abalo, M. A., 144–46, 151, 171
Acme, 124
Acree, William M., 95, 171
Acton, 107, 110
Adams, Albion H., 85, 93, 142, 148, 170–71, 188
Adams, Sherman, 90
Adams House, 93, 98, 103, 107, 142, 146
Addison, W. H., 182
African Americans: as Civil War soldiers, 47–50; presence in Civil War aftermath, 52–53, 76–78; and the phosphate industry, 122, 127; and the building of the railroads, 126; businesses of, 127–28. *See also* Slaves and slavery; Fort Meade; Homeland; Churches
African Methodist Episcopal (AME) Church, 129; ministers of, 169. *See also* Saint Paul AME Church
Alafia, 2, 15–16, 48
Albritton, H. M., 172
Albritton, J. L., 172
Alexander, J. S., 172
Alexander, James, 130
Alfred, P. E., 166
Allen, Eliza Davis, 77, 129
Allen, Hannah, 161
Allen, Moses, 77, 130, 172
Allen, William, 159
Alleyne, Cecil H., 104, 107–09, 123
Alleyne, Mrs. Cecil H., 109–10
Altman, Ann, 161
Altman, G. L., 171
Altman, Jesse, 180
Altman, John, 159, 180
Altman, William, 161
Anderson, Anna S., 170
Anderson, John L., 191
Anderson, Thomas W., 85, 89, 119, 123, 170, 172
Arcadia, 64, 121
Armstrong, J. M., 188
Arnold, Daniel, 161
Arnold, Lewis G., 19, 158
Arnold, M. O., 85, 95
Ashton, D. E., 114, 167, 171
Atkins, Thomas A., 116
Atkins, W. S., 95, 171, 185
Auburndale, 95
Aunt Line, 29
Austine, William, 157

Averra, John, 161
Avon Park, 107
Axlin, W. J., 172

Bainbridge, Henry, 5, 157
Baine, Tillie, 76
Baker, Isaac, 171
Baker, Julius, 161
Baker, R. O., 116
Ball, W. G., 85
Ball, W. M., 94
Ball & Co. store, 94, 104
Ballyhooly (private home), 110
Banks, R. T., 116
Banks and banking, 124
Baptist church, 66, 119–20. *See also specific churches*
Barnes, Milton, 171
Barnett, C. E., 172
Barry, William F., 17, 158
Bartow, 52, 70, 83–84, 94, 118; as county seat, 54; telegraphic communications at, 55; railroad at, 95–96; as county's first incorporated town, 96; and 1887 temperance vote, 127; Roman Catholic Church organized at, 132
Bates, W. H., 169
Battles: of Black Point (1835), 178; of Peace River (1856), 25–30; of Olustee (1864), 43
Beard, W. K., 127
Beddoes, William, 114
Belcher, Edmund C., 130, 169
Bell, John, 39
Bellamy, William, 160
Benedict, James, 85, 115–16
Benedict, Mrs. James, 115–16
Benedict, Robert, 191
Bennett, Allen, 130
Benson, Henry, 20
Benton, George, 161
Berry Hendry Branch, 16, 123
Best, A. W. J., 142, 168, 191
Best, Peter, 171
Bethel. *See* Homeland
Bethel Academy, 76
Bethel Methodist Church, 75, 119
Bettis, J. L., 92
Big Charlie Apopka Creek, 3
Billy Bowlegs War, 24–35
Black, George W., 95, 115
Black, Mrs. George W., 115, 143, 164

Black, J. F., 95, 102
Blackburn, ———, 164
Blackburn, Thomas A., 145, 171
Blackburn, W. H., 171
Blacks. *See* African Americans
Blangwaer (private home), 110
Blanks, S. L., 172
Blockade running, 40, 42
Bloom, Daniel, 161
Bloom, James, 161
Bloom, William, 161
Blount, Nathan S., 182
Blount, Oregon Hendry, 29, 32
Blount, Owen R., 38
Bloxham, William D., 86
Blume, D. P., 171
Blume, Lafayette, 171
Boatwright, R. B., 171
Bobbett, A. E., 113, 171
Boggess, Francis C. M., 23, 26, 29–30, 38–39, 46, 50, 52, 159, 163–64
Bone, Thomas, 171
Bostick, B. B., 149
Bowen, W. M., 171
Bowlegs, Billy, 24, 30, 179
Bowlegs Creek, 5; as boundary of Indian lands, 3; Civil War engagement at, 46
Bowling Green, 1–2
Boyd, J. W., 85–86
Boyd, McLeod, 191
Boyd, Wesley, 162
Bradley, Ben, 56
Brandon, Jared W., 168
Brandon, John W., 58, 160, 162
Brandon, Wesley, 64
Breckenridge, John C., 39
Brewster, William, 130
Bridge End (private home), 110
Bridges, 35, 52, 54, 61, 68, 81, 92–93, 145
Broad Street, 55, 98, 103, 133, 149–50. *See also* Main Street; Wire Street
Broadway, 55
Broderick, George L., 113, 191
Brooker, Margaret, 159
Brooker, William P., 23, 28, 32–34
Brooks, Alonzo, 172
Brooksville, 51
Brown, ———, 127, 189
Brown, D. H., 128, 169, 189
Brown, Edward M., 86, 125
Brown, Harvey, 13–14, 157–58
Brown, W. B., 185
Brown, William, 161, 180
Brown, William M., 189
Brown Street, 101
Bryan, A. B., 171
Bryan, A. L., 171
Bryan, Frank, 171
Bryan, T. J., 171

Bryan, Travis, 171
Bryant, Francis, 161
Buck, A. H., 171
Bulloch, A. J., 115, 166, 188
Bulloch, Alfred T., 165
Bulloch, Cora Lee, 165
Bulloch, Henry, 116
Bulloch, Lucie, 165
Bulloch, Mrs. A. J., 93, 107
Bunch, D. S., 183
Bunch, J. J., 172, 183
Burdine, William M., 142
Butler, C. E., 136, 169

Caloosahatchee River, 7, 20, 26, 47, 49, 83
Campbell, Mary, 161
Campground Branch, 38, 49, 123
Canter, Arthur Benjamin, 85, 107, 114, 166, 171, 191
Canter, Sterling, 85, 191
Canter & Stansfield, 134
Carlton, A. T., 171
Carlton, Alderman, 22–23, 27, 163
Carlton, Daniel, 27
Carlton, James, 160
Carlton, John W., 168
Carney, H. C., 164
Carney, William, 159
Carpenter, W. T., 75
Carroll, W. J., 182
Carter, Evans, & Company, 114, 124, 133, 135–36
Carter, James G., 94, 97, 103, 114, 126, 136–37, 147, 166, 171
Carson, Robert A., 159–60, 168
Carson, Samuel W., 69, 72, 168, 189
Carwan, Mary, 161
Casey, John Charles, 2–3
Cason, John, 159
Cattle business, 73, 78–79; ranges in 1849, 2; herds moved east of Peace River, 16; during Civil War, 42–51; post-Civil War, 53, 56–57; and the Hurricane of 1878, 80
Cemeteries, 64
Cemetery Street, 64
Chamber of Commerce. *See* Fort Meade Board of Trade
Chandler, S. M., 182
Chandler, W. W., 182
Chaney, Jacob, 161
Charleston Avenue, 98, 153
Charlotte Harbor, 43, 65, 118
Childers, E. R., 85, 95, 123, 167, 171, 189
Childers, Lula Marsh, 118–19, 164
Childs, Jonathan W., 47, 160
Childs, Thomas, 8
Chokonikla, destruction of Indian store at, 1–2

of garrison, 20; purchased by John I. Hooker, 20–21; during Third Seminole War of 1855–58, 24–35; beginnings of town life, 30–35; violence and Regulator activities at, 36–37, 53–54, 66–67; Civil War, 39–51; Confederate occupation of, 40; Unionism at, 43–44; Union army burns in 1864, 45–48; telegraphic communications at, 54–55, 70–71; post–Civil War economic revival, 56–62; town platted and initially subdivided, 62–64; isolation of, 65, 78–79; land title problems, 66; failed attempt at incorporation, 66; temperance movement at, 72–73; northern and midwestern immigration to, 84–86; subsequent subdivisions, 87–89; incorporation of, 96–97; arrival of the railroad at, 100–04; English settlers at, 107–14, 133, 148–49; impact of phosphate industry on, 121–26; beginnings of substantial black community, 126–27; race relations at, 127–30; and economic troubles in 1890s, 132–38; impact of the Great Freeze of 1895 at, 139–42; and the influence of Cuban tobacco growers and cigar makers, 144–53; and Spanish-American War, 151; incorporation repealed, 153; shift of business district toward railroad depot, 153–54; postmasters, 170; registered voters in 1896, 171–72; school trustees, 163; teachers at, 164; town officers, 166–67
Fort Meade Academy, 97, 115–18
Fort Meade AME Church Circuit, 129
Fort Meade & Plant City Railroad, 102, 106, 113
Fort Meade Board of Trade, 126, 133, 189
Fort Meade Fertilizer Company, 122
Fort Meade High School, 117–18, 145
Fort Meade Hotel, 93–94, 107
Fort Meade Jockey Club, 110–12, 127, 133
Fort Meade, Keystone and Walk-in-the-Water Railroad Company, 84, 96, 185
Fort Meade Land Agency, 86
Fort Meade Methodist Circuit, 90
Fort Meade Phosphate, Fertilizer, Land and Improvement Company, 122
Fort Meade Publishing Company, 150
Fort Meade Silver Cornet Band, 143–44
Fort Meade Street Railway Company, 103–04, 126, 150
Fort Meade String Band, 73
Fort Meade Tobacco Growers Co., 145
Fort Myers, 7, 43–48, 57, 113; Confederate attack upon, 49–50
Fortner, Mitchell G., 183
Fort Ogden, 52, 57, 71
Fort Thompson, 20, 47, 49–50
Foster, E. K., 86
Fourth of July celebrations, 74

Fox hunts, 110
Francis, William H., 114, 171
Francis Street, 98
Frasier, J. C., 39, 159
Freezes and heavy frosts: in 1851–52, 13; in 1878, 81; in 1886, 91–92, 101; in 1894–95, 139–42; in 1899, 152
French, A. J., 97, 166, 189
French, Alex V., 104
French, Seth, 88–89, 92
French, William F., 8–11, 14, 157
French House, 92–93, 95. See also Fort Meade Hotel
Fries, Charles L., 97, 104, 166
Frostproof, 84
Fuller, M. W., 172

Galilee Baptist Church, 128, 130, 132; ministers of, 169
Gandy, Green, 160
Gant, G. W., 182
Garden of Eden Land Agency, 86
Gardiner, H. A., 85, 89
Gardner, Belton C., 142, 166
Gardner, John W., 191
Gardner, W. B., 85, 171
Gardyne, J., 123
Gartner, A. F., 147, 171
Gates, E. J., 130, 168
Gay, Herman, 166
Gay, Hiram, 171
Giles, Enoch H., 168
Gill, A. J., 172
Gillespie, F. C., 171
Given, O. M., 164
Glover, Charles, 77
Godwin, Aaron Elijah, 160
Godwin, Mariah, 42
Godwin, Solomon, 42, 66, 159–60, 182
Godwin, Thomas, 160
Gonzalez, J. E., 189
Goodman, William, 172
Good Templars, 72. See also Temperance movement
Grafton, Henry D., 157–58
Graham, S. W., 164
Grand Army of the Republic (GAR) chapter, 143, 191
Grandy, William, 160
Gray, W. T., 171
Great Freeze of 1895, 139–42
Green, Delia, 160
Green, James Dopson, 43–45
Green, John, 23, 42, 159, 163, 180
Green, Lewis, 160
Greenwood, Robert, 102
Griffin, Stephen L., 166
Griffin, Thomas, 180
Gristmills, 38, 58–59

About the Author

CANTER BROWN, JR., winner of the Florida Historical Society's 1992 Rembert W. Patrick Memorial Book Award for his *Florida's Peace River Frontier*, has a background in both law and history. He served in government for more than fifteen years, working in research, legal, and administrative positions in the Florida Legislature, Georgia General Assembly, and United States Congress. Brown earned Doctor of Jurisprudence and Doctor of Philosophy degrees from Florida State University. He currently teaches in the History and Political Science Department at Florida A&M University. His other awards for historical writing include the Governor LeRoy Collins Prize of the Florida Historical Society and the Southern Jewish Historical Society's Benjamin H. Levy Prize. Brown is a native of Fort Meade, Florida.